Praise for *Your Successful Real Estate C...*

"At last, there is a quality book I can confidently recommend to people considering careers in real estate."

—Robert J. Bruss, syndicated real estate columnist

"Your Successful Real Estate Career is as good a take on our business as I've ever seen . . . inspiring, clever, and factual, with a good sense of humor. I've got it at the top of my recommendation list. That's a great compliment, since I've been in this business over 30 years."

—Ed Willer, Realtor, York Simpson Underwood Realtors; Past President, Raleigh, N.C., Regional Association of Realtors; Realtor of the Year, Raleigh, N.C., Regional Association of Realtors

"This book should be required reading for anyone in the pre-license course."

—John Reilly, DREI, attorney, author, educator

"Written by the master. If real estate is your career, this is your book."

—Oliver Frascona, attorney, author, educator, Boulder, Colorado

"Doctor Ken's comprehensive guide for newcomers and refresher course for old pros should be on every real estate bookshelf in the Free World. It will always be on mine."

—Joe Klock, real estate author; former Dean, Coldwell Banker University

YOUR SUCCESSFUL REAL ESTATE CAREER
Fifth Edition

Kenneth W. Edwards

AMACOM

American Management Association

New York • Atlanta • Brussels • Chicago • Mexico City
San Francisco • Shanghai • Tokyo • Toronto • Washington, D.C.

REALTOR® is a registered collective membership mark that identifies a real estate professional who is a member of the National Association of REALTORS® and subscribes to its strict Code of Ethics. AMACOM uses these names throughout this book in initial capital letters or ALL CAPITAL letters for editorial purposes only, with no intention of trademark violation.

This publication is designed to provide accurate and authoritative information in regard to the subject matter covered. It is sold with the understanding that the publisher is not engaged in rendering legal, accounting, or other professional service. If legal advice or other expert assistance is required, the services of a competent professional person should be sought.

Library of Congress Cataloging-in-Publication Data

Edwards, Kenneth W. 3
Your successful real estate career / Kenneth W. Edwards. — 5th ed.
   p. cm.
   Includes bibliographical references and index.
   ISBN-10: 0-8144-7319-9
   ISBN-13: 978-0-8144-7319-1
1. Real estate business—Vocational guidance—United States. 2. Real estate agents—United States. I. Title.
HD1375.E33 2007
333.33023'73—dc22   2006019309

Printing number

10 9 8 7 6 5 4 3

Contents

Preface to the Fifth Edition

Over the life span of this book, the real estate market has changed dramatically, and the only thing we can say for certain is that it will change dramatically in the future. My challenge has been to provide the guidance needed for the prospective real estate professional to best prepare to meet those challenges. Here are some the new or updated features you will find in this edition to help you accomplish that goal.

- An emphasis on the importance of understanding that as a licensed real estate professional you will be an entrepreneur, not an employee. There's a huge difference.
- Guidance on how to transition from a newbie to a seasoned, highly successful agent, including picking and working with a compatible mentor.
- Information to help you look down the road toward the time when you may wish to employ an on site personal assistant or a virtual assistant.
- Introduction to a client prospecting plan labeled "Focused Fandango Farming", designed to produce so much business you'll be dancing all the way to the bank.
- An overview of an ever expanding array of incredible educational opportunities, including the National Association of Realtors Graduate Realtors Institute (GRI) and their technology based course which results in the ePro professional designation.
- Recommendations on how to market yourself to the Hispanic, Asian, African-American and military communities, since these have traditionally been underserved demographics.
- Specific directions on how to "find a niche and fill it", since there are an incredible array of exciting, and potentially profitable market segments. Farms, luxury homes, vacation properties, wineries and orchards are just a few examples.

Few things you can do to earn a living are as challenging and exciting as a career in real estate. It is an activity with widely diverse opportunities and exceptional income potential. There has been a continuing interest in it among people searching for meaningful and well-paying work and among educators who respond to those trends. Almost every community college in the country, for example, offers courses in real estate licensing, as do an increasing number of four-year colleges and universities. Several states sponsor real estate education and research centers. In every part of the United States, scores of private real estate schools present quality instruction both in the class room and through distance education programs. Each year thousands of individuals receive their licenses to sell real estate.

Many who enter the field enjoy long, satisfying careers. Unfortunately, many others do not. Historically, the dropout rate has been extremely high, primarily because all too often people enter the field with an inaccurate or distorted perception of what the business is all about and what it takes to do well in it on a long-term basis. My primary goal in this book is to provide you with that information.

WHO SHOULD READ THIS BOOK

If you are considering real estate as an occupation, I have written this book for you. When I entered the profession a couple of decades ago I looked for a source of information that would give me a straightforward and reliable insight as to what the business was all about and what I would need to do to succeed in it. Most of what I encountered was basically recruiting information designed to reassure anyone who wished to become a real estate agent that they could succeed and make big money. That convinced me there was a need for a book of this nature. When I submitted my original manuscript to one publisher, the reply was: "Sorry, I doubt there's a market for an honest book about selling real estate." Fortunately, folks on the Editorial Staff of the American Management Association (AMACOM Books) believed there was a market, reader response has been extremely positive, and we're now in our fifth edition.

If you have recently entered the field, the book should help get you headed in the right direction and ensure that you stay on track. If you have been in the profession for a while, it can provide a helpful "return to the basics" review. It is a comprehensive, candid, and practical career guide that will assist you in deciding whether to enter the field and will help you to be successful if you do. It deals with the opportunities and obstacles you are likely to face, presented in the order you are likely to face them. I describe an effective method of conducting your business affairs that emphasizes professionalism, hard work, long-term achievement, and personal satisfaction.

The overwhelming majority of people who work in real estate concentrate their efforts on listing and selling residential property, because that is where most of the opportunities for employment exist. Therefore, I have organized this book to be of maximum assistance to people who are starting out as residential sales agents in general real estate brokerage companies. That will means that in all states and the District of Columbia, you will need to be licensed, which entails passing a written examination and formal course work. I provide detailed guidance on getting your license and starting your career, and I discuss extensively the opportunities available for specializing or broadening your career as you gain experience.

One thing that makes real estate such an interesting field in which to work is the widely divergent backgrounds of those who enter the profession. Real estate is truly a melting pot of practitioners. You will encounter everyone from former plumbers to Ph.D.'s. At the outset, however, everyone needs reliable career information. If you have extensive previous business experience, you may not require as much information as I present on some topics, but my aim is to be as thorough and helpful as possible and take nothing for granted.

I had three specific groups in mind as I wrote this book. One is composed of those who are entering the general job market for the first time. I have tried to be particularly sensitive to the needs of these individuals. Although they represent a distinct minority of the total workforce in the profession, more and more new workers are choosing careers in real estate, resulting in the general upgrading of the profession and the expanding availability of quality licensing programs.

The second group consists of women reentering the workforce after an absence, often one of an extended duration. For these individuals, real estate has traditionally been a very popular occupation. Licensing programs can be rigorous, but otherwise the field of real estate is comparatively easy to enter, offers true equality of opportunity, permits a flexible work schedule, and promises good income potential. In writing for women readers, I drew heavily on knowledge of my wife's experience as a real estate professional and those of several of my female associates and former students.

The final group for whom I wrote this book includes those who are in some other occupation and are now considering real estate as a career change or as a second career after retirement. Real estate was a second career for me, so I have a good understanding of the attraction it holds for people looking for a new field to enter.

In Chapter 16, "Special Messages for Special People," I offer specific suggestions to individuals from each of these groups to make their entry into real estate as smooth and productive as possible.

While the book is written as a career guide for people considering real estate as a profession or for those already in it, I've received positive feedback from readers who simply want to learn as much as they can about the real estate profession and how it operates to make them better investors, but who do not want a real estate license. That's a plan I've seen implemented very successfully by several students who have taken my real estate courses, so I will elaborate on that in Chapter 16.

HOW TO USE THIS BOOK

First, I suggest you skim the entire book. This will give you a good overview of typical job-related activities and long-term opportunities. Do not become overly involved with specific details. Concentrate on subjects that are of the most immediate interest to you and will help you to make a sound career decision. If you then enroll in a license-training course, use the book to help you understand how the subject matter you are studying relates to real-life real estate. It is widely used as a supplementary licensing text for that specific purpose. When you start looking for a company with which to affiliate, study Chapter 3 thoroughly *before* you begin your search. If there is no formal training program where you work, you can use this book to structure an effective one of your own. If there is a training program, this book can serve as a valuable adjunct, offering a perspective and alternatives you are not likely to encounter elsewhere. However you use the book, I trust you will come to regard it as your "career companion."

WHY THERE ARE A FEW DISCOURAGING WORDS

As I thought about the content and tone of *Your Successful Real Estate Career*, my challenge was to be candid enough to be helpful, yet positive enough to reflect my genuine enthusiasm for real estate as a career. When I focus on disadvantages of the job and on disagreements among those in the field about the professionalism of certain practices, my intent is to be constructive. If you have a clear idea of what to expect in the workplace, good and bad, you will be much more likely to adapt successfully and be better prepared to develop your own personal philosophy of doing business by having been exposed early to divergent ideas. Leigh Robinson, author of the best-selling book *Landlording,* put it in these colorful terms: ". . . *Your Successful Real Estate Career* portrays the work just as it is, hemorrhoids and all."

My objective is certainly not to discourage people who are suited for real estate from entering it. On the contrary, it is to encourage serious-minded, career-oriented individuals who appreciate candor and objectivity. From the standpoint of those in the profession, it is expensive and time-consuming to recruit and train real estate agents. It is clearly in everyone's best interests to provide information that is balanced and effective in attracting those who are most suited for the field.

If you are reading the book to help you decide whether to pursue a career in real estate or not, let me suggest this: If, after you have read the book, you are still enthusiastic but have not yet made up your mind, enroll in a pre-licensing course, complete the requirements, and take the state licensing exam. I will have plenty of guidance for you on achieving that goal. At that point, you will be able to make the best informed career decision possible.

RESEARCH METHODS AND WRITING STYLE

My primary research methodology was based on direct personal observation. I was a very successful residential real estate sales agent for several years, after a career in the U.S. Air Force. I currently have my Oregon real estate broker's license, although I devote most of my time now to teaching and writing. I have taught real estate licensing courses at an Oregon community college for over a decade. I have remained active as a member of the National Association of Realtors and have served on the local ethics and arbitration panel. I have also been Book Review Editor for *Real Estate Professional* magazine for many years and frequently write feature articles for the publication. For several years I wrote a Realtor career advice column titled "Ask Doctor Real Estate". During the early years of my real estate career, my wife was also a licensed salesperson, and we worked together as a team in the same office.

To secure background information and to help me achieve a national perspective, I conducted a written survey of several hundred experienced real estate brokers and salespeople from around the country (see Appendix A). I wanted to find out why people leave the profession prematurely. If I knew what caused difficulties for some, I believed, I could do a better job of advising prospective salespeople. I refer to the results of the survey and quote survey respondents throughout the book.

At the present time, there are just over two million real estate licensees in the United States. Of those, roughly one million are members of the National Association of Realtors (NAR). The word *Realtor* is a registered trade name that may only be used by those who are members of NAR. While comprising a minority of the total force, the Realtor organization is the dominant professional real estate entity in the country. For a variety of reasons described in this book, I strongly recommend real estate professionals become Realtors.

I have included several real estate "war stories" and personal experiences to illustrate some particularly important points. As you will see, my former students have provided me a wealth of information in this regard. Real estate is an exciting and dynamic profession, and any book describing it that does not capture that spirit does not do the profession justice. What you will *not* find are lists of sure fire success techniques and formulas guaranteed to produce instant fame and untold riches. What specific advice I include I have followed myself, or I have watched others follow, and the suggestions do work. However, only you can decide what is best for your situation and your personality.

I have tried to cover the subject matter itself in a way that applies to all areas of the country. But although there are marked similarities in the practice of real estate in all states, there are also important differences. What is permissible in one place might be improper or even illegal in another. Because no one can be licensed to sell real estate without demonstrating knowledge of local rules and regulations, you should be able to judge where practices I discuss differ from what is followed in your state. In all matters covered in this book, your current state law is your absolute guide.

Real estate prices also vary markedly from one region to another. What buys a mansion in your hometown may purchase only a modest bungalow (or a lot upon which to build a modest bungalow) somewhere else. When I present examples that mention home prices or income levels, adjust the figures as necessary to bring them in line with what you know to be the case where you live.

Although this is not a formal research report, you will find an extensive bibliography in Appendix C to use for further study.

A FARMER'S PHILOSOPHY

One fellow outside of the profession who read my manuscript made this comment: "You certainly do expect a lot out of a new real estate agent!" At first reading, you might have the same impression, but if you take the contents one small chunk at a time, you will find that it is not that imposing. And, of course, there is the argument that anything worth doing, is worth doing well. When I was the commander of the Air Force ROTC unit at Cal Berkeley, I had a student in our program from Nebraska who was studying to be an attorney. His father was not thrilled with his son's choice of occupation. The boy said that as he left the family farm, his hardworking dad's last words to him were, "Son, if you are determined to be a lawyer, be an honest one and be a good one." That's not bad advice, no matter what profession you enter.

YOUR INPUT IS WELCOME

I have received excellent feedback from readers of previous editions, and I am anxious to have yours. In teaching my real estate licensing class I ask my students to give me a written answer to the question: "What is there about a potential career in real estate that concerns you the most?" Since I have dozens of former students who are currently real estate professionals, I ask them the question: "What has been the most serious challenge you have faced in your real estate career, and how have you responded to it?" Depending upon your individual situation, I would appreciate your response to those questions. My contact information is below. E-mail is the most effective.

I am particularly interested in suggestions from those of you who are new to the field, since you will be facing the challenges that I discuss in the book. I would also like to hear from brokers about what might be included to be of more help to you in working with new agents. If you are using the book in teaching formal real estate courses, I would be grateful for suggestions on how the material might be expanded or altered. Please direct your comments to:

Dr. Kenneth W. Edwards
Professional Associates
7990 NW Ridgewood Drive
Corvallis OR 97330
e-mail address: DoctorKenisin@aol.com

Acknowledgments

I had two primary objectives when I entered the real estate profession after my Air Force career. The first was to succeed while using the type of business practices I describe in this book. The second was to gather the research material and gain the practical experience I needed to write a real estate career guide. I had a lot of help in achieving both goals.

Early in my real estate career, my wife, Judith McVay Edwards, got her real estate license and we worked together as a team. She did most of the hard, unglamourous work, while I generally got the credit. In my writing efforts, she has been my constructive and gentle critic and has given the loving support I needed to see the project through. My original broker, W. Dale Dyer and his partner/wife Carolyn Dyer, provided the perfect environment for learning about the real estate profession. The experience was made all the more enjoyable by their constant and friendly encouragement.

For the past several years, I have taught real estate licensing at Linn Benton Community College in Albany, Oregon. Many of my students have gone into the real estate profession and continue to give me extremely valuable feedback on the challenges and opportunities they are encountering.

One of my most enjoyable and rewarding real estate-related writing experiences was working as the consulting and contributing editor for the State of Oregon's award winning official *Real Estate Manual*. I have greatly appreciated the continued support and encouragement of the staff at the Oregon Real Estate Agency over the ensuing years.

As the Book Review Editor for The Real Estate Professional magazine I've had the opportunity to review just about every book that relates to the real estate profession, which has helped immensely in my writing activities. The Publisher of The Real Estate Professional, Ed DesRoches, has provided constant encouragement and support, not to mention my editorial contact at the magazine, the patient and understanding Judy Farren.

Since the first edition of this book came out roughly two decades ago,

I've worked with the editorial and marketing staff at AMACOM Books in New York City, the trade book division of the American Management Association. I owe a particular debt of gratitude to my original Acquisitions Editor, Karl Weber. I'm certain that his guidance to go through my original manuscript and add "real estate related 'war stories' to each chapter" accounts in large part for the book's long term success. AMACOM staffers Ellen Kadin, Irene Majuk, and Christina Parisi have all provided incredible support and encouragement over the years.

I am grateful to the following organizations for assisting me in my research: the Real Estate Educators Association, the National Association of Realtors, the National Association of Real Estate Editors, the Association of Real Estate License Law Officials, and the Military Officers Association of America.

Finally, special thanks to my past and current clients, customers, and associates, all of whom have contributed to making my time in real estate such a pleasant, memorable, and profitable experience.

1

Is Real Estate For You?

It's a Great Life . . . If It's the Life For Which You're Suited

Choosing your occupation is one of the toughest decisions you will ever make, and clearly one of the most important. That is true whether you're a young person looking for your first full-time job, or someone embarking on a second or third career later in life. For you to make the best choice, you need to find out as much as you can about your possibilities from reliable and unbiased sources. You need to know what kind of person is most likely to succeed, and you need to find out how much money you can expect to make. It isn't always easy to get the kind of information you require. In real estate, for example, my research indicated that *lack of objective information about the career field before they enter it* is a major reason why people drop out of the profession (see Appendix A).

There is no question that residential real estate sales can be exciting and tremendously rewarding-for the right person. My purpose in this chapter is to help you decide whether *you* are that person or not.

THE NATURE OF THE JOB

First, let's take a brief look at some of the basics. In legal terms, an agent is someone empowered to transact business for another person. Real estate agents perform that function. I discuss the subject of agency as it relates to real estate in depth in Chapter 5. As a *licensed real estate salesperson* (the most widely accepted official term) you will work for a *real estate broker*. A broker has spent a prescribed amount of time in the profession, has received additional training, and is subject to separate licensing procedures. Your broker will provide you with desk space and certain support items, and she is obliged to supervise your professional real estate activities for as long as you are together. In return, you share your income with her. There are variations to this arrangement which I will cover, but this is the most common arrangement. Several states, including Oregon where I have my license, have gone to what is known as a single licensing system, in which the salesperson designation is eliminated. Everyone is licensed as a broker, and the supervisory relationships may be altered slightly. Colorado was the first to adopt this system. But let's be honest. Whether you are called a salesperson or some variety of broker, your challenges and opportunities will essentially be the same. The system in place in your state will, of course, become clear to you as you pursue your license training. Contact information for each state's Real Estate Agency is included in Appendix B, as well as contact information for the Association of Real Estate License Law Officials (ARELLO). The ARELLO web site contains the web site links to each state agency. You'll find an incredible amount of useful career information there, so it would be wise for you to log on and check out your state's site as an essential first step in your real estate career exploration.

Almost all real estate agents are paid solely from commissions (brokerage fees paid to their supervising brokers and shared with the agents), which result either from property they sell or from the sale of their listings (contractual agreements with owners to market property) by other agents. This is true whether they are among the approximately 95 percent who are independent contractors or whether they are employees. In real estate sales, the term *independent contractor* is used to describe the nature of the supervisory relationship between broker and agent, and has specific legal and income tax implications. Rarely are real estate salespeople paid a set salary. I describe these basics more fully in Chapter 3. Some alternate business formats are evolving, which I will cover in Chapter 17, but commission sales are still the dominant model.

The point is that selling real estate is a job in which you survive and prosper by producing results. How you do that will be left largely to you. Whatever works, within the bounds of common sense, legality, and reason, will be acceptable. Within the profession, even among coworkers in the same office, there can be a remarkable diversity in the way the role of a real estate agent is interpreted. Many successful agents rely heavily on traditional sales techniques, such as door-to-door solicitation and telephone canvassing. Others who are equally productive either do not employ any "standard" approaches or modify them greatly. One of the real attractions of the occupation is that you are able to pursue your career in a manner that is compatible with your own personality and values.

TRAITS AND SKILLS YOU'LL NEED

How well you do as a real estate agent will be determined by how well adapted you are to the demands of the profession. Here are some of the personality traits and job skills you will need in real estate. No one will possess all of them, nor is everyone equally thrilled with all parts of the job. Further, a real strength in one area can compensate for average abilities in another.

■ *You need to like the lifestyle.* Most successful agents I know treat real estate more as a fascinating hobby than a job. They're never happier than when they are in the middle of putting a transaction together. They do not watch the clock and they are ready to spring into action when the bell rings (or the beeper beeps), whether it's day or night, weekday or weekend. The more astute agents discipline themselves to ensure they have balance in their lives, but the fact remains that they love their work and typically immerse themselves in it. You don't need to be quite that passionate about the profession to succeed, but it needs to be more than "just a job" for you to put up with the demands on your time. People expect you to respond at *their* convenience, not yours. For many, evenings and weekends are the only time they can look at property or talk to you about selling their home. If you are the type who dislikes a nine-to-five, Monday-through-Friday routine, then the real estate lifestyle will appeal to you. I'm amused, however, when I hear a prospective real estate professional indicate that the reason a real estate career appeals to them is that they can "set their own schedule". Trust me, it doesn't work that way.

■ *You need to be a self-starter.* If the concept of individual accountability for achievement—judged almost exclusively by the number of business transactions you successfully consummate attracts you, you will find real estate to be an invigorating experience. You will either succeed or fail almost entirely based on your own individual efforts. You need to understand that fact very clearly. No matter how effective the training program of the company with which you affiliate, and no matter how enlightened and supportive the broker with whom you work, you must have the desire and the ability to do it on your own. In my survey, *lack of "self-starter" and "self-motivator" personality* emerged as *the* most important reason people leave real estate prematurely (see Appendix A). A national franchise broker from California summed it up well in his survey reply: "Unless you are strong on self-discipline and do your own motivation, you should forget about real estate." Many people thrive in this atmosphere and would be uncomfortable in a more traditional environment. Others feel neglected, become lost and discouraged, and give up. You need to have a hearty amount of the rugged individualist in you.

■ *You Need to Know Who You Are.* Here's what I mean. In a recent survey I did of my former students who are now active in the profession I asked them to identify the greatest challenge they have faced in their real estate careers and what they did to respond. Here's a direct quote from a woman who is now a very successful agent: "The greatest challenge I faced was to understand that I was an entrepreneur, not an employee. One word describes what I had to do that was different than when I was salaried—'prospect'."

Webster's New World Dictionary describes entrepreneur as: "a person who organizes and manages a business undertaking, assuming the risk for the sake of the profit." Although the trappings may look somewhat different, that's essentially what you will be—a one person business. To make a profit you're going to have to come in contact with potential clients. For the most part they will not come to you. You will have to find them. Peter Drucker is credited with this apt quote: "The purpose of a business is to create a customer".

■ *You need to be a hard worker.* It is not uncommon to encounter someone prospering in real estate who seems to lack all the prerequisites generally thought to be essential for success. Examples abound of people who violate every widely held sales precept and yet do quite well—sometimes amazingly well. But big money without hard work? No. Absolutely, positively not. Hard work is an indispensable, unconditional prerequisite. Formal research by the National Association of Realtors confirms what common sense would suggest: a direct, positive correlation exists in real estate sales between average hours worked per week and income. Those mavericks making the big bucks might be marching to a different drummer, but they're all working hard in their own way. A Wisconsin broker summed it up well in this survey comment: "Those who don't do well are those who just can't seem to get to work early and stay late, working effectively while there. Many new people think real estate is an easy job with easy money. Real estate success takes training, dedication, and an ability to work long hours, weekends, and during summer vacation periods."

Let me give you a personal example that exemplifies perfectly the correlation between hard work and success. One summer day several years ago, I got a call from a young man inquiring about the upcoming real estate licensing sequence I was teaching in the evenings at the local community college. I had trouble hearing what he was saying because of background noise. I asked him what the noise was, and he informed me that he was on break from his summer construction job. It turned out he was Bryan Martin, a full-time senior engineering construction student at Oregon State University, who was taking roughly eighteen credit hours per quarter.

He told me he had always been interested in real estate and wanted to get his license. He enrolled in my year-long course while finishing his bachelor's degree requirements. I attended his graduation and have kept in touch with him since. Bryan got his real estate license and affiliated with a brokerage in Bozeman, Montana. He specialized in working ranches and hunting properties, and closed over $11 million in sales in his second year. Shortly thereafter he moved on from real estate to his first love and now runs his own hunting and guide service in Canada. He owns and operates Canadian Mountain Outfitters, Ltd. You can check out his operation at www.canadianmtnoutfitters.com. Click "The Guides" link and you'll meet Bryan. My point is this: I doubt that he would say he's a particularly hard worker, whether in real estate or hunting, because much of what he does he enjoys so much. I guess the question to ask yourself is, "How committed am I willing to be to my real estate career?" Incidentally, the last time I talked to Bryan he was on his cell phone driving in his automobile somewhere in the Great Plains. He informed me that he'll eventually get back in to real estate, but he loves what he's doing now so much he can't leave it.

Here's another example. Several years ago a fellow by the name of John Tacke took my real estate licensing course. It was an academic year long course. At the time he was a collection driver for the local disposal company. I often saw him around town, and at our home, driving huge trucks plying his trade. For approximately three years he transitioned from his regular job to his real estate career. In the final phase, for about a year, he worked the midnight to ten a.m. shift with Corvallis Disposal. After a quick one hour nap he headed to his real estate office for roughly an eight hour stint, then home for dinner and a few more hours shut eye. Bottom line: roughly eighteen hours work, six hours sleep. John is now a full time, successful real estate agent. You can visit his company's website at www.northwestrealtyconsultants.com and check out his bio at the "About Us" link. When I talk to him on the phone he always thanks me for providing him the key to a job he loves.

It's entirely possible that I am preaching to the choir with this sermon on hard work. If you're like many agents, your problem will be just the opposite. You will need to be dragged away from your desk at night and threatened with bodily harm by your broker or your mate to get you to take a vacation. You could even develop some detrimental personal habits. For example, I frequently encounter a friend of mine, one of the most successful agents in our community, hastily wolfing down a fat-laden hot bratwurst at the stand in front of our local supermarket. He figures he can't afford to take the time for a sit-down lunch. He likely still doesn't know how his lovely wife learned of his less than exemplary dietary practices.

■ *You need to be a smart worker.* Although hard work is essential, you are paid for the results you achieve, not the hours you put in. This means that you must spend your time doing those specific things that have the highest potential for paying off. It also means that you should organize your business affairs to be efficient and productive. The ability to "work smart" has little to do with native intelligence. Fortunately, for most of us, you do not need to be intellectually gifted to be a successful real estate agent. It is far more important to have common sense and knowledge of human nature.

It also will help if you have a creative streak in you. Let me give you an example. During one of my real estate licensing classes, we were discussing the topic of listings. One of my students inquired whether checking out obituaries in the local newspaper would be a good source of possible listings. The woman has done remarkably well in her real estate career. I frequently refer current license students to her for career counseling.

■ *You need to enjoy solving "people problems."* Excuse the old cliché, but you absolutely must be good at "working with people." You must enjoy the challenge of helping people to solve complex, often highly emotional, problems. Every transaction in which you are involved will have difficulties. Although you try to ensure that nothing serious goes wrong, you will sometimes need to deal with situations you could neither foresee nor forestall. Those who do well acknowledge the inevitability of obstacles and appreciate the fact that they will be paid in direct proportion to their ability to anticipate and resolve them. They are also able to detach themselves enough from the situation to maintain the objectivity that is vital to effective problem solving, and they seem to genuinely enjoy the challenge of handling situations that are particularly complex or sensitive.

■ *You need to be able to work with all kinds of people.* The longer you are in real estate and the more successful you are, the more you will be able to control your clientele. Your reputation will attract people who share your general business philosophy. But that will not be the case initially, so you must be prepared to work with all types of people. When I counsel prospective students for my real estate licensing classes, I typically ask what attracts them to the real estate profession. One of the most frequent responses is, "I like to work with people." What would probably be more accurate is, "I like to work with people I like." If you have never had the experience of dealing with the general public in a service or sales job, it will be difficult for you to fully appreciate how challenging it can be. Humility, an ability to keep things in perspective, and a healthy sense of humor are vital.

■ *You need to be a good listener.* If you are worried that you are not good with words, relax. The perception that the effective real estate salesperson is one who overwhelms the prospect with a steady stream of clever conversation is seriously inaccurate. Experienced brokers agree that the most important communication skill an agent can have is the ability to keep the mouth closed and listen—I mean really listen. There is a big difference between effective and truly empathetic listening (putting yourself in the position of the other person) and simply remaining silent while someone else is talking. If you are interested in a successful career, you must have this talent, or be willing to develop it.

■ *You need to be emotionally stable and mature.* You must be able to gain the trust and confidence of other people while maintaining your own sense of balance and fairness. More often than not, the people you encounter will be honest and forthright, but there will be enough exceptions to try the patience of the most steadfast and optimistic person. The purchase or sale of a home is typically the largest single monetary transaction that a buyer or seller will ever be involved in, and in dealing with such large sums of money, you may rustle up the dark and seamy side of an otherwise sweet and sunny disposition. You will need to be the emotional bellwether.

■ *You need to know your product.* You will not be expected to be an expert electrician, plumber, or carpenter, or to have an intimate knowledge of architecture or construction. But you do need to be familiar with the practical matters that are of primary concern to home owners. If you are a home owner yourself, that helps immensely. If not, I strongly recommend that you place "buy my own home" at the top of your list of economic goals. Whether you educate yourself through self-study, formal courses, or a combination of the two, you will list and sell more homes—and make more money—if you know your product and can talk intelligently about it. Something I've never been able to fully comprehend is that there is typically absolutely nothing about the product we sell (houses) in our pre-license classes. I was fortunate in that my broker was also a builder and we got many educational sessions on the basics of construction.

■ *You need to be convinced of your product's value.* For most people, home ownership remains the best investment they will ever make. It also fulfills a basic human need for shelter. Every survey ever done in the United States shows that more than 90 percent of renters would prefer to be home owners and are working toward that goal. Who could ask for a better product to sell? It is also hard to overstate the economic and social value that real estate ownership provides for the community and the nation. It should be easy to be enthusiastic about your product—but if you are *not,* that will become clear to those with whom you work. There are people who can sell anything, whether they believe in it or not, but most of us must first be honestly convinced ourselves.

■ *You need to know the territory.* For practical considerations, each real estate company has what it considers to be a normal geographic area of operation. In some small communities, it may be the whole town and the surrounding countryside. In large metropolitan areas, it might be a particular section of the city. Wherever you work, you must know intimately the structure of the community. You must be knowledgeable not only about residential housing but also about shopping centers, hospitals, crime rates, and schools. It may sound trite, but "you gotta know the territory."

There's also some practical considerations. I once had a very promising student who lived roughly 20 miles from the company with which she affiliated. It turned out to be just too much of a logistical challenge for her. When prospective clients would call her at home during other than normal business hours when she was in her office, it meant a thirty minute trip from home to meet them. It just turned out to be too time consuming and unpredictable. She became a licensed real estate assistant where she could depend upon a certain schedule.

■ *You need to be flexible.* The profession of real estate has undergone tremendous change in the past few years, and the future looks to be even more challenging. Part of the upheaval has been the result of technological advances and part has been caused by fundamental challenges to traditional ways of doing business. You must be willing to adapt to new technologies and to new methods of operation. It's not always easy.

■ *You have to persevere.* I am familiar with several successful agents in our local community (we're talking roughly $100,000 net income per year) who, if you asked me to name the character trait most responsible for their success, I would unhesitatingly respond: dogged perseverance. Yes, they work hard, they have integrity, and they relate well to people, but they would be the first to admit that they are not inherently gifted. I worked with them in the early 1980s when I was actively selling residential properties and the average price of homes in our community was in the $60,000 range. Here we are roughly thirty years later and the average price of a home is near $200,000. They stuck it out when mortgage interest rates hit double digits and qualified buyers were as rare as a sunny day in Oregon, and they are now reaping the harvest. The word *quit* is simply not in their vocabulary.

EXTERNAL FACTORS THAT INFLUENCE SUCCESS

The environment in which you work makes a big difference in how well you will do in real estate sales. Here are three factors that play an important role:

1.   The state of the nation's economy. Those who work in salaried jobs, particularly in the public sector, can generally expect a reasonably stable income history. In the business world it's different, and as an independent contractor in real estate, your income can fluctuate with the health of the economy in general and the housing market in particular. Of course, there are agents who continue to do well when things start to go sour (there are even special opportunities in such an environment), but the fact remains that there

is a relationship between your potential income and national economic factors.

2. The part of the country in which you work. It doesn't take any more ability or effort to sell a $300,000 house than it does to sell one that costs $150,000 (actually, often it takes far less), but you make roughly twice as much when you do. If you successfully sell residential real estate in an area where housing prices are traditionally high, you will earn a very impressive income. The obvious counterpoint is that it will cost you a lot to live there. Where you work will make a big difference in how much money you make. In most instances, you will be much better off working where you know the territory (and are known in the territory), but there are greener, high-paying pastures if you have wanderlust. For example, early in my Air Force career, I was stationed for a short time in New Rochelle, New York, which is in Westchester County. The last figures I saw on the median price of homes, they were around half a million dollars. The San Francisco Bay area is another area with high-priced neighborhoods. If you were to establish yourself as a successful real estate professional in either of these markets, or ones similar to them, you would definitely be in the high tax bracket category.

If you consider relocating, you need to be current on your demographics. Those areas with healthy growth tend to have robust real estate markets. Those with economic woes will have many sellers and few buyers—not a fun or profitable environment in which to work.

3. The quality of the company for which you work. Given the individualistic nature of the business, it is entirely possible for a strong agent to do well with almost any company. However, if the office you choose is vigorous and successful and has a genuine commitment to the training and development of new people, your income potential (not to mention your longevity) will be substantially enhanced. Activity generates activity, success is contagious, and positive role models will be there for you to observe and emulate. It doesn't necessarily have to be a large office or one that has been in business a long time, but when you are new and striving mightily for direction and business contacts, it helps greatly to be part of an energetic and caring brokerage.

HOW MUCH MONEY CAN YOU MAKE SELLING REAL ESTATE?

There are few fields in which people doing basically the same work earn such widely divergent incomes. The saying in real estate is that "20 percent of the agents do 80 percent of the business." That's really a derivative of an observation made a couple of centuries ago by an Italian scholar to describe distribution of wealth in nations. Give or take a few percentage points (some would say "10 percent of the agents do 90 percent of the business" would be more accurate), the generalization is essentially correct. A minority of agents do extremely well, during the best of times and during the worst of times. The idea, of course, is to be among that 20 (or ten) percent. If you are right for the job, if you are willing to work, and if you persevere, it is an entirely realistic and achievable goal.

When you hear that your earnings potential in real estate is unlimited, it's not all hype. The elite among the top producers earn whopping incomes. When NAR did a study a couple of years ago of what they defined as "top producers" it revealed they had a median income of $177,400. That means some earn several hundred thousand per year, and adjust that figure for the inflation and the hot nature of the real estate market in the ensuing years. But super achievers aside for a moment, let's consider some numbers about average earnings. The best income information is published periodically by the National Association of Realtors. Their most recent information revealed that median (half above and half below) gross income for all full-time Realtor salespersons was $37,600—hardly the stuff of which lifestyles of the rich and famous are made, particularly since we're talking gross, not net. And I hope you're sitting down for this one. The median income for first year Realtors over the years has averaged out at just about minimum wage.

A closer look suggests that the news is not all bad. First, when you use a median income figure it means that half make less than that and half make more. Further, those in the top 20 percent (the ones doing 80 percent of the business) earn a very decent income. Second, it is almost certain that many who say they are full-time are really not in spirit and motivation. For example, in many households the money earned in real estate is a second income. Although the spouse earning it may work hard, the pressure to produce is not the same as if a family-supporting wage had to be earned. Some retirees with incomes from their previous professions also fit this category. Rest assured that if real estate provided their only source of income, most would earn a lot more at it.

We have to acknowledge, however, that many people enter real estate sales who are simply not suited for it. They earn an embarrassingly low income, become discouraged, and quit. In addition, a small minority apparently looks upon real estate as a way to earn a lot of money in a glamorous job without much effort. They're history in a hurry. Of course, it is disheartening that a large number of people are in real estate sales who should not be. Viewed selfishly, however, if you *are* suited for the profession you may conclude that it is to your distinct advantage to compete in such an environment.

How much can *you* make your first year? It's probable that it will take about six months for you to hit the break-even point—where your income is paying for your expenses—so we'll allow that time as a "break-in" period.

From that point on, if you are temperamentally suited for a real estate career, have affiliated with an active company, and approach your job in a businesslike and entrepreneurial manner, you can far exceed normal income expectations. For someone with the right qualities and attitudes, earning between $35,000 and $45,000 net would not be an unrealistic first-year expectation.

Not spectacular, but comparable to entry-level jobs in some very reputable professions. If you have been successful in another field and have extensive local contacts, you should be able to earn substantially more, again allowing for break-in. As a successful agent, the longer you stay in the business, the more money you can anticipate earning, because your referrals will increase, your contacts will expand, and you will be able to better identify where to direct your efforts to get results.

Finally, if you become established in one of the areas of the country with high housing costs, you can upgrade all my estimates dramatically. For example, I sold real estate in a small university town in Oregon where housing costs at the time were very modest. In my first year, after that initial training and shake-down period, I earned about what a professor at a mid size college would make. If I had sold exactly the same number of comparable properties in, let's say, the San Francisco Bay area, I would have made about what the president of the college would have earned. My income increased each year.

THE PART-TIME OPTION

For those who wish to choose a middle path and enter real estate part-time, there are some special considerations. First, it will be somewhat more difficult to find a broker with whom to affiliate, since many do not accept agents who are not prepared to work full-time. The brokers' rationale seems to be that the field is complex and demands total attention. Further, many brokers believe that they invite potential legal difficulties by having part-time agents, since they fear that those who do not constantly stay in touch with the marketplace are more likely to overlook legal requirements.

However, many brokers throughout the country accept part-time salespeople. Thirty six percent of all Realtors classify themselves as part-time, meaning they work 39 hours a week or less. Among non-Realtors, the figure is probably higher than that. Many have worked out satisfactory relationships by carefully defining their roles and making themselves available on a predictable, but reduced, schedule. I had one broker tell me, "I've had a few part-time agents who accomplished more in an abbreviated work week than some of my full-time people."

There are even some spectacular part-time success stories. While still on active duty with the U.S. Air Force, Ron Rush reportedly closed more than $7 million in transactions one year while working as a part-time agent with Long & Foster Realtors in Fairfax, Virginia. He really got hot after he retired from the Air Force and started selling full-time. He's still with Long & Foster and has his two sons working with him on the Ron Rush team. You can check out his operation at www. ronrushteam.com. The last time I visited the site Ron's team had over a hundred listings with an asking price of over a million on two of them.

Despite such impressive examples, it would be unwise to become lured by the work-part-time-and-make-big-money pitch. It just doesn't usually work out that way. As should be expected, those who work an abbreviated schedule earn substantially less, on the average, than their full-time counterparts. Of course, that is fine if it fits your monetary and personal goals.

DECISION TIME

Is real estate for you? If you truly enjoy solving people problems, if you like running your own affairs, if you are genuinely excited about having the amount of money you make directly related to how hard and how creatively you work, and if you're ready, willing, and able to withstand those predictably lean first six months or so, then the answer is yes. I suspect that for many of you, it is not a case of, "Is it for me?" but rather, "How do I get started?" Step one is to get your license.

2

Getting Your License

Fun Or Folly: Your Choice

Getting your real estate salesperson's license can be either an invigorating experience that you will recall fondly for as long as you are in the profession or a stupefying, mind-numbing bore. The difference will depend not as much on the particular licensing program you chose as on your attitude toward that program.

Some look upon the whole process as a necessary evil, to be concluded with as little pain, strain, and expense as possible. That's unfortunate, because it is incontestably the most important step you will take in pursuing your real estate career. No matter how talented you may be, no matter how enthusiastic you might be, no matter what your potential, you must meet this challenge to enter the field.

My objective in this chapter is to help you understand the testing and licensing procedure, to assist you in selecting the program that best fits your needs and your personality, to suggest appropriate study techniques, and to encourage you to participate in the entire process in a way that will help you to get the most out of it.

REQUIREMENTS OF INDIVIDUAL STATES

In all fifty states and the District of Columbia, you must have a license issued by the state (or the District) before you can engage in professional real estate activity. That's a broad term that most states define to include anything from selling real estate to counseling—presuming you do it with the expectation of being compensated. You need to determine the requirements of the state in which you wish to work, because there are substantial differences. All require the completion of specific course work, but there are typically a variety of educational options available. Some have provisions for a waiver of course requirements for those with special backgrounds. *All* require that you pass a written, objective test (multiple choice). Sorry, sociology majors, no essay questions. There is an office in each state that supervises all real estate activity, including licensing. I have included a list of these with contact information in Appendix B.

Please understand that the states take their real estate licensing and testing responsibilities *very* seriously. It is definitely not a fill-in-the-square type of operation. Even if you have a Ph.D. in real estate from Prestige U., you must take, and pass, the test to sell real estate. Just to motivate you, let me pass on some information that's contained in the annual *Digest of Real Estate License Laws* published by the Association of Real Estate License Law Officials (ARELLO). (See "Real Estate Industry Statistics and History" in Appendix C.) I've followed the trends in licensing pass rates, and they've been as low as 30 percent in some states in some years! Oregon is more typical, in that the pass rate has stayed at approximately 75 percent. That still means that roughly a quarter of the people taking the exam fail! Retesting is possible, but it would clearly be preferable to recognize the magnitude of the challenge early and prepare accordingly.

THE NATURE OF THE TESTS

Some states prepare their own tests, whereas others use national testing services. There is a great deal of similarity among all of them in terms of test construction and subject matter. All have two major parts: one covering national material and one dealing with subject matter related specifically to the state. A certain percent of the entire test requires arithmetic computations. The exact percentage varies. These questions are typically scattered throughout the test. To set your mind at ease, if you've had high school algebra you've got the basics needed to meet this challenge. (I offer further guidance on handling the math in this chapter's section on study techniques.) The state portion contains material that pertains to its specific laws, rules, regulations, and procedures. It is not unusual for the failure rate of the state section to be higher than that for the national, since the material is typically very specific and sometimes rather obscure. My advice, therefore, is to bear down hard there, since you need to pass both portions.

YOUR STUDY OPTIONS

When I was studying for my salesperson license, our state used a national testing service. I found that its *Applicant's Bulletin* was very useful in structuring my own self-study program to supplement my formal training. A recent review of current material from the various testing services and states convinced me that this is still the case. I strongly recommend, therefore, that you secure everything available. Some provide practice tests, for which there is a charge. Your state real estate agency will have contact information, including the testing service web site, if applicable. Oregon may be setting a trend, in that they sell a *Question and Answer* book that contains more than three thousand questions from its official test bank (there are plenty more in their test bank that they don't provide).

A variety of alternatives will be available to you which will satisfy your pre-license educational requirements. Your best bet is log on to your State Real Estate Agency's official web site. There will be information on license requirements and approved educational providers. As you explore your options you're likely to find you can attend a live classroom program, sign up for a self study course by using a handy little compact disk (with additional print material), or do it all on line. One web site you may wish to visit is www. RealtyU.com. It's the official web site of Realty U, the largest national organization of real estate educational providers with over 200 real estate schools nationwide in 42 states.

Almost all community colleges and many four-year institutions offer courses in real estate. You need to investigate to determine the actual relationship of each to the state licensing requirements. Many institutions have programs tailored to satisfy state standards and prepare students for the exam. They might even be offered in the evenings to permit maximum community participation. These courses may be taught by permanent members of the faculty or by active real estate professionals with acceptable academic credentials.

As real estate has become increasingly popular as a profession, a whole industry of private real estate schools has developed. Some are educational franchises, while others are independent activities run by educators, attorneys, real estate brokers, or real estate companies themselves. Many are small mom-and-pop operations, while others are large complex businesses. These private schools are typically very closely monitored by the real estate regulatory agency, both as to course content and instructor qualifications. As private businesses, the schools must keep informed about what is going on in the field in order to survive. In most cases, they have a neatly packaged and lively program, taught by highly qualified instructors, often in modern facilities. You will also likely have the option of completing the program completely on your own in a self study program. Quality and cost vary, however, so it's smart to check them out thoroughly before you commit yourself.

You can do some investigation over the telephone. Call the sales managers at several local real estate companies and explain that you are planning to enter real estate and would appreciate advice concerning the best way to study for your license, including an assessment of specific local options. You will most likely get a helpful, enthusiastic response, for brokers naturally see prospective licensees as the prime source of new agents. At this point, don't become caught up too much in the quality of various real estate companies, because it will all be academic if you don't pass the test. Your personal interviews will come after you clear your first hurdle—getting your license.

In some states, it is permissible for real estate brokerages to run their own real estate licensing schools. Some even offer tuition assistance (or even free tuition) if you will commit to come to work at that brokerage after passing the exam. Some people have criticized that practice, because they believe that the major motivation of the school is to provide a recruitment pool of new agents for the brokerage. Keep an open mind if that option is available to you. I recommend that you judge the schools based upon the quality of the instruction you believe you are likely to receive, rather than any monetary incentive.

If you have tentatively decided to go into real estate but still have some unresolved doubts, you may want to test the waters by enrolling in a single course at a local community college or take a specific segment of a real estate school's curriculum, if that's possible. A taste of real estate practices, real estate law, or real estate finance might help you to decide. In my own case, I took a course in real estate practices at the local community college while I was still on active duty with the Air Force. The instructor was an active local broker. He did an excellent job of teaching the material, and I also learned about practical job-related matters. After that, I enrolled in a private real estate school taught by an attorney for my formal license training.

Programmed learning courses in real estate are becoming popular, and many have enjoyed a high degree of success, as measured by the pass rate of their students. They come in a variety of formats from audiotapes to videos to computer programs. There are even distance learning programs now with the advent of computer technology. All these types of courses offer flexibility in scheduling and permit you to work at your own pace. They also eliminate one of the most troublesome aspects of classroom teaching: the inordinate amount of time often spent on tangential discussions. These courses might be ideal for you, particularly if you have a considerable amount of self-discipline and willpower. For other people, the stimulus of a classroom situation as well as the built-in demands of a regularly scheduled class meeting might prove to be more practical. You should also be aware that in some states it is permissible for individuals who have no real estate experience themselves to operate real estate licensing schools that offer programmed instruction. That would make it difficult to receive real-time answers to your questions as you proceed through your course work.

YOUR IMMEDIATE GOAL: PASS THE TEST!

Regardless of the choice you make, you need to reach peace with yourself on one important matter: You will study theoretical material that you will almost certainly never use in your active real estate career, while you will not cover a great deal of specific matters that you could use. A common sentiment among my survey participants was that licensing courses often fell short in providing immediately useful information. About 60 percent of the respondents felt that *inadequate preparation in practical real estate matters during pre license activities* was *very important* or *important* in explaining high attrition. This comment by a broker-builder from Michigan was typical: "Schools should instruct people on how to conduct their business as well as how to pass the examination. Too many newcomers simply do not know the mechanics of a real estate transaction."

I do not make this point to denigrate the quality of the instruction in real estate licensing programs. In both private real estate schools and college classrooms, you will frequently find dedicated instructors who teach not only the theoretical material thoroughly but also relate it to "real world" real estate. But you should be prepared for some disparity between what you must know to pass the licensing test and what you need to know to succeed in the profession.

It will be much better for your mental health and peace of mind if you do not fight the problem. The content of these programs is typically tightly controlled by state regulatory agencies. The schools can teach only what they are told to teach, so if you don't like the message, don't fuss at the messenger. The theoretical background will give you a better perspective of the general field and confidence in your role as a professional in it. Even if that were not true, you have to master the material to pass the test, and you have to pass the test to get the license. If you understand that, and proceed accordingly, you will be less likely to share the frustrations of the survey respondent who complained, "Real estate school was an exercise in futility. No nuts and bolts!" If it is any consolation to you, students of law and medicine, and every other known profession, have always had the same kind of complaints. These requirements of dubious utility are known as rites of passage, so take a deep breath, swallow hard, and press on.

In teaching my real estate licensing classes I rely somewhat on my military background and we go through a little ritual early in the course. It's called, "smile, click your heels, and salute." That's what we do in unison when we get bogged down on learning material we all recognize we'll likely never need in the real world of real estate.

STUDY TECHNIQUES: BACK TO BASICS

If you have been away from the books for a few years, don't worry. Many people with *very* average academic aptitudes pass the real estate test every year. Taken one small bite at a time, and presuming a fair amount of grit and gizzard on your part, it will not be too difficult. On the other hand, I have known people with advanced degrees who have failed the exam, at least the first time. Knowledge of quantum physics won't help you one bit in answering questions about the Federal Fair Housing Law. If you have a study system that works for you, then use it. But if you don't have a system, or if it has been a while, consider these suggestions:

■ *A few hours of study each day is preferable to longer, infrequent sessions.* Find a quiet place that is conducive to study—preferably somewhere *without* a TV, radio, stereo, or bed. If you are a morning person, two hours of study before the rest of the household starts rustling about will be better than twice that amount of time later. Some people concentrate better and accomplish more late at night, so do whatever works best for you.

■ *I have found that group study sessions can be very productive if they're properly organized.* They will be most helpful if the number of participants is kept comparatively small and everyone is prepared to contribute. What I've found as an instructor is that I get valuable feedback as a result of these sessions, since quite frequently it will become apparent that something we've covered was not clear to the class.

■ *An individual study technique that has proved to be successful for some people involves preparing sample test questions.* From using the course material and study guides, you will quickly become familiar with the format of exam questions. (For ease of scoring, questions are of fairly standard construction.) As a culmination of your study efforts and in preparation for the test itself, you might try your hand at preparing some questions on your own. You will be surprised at how well you must understand the material to be able to write questions about it. If you find yourself becoming bogged down with the process, rather than the material, switch to a more traditional approach.

■ *There is one area of real estate licensing preparation that strikes terror into the hearts of many: mathematics.* For some people, the fear of anything to do with numbers induces an emotional and mental paralysis. Let's face it: math *is* a requirement, and it *is* difficult for some people. But it is manageable. Here is a suggestion. First, find out exactly what your math skills are. You may know a great deal more than you give yourself credit for. On the other hand, your fears may be well founded. You can get a copy of a basic real estate text or a real estate math book at the local library or bookstore (see Appendix C for suggested titles). Almost all will have enough information in them to let you know exactly where you stand in math. If you need to, you can then devise a study plan to bring yourself up to speed.

■ *You also need to become adept at using a handheld calculator.* It is impractical to consider taking real estate licensing courses without that skill, even if you use it only for basic arithmetic functions. It is even more impractical to think you could compete effectively as a sales agent without knowing how to do things such as computing monthly mortgage payments on a home loan, for example. There are several moderately priced instruments on the market. You can learn to operate a calculator with only a moderate amount of self-study, using nothing more than the manufacturer's instruction manual. Additional study, individual or formal, will be time well spent.

SELF-STUDY: PROCEED WITH A PLAN

In the event you decide to pursue a study program on your own, either as a self-directed effort in preparation for the licensing examination (if permitted by your state) or simply to supplement the instruction you get in a formal program, you will find a list of reference books in Appendix C. I have indicated which ones are the basic, standard texts that are in widespread use. I've used several of them in teaching real estate myself, and have reviewed most of the others in conjunction with my job as book review editor for *The Real Estate Professional* magazine. There is a marked similarity in basic content among the books. If you are merely browsing to decide whether to start the whole process or not, some time spent with one of these books will give you a good idea of what to expect in the classroom.

There are a handful of books that I would like to suggest to you as being particularly helpful. One is *Modern Real Estate Practice* (see Appendix C under "Principles and Practice"). It's in its seventeenth edition and gives a comprehensive overview of the material ordinarily covered on the national portion of all exams. I've used it, and previous editions, for over a decade, and student response has been very positive. You will also find an abundance of actual practice exam questions in it. Another excellent basic reference is *Real Estate Principles* by Charles Jacobus, a Texas attorney and real estate educator. There are also a number of solid real estate licensing exam guides. Among those I've personally used and can highly recommend are *Real Estate License Exams for Dummies* by John Yoegel and *Questions and Answers to Help You Pass the Real Estate Exam* by John Reilly and Paige Bovee Vitousek (see Appendix C under

"Examination Preparation Guides"). *The Language of Real Estate* by John Reilly, an attorney/real estate broker with an ability to communicate, is the definitive basic real estate reference book (see "Real Estate Reference" in Appendix C). I refer to it more than any other book in teaching my real estate class.

No self-study program would be complete without coverage of state rules and regulations. Your state agency can provide study references. Often, there are commercial guides available.

WE'RE TALKING "TOTAL IMMERSION"

You will invest a great deal of time and effort, not to mention a fair amount of money, in your license program. In a sense you will be learning a completely new language. The phrase I mention frequently throughout my licensing class is "total immersion". That's what it will take to accomplish your goal. What I've also found is that those students who approach the course work seriously and who take the exam immediately after they finish almost always pass on their first effort. I attribute that not only to their attitude and work ethic, but the fact that much of the material is so unique that it will rapidly evaporate from your memory cells.

IF AT FIRST. . . .

It is not unusual for some people who turn out to be successful real estate professionals to have trouble passing the licensing examination. If you fail on the first try, don't get discouraged, get determined. Retrench and try again. Sit down in a brainstorming session with other classmates who took the test with you and try to recall as many specific questions as you can. Then review your course notes and isolate the areas that caused you difficulty. Bear down on those and give it another shot—preferably while the information is still fresh in your mind.

BUT FIRST, A HOMEWORK ASSIGNMENT!

Early in my Air Force career I attended the first level of professional education, called Squadron Officers' School. It was a 13 week course composed both of academics and leadership training. On our first day the entire class of roughly 800 students sat in a large auditorium and took what was labeled a "Pre Test". It was actually the final written exam from the preceding class. Of course, we were bewildered and clueless as to how to answer the endless pages of objective test questions. We were told that the objective was to give us an overview of what to expect in the ensuing academic program. It was really quite effective. I recall that as the class proceeded I kept recalling questions that had been asked and relating them to material we were studying. So, for you I've prepared a Pre Test. Your home work is to go to Appendix D and take the objective exam. Answers are provided, but check them out after you've done the exam. These questions are from the State of Oregon's official test bank. Oregon is the only state that actually publishes a Question and Answer Book with hundreds of questions that are used on the licensing exam. Of course there are hundreds of others that are not included. I use the book extensively in teaching my real estate class and have been given the OK by the folks at the Oregon Real Estate Agency to include a sample of them for your Pre Test. Good luck!

THE LIGHT AT THE END OF THE TUNNEL

If you pursue your goal with a serious purpose and persevere, you will enjoy the academic program, make some good friends and great contacts, and pass the test. When the excitement of receiving the good news subsides (in many jurisdictions you get the results immediately after completing the exam on a computer), you will be ready to step out into the glare of the "real world." How well you actually do in it will be greatly influenced by the quality of the company with which you affiliate.

3

Choosing a Company

For Better or Worse, for Richer or Poorer . . .

Deciding where you are going to "hang your license" may not be *as* important as selecting a mate, but it ranks right up there. If you work in an environment in which you are comfortable and for a broker with whom you are compatible, you are likely to have a long, happy, and prosperous career there. If you make a hasty emotional choice, it could mean an early split because of irreconcilable differences. The key is to research carefully and decide ahead of time what it is you are looking for.

First, don't worry about getting a job in real estate once you get your license. The personnel situation is volatile, so most companies are constantly recruiting. However, there are wide differences among offices in structure, operation, and philosophy, and the most successful are, of course, the most sought after. Your goal is basic—to find the company and broker with whom you would like to affiliate and who in turn wants you. How do you begin? Whom do you see? What questions do you ask?

JUDGE AND BE JUDGED

Your first step is to package your most important product—the one and only you—in the best possible way. The outcome you want to achieve is to have every broker in town anxious to have you join the team. Don't be surprised if that happens. If you come across as someone who is going to succeed in real estate, brokers will be looking at you, but they'll be seeing dollar signs, because if you make money they make money.

I had a boss in the Air Force once whose advice to junior officers who wanted to become senior officers was, "Keep your mouth shut and your shoes shined." He was half right. Appearances do count, and you need to put your best foot forward (with a shined shoe on it). You will also want to be dressed in neat, conservative business clothes and drive up in a freshly washed car. If it has been some time since you've interviewed for a job (or if you never have), do a little research on how to prepare a resume and how to handle interviews.

And here's a quick personal note. Grooming standards among the different generations clearly vary. For example, in wandering around the campus of a nearby major university, I have observed that it is not unusual for young men to let their hair grow long, sport a scruffy beard, and wear clothing that has apparently not been pressed or cleaned for a very long time. While that may be accepted practice in peer circles, be advised that many people, fair or not, will be turned off and simply not do business with people whose personal appearance bothers them. I must admit that I've had students in my real estate classes to whom I would have loved to give this guidance, but simply couldn't work up the courage. Hope they're reading this.

When interviewing, put yourself in the position of the person on the other side of the desk and try to see yourself as others see you. Real estate brokers are looking for results-oriented individualists who can also function effectively as team players. Yes, it would be appropriate to prepare a resume. It need not be elaborate, but it should be typed and free of errors. One page is long enough. There's plenty of literature on how to prepare resumes, and several easily followed computer software programs are available.

When you are ready to be judged, you can start doing some judging of your own. As you read what follows, I think it only fair to point out that if you follow my advice, you will be in a distinct minority. Few other fledgling real estate agents who are looking for that first broker with whom to affiliate will conduct their search as seriously and conscientiously as you conduct yours. From your standpoint, I would think that would be a *very* encouraging sign.

STARTING YOUR SEARCH

You can learn a lot about a company on the basis of some simple observations. Assume you are a buyer from out of town. Drive around the community and inspect the real estate offices from the outside. Ask these questions about each: Does it present the type of appearance that would motivate you to stop and do business? Is it conveniently located and is there ample room to park? On the inside, does the office present an orderly, pleasing appearance, and does it have the look of a successful business operation? That is the way potential clients and customers will evaluate the firm, so it is critical that you develop that perspective. Second, review the company's print advertising. You can get a good feel for the broker's business philosophy by the tone. Would you feel comfortable having your name listed in the advertisements as an agent? Many brokerages prominently feature the sales staff in their advertisements, including pictures and features such as "Our agent of the week." Others rarely mention the names of the agents.

Next, visit the web sites of various brokerages. Are they easy to navigate? Do they have up-to-date information about various properties, including those of other brokerages? Local rules differ on this, but the trend is clearly to give consumers the information they want, as opposed to giving them just enough to motivate them to call the office. Is their community information current? School information is particularly critical to many buyers. Almost all company web sites will have an "Our Agents" link. How are these presented? Are there individual pictures with well written bios? Incidentally, when you have your picture taken for promotional purposes, have it done by a professional. People will be forming first impressions based on it. With each passing year, the Internet will become more important in the marketing of real estate, so you will want to affiliate with a broker who is on the cutting edge, rather than one who is merely going through the motions.

TALK IS CHEAP—AND HELPFUL

The next step is to talk to people, the more the better. Start by talking to active agents in different companies—not the supervising broker at this point, but someone who is "in the trenches" doing the same basic things you will be doing. It helps if you already have some contacts, but that isn't really necessary. On several occasions, people called our office and asked if it would be possible to meet with an agent to discuss a possible career in real estate. You will likely meet with an agent who is successful, enthusiastic, and articulate. These informal, open exchanges with a working professional will be invaluable to you. The direct, honest approach is best. Tell her you have passed your real estate exam and that you are looking for a broker with whom to affiliate. Plan to spend only about twenty to thirty minutes in this meeting, for a good agent's time is valuable. Find out which companies, other than hers, she considers the best in town. If you hear the same two or three mentioned in several interviews, you will know that they enjoy a favorable reputation among those who know them best—their competitors.

At some point in your investigative process, you will also want to talk to people outside of real estate who can give you an idea of the reputation of the various companies within the community. This can be a little awkward because they might be reluctant to express an adverse opinion, but you will be able to learn as much by what they don't say as what they do. If possible, talk to local attorneys who specialize in real estate, real estate loan officers at banks and savings and loans, officers at local escrow and title companies, and insurance agents. They know which of the local agencies are the most respected. Ask them whom they would go to work for if they were getting into real estate sales.

Finally, you will need to talk with the principal broker, for that is the person under whose supervision you will actually work, and who decides how the company will operate. In some instances, the broker has an ownership interest. Among NAR brokers, for example, almost half have some type of ownership interest in the company with which they are affiliated, with over a quarter of them as sole owners. Brokers vary in managerial style just as salespeople vary in selling style. Some are detail-oriented people who also sell, while others are strictly "big picture" managers. Some have characters that are, as they say, above reproach. Others have characters that are very definitely reproachable. It would be hard to overstate the importance of working with a broker with whom you can develop personal and professional compatibility. On occasion former students of mine, whom I thought would unquestionably succeed big time in real estate, get off to a fast start but then after about a year become disillusioned and drop out of the profession altogether or change offices. When possible, I follow up to see whether I can determine the reason. A recurrent theme is, "I just couldn't work for that broker—his business philosophy and mine were just not compatible."

How many companies should you contact? Talk to as many as is practical, but try for a minimum of three or four. It will be tempting to stop your search if you encounter a company with which you think you would like to affiliate and who is definitely interested in you. That could be a serious mistake. The next one on your list might be an even better choice.

As you interview have specific questions in mind and be prepared to take notes, for after several meetings things will begin to blur. Figure 3-1 is a sample checklist that you can adapt to your own situation. If you talk to a sales agent in the company, do not assume that the answers you get commit the company. That's not likely to be a problem if you are dealing with an agency with a good internal system of communication, but remember that the broker is the boss and sets policy.

There's another outcome you want to achieve as a result of your interviews. You can obviously go to work for only one broker, but you will be working on cooperative transactions with all of them at some time in the future. In real estate, unlike most other professions, you have to be able to work in harmony with your fiercest competitors. You therefore certainly don't wish to cause any hard feelings when you go through your interview process. A friendly note to the brokers you did not select thanking them for their time and indicating you look forward to working with them in the future would be appropriate.

Don't be surprised, and don't take it personally, if you occasionally en-

Figure 3-1. Checklist for evaluating a real estate firm.

Company _____

Broker _____

1. *Before the interviews.*
   A. Drive by the office.
      (1) Convenient location? _____
      (2) Ample parking? _____
      (3) Attractive exterior? _____
   B. Visit the office.
      (1) Businesslike atmosphere? _____
      (2) Diverse, high-quality sales staff? _____
   C. Tone, quality, and quantity of ads? _____
   D. Quality of Web site? Individual agent links? _____
2. *Interview with the active agent.*
   A. General guidance offered. _____
      _____
   B. Comments about other companies. _____
3. *Interview with the broker.*
   A. Share of market/range of agent incomes. _____
      _____
   B. Written office instructions? Clear? Comprehensive? _____
      _____
   C. Independent contractor or employee? Copy of contract? ____
   D. Training program? Length? _____
   E. Multiple Listing Service (MLS) membership? _____
   F. Support facilities? _____
   G. Realtor affiliation? _____
   H. Office ethics? _____
   I. Commission splits? _____
   J. Errors and omissions insurance? _____
   K. Obligations to firm? _____
   L. Benefits? _____
   M. Special functions (property management, escrow, building)? ____
   N. Relocation operation? _____
   O. Part-time option? _____
4. *Expenses (indicate one time or periodic).*
   A. Office start up fees $ _____
   B. New license $ _____
   C. Realtor dues $ _____
   D. Lockbox key fee $ _____
   E. Start up training $ _____
   F. Business cards $ _____
   G. Multiple listing service $ _____
   H. Other. _____
5. *Overall impressions and remarks.* _____
   _____
   _____
   _____

counter brokers who treat you rather brusquely when you make your initial contact. For example, there are occasions in which I will contact several local brokers on behalf of students of mine who might have either very special talents or a unique set of circumstances to inquire as to the possibility of a job interview. "No, we simply don't have any empty desks so I really don't even want to talk to any prospective agents" is the response I once got when engaged in such a mission. Oh, right. It's as if you were the coach of a basketball team and Kobe Bryant called asking for a job interview, but you said, "Sorry, Kobe, I'd love to chat, but we don't have an empty locker right now."

On the other hand, when you get an interview, and when you come across as a desirable possible addition to the team, here's a final word of friendly caution about talking to successful real estate salespeople and brokers. They are incurable optimists and are simply not wired to say anything negative about the profession. Most are masters at the art of putting the best face on things. Be an attentive and discriminating listener.

FACTORS TO CONSIDER WHEN CHOOSING A COMPANY

There are a number of important factors that you should take into account as you decide where you'll best fit in and where you'll be the most successful. These are the most critical:

■ *Local Market Share and Agent Income.* Most brokers maintain a detailed accounting of how they are doing in relationship to their competition. They also know how much each sales agent in their organization is earning now, and how much each earned in past years. Don't expect to be given company secrets or to be told exactly what each person in the office is making, but it is not unreasonable to anticipate being told how the company stacks up in the marketplace and the general range of agent incomes.

■ *Composition and Quality of Sales Staff.* If practical, most brokers try to maintain a mix of ages, races, sexes, and experience levels among their staff. Diversity is an advantage, for you want exposure to as many ideas and perspectives as possible. If the company is large and successful, it is likely that some of the more experienced agents specialize in areas like investments, exchanging, or rural and farm property. This is an ideal environment. Nothing is more stimulating and educational than being exposed to a variety of transactions actually being consummated in the marketplace. Another definite plus is that the first time you encounter an area that's new to you, you're likely to have someone in the office who will be able to offer guidance and support.

Some brokers who run small offices make up for a lack of numbers by injecting their own personality, background, and expertise through a hands-on managerial style, particularly with new agents in need of guidance, direction, and encouragement.

Pay attention, too, to the ability of the office secretary or office manager. If you are treated with courtesy, good cheer, and efficiency when arranging for your interview, your clients will most likely receive the same kind of welcome. On the other hand . . .

One sign of how well an office is managed is the length of employment of the sales staff. Large office or small, if there has been an extremely high turnover rate, be cautious. There may be a logical explanation, but it pays to investigate.

■ *Recruiting and Retention Philosophy.* A few brokers subscribe to the "cannon fodder" method of recruiting. They enlist more salespeople than they can reasonably expect to accommodate, train them intensely in the art of pressure selling, send them into battle, and keep the occasional survivor. One of my survey participants called these firms "body shops." Unless you are fully combat ready, you are well advised to avoid them.

A veteran broker explained his personal recruiting and retention philosophy to me this way: "Some real estate companies will bring aboard ten new agents, throw them all hard against the wall, and keep the one who sticks. We screen carefully, select one, and keep throwing her against the wall *until* she sticks."

■ *Office Esprit de Corps.* This could be tough for you to judge when you're doing your company research, but here's a quick personal observation that illustrates my point. Having taught real estate licensing at a nearby community college for several years, I have active agents in just about every real estate brokerage in the local area and nearby communities. I visit the different offices on occasion for various purposes. Recently I was in the local Kellar-Williams office talking to their Director of Training, Trish Reinert. All of a sudden I heard cheering that sounded like a high school football crowd. Trish jumped up and excused herself. When she returned I asked her what was going on. "Oh, when any of our agents gets a listing or makes a sale we all gather and celebrate", she replied. I was impressed.

■ *Agent Status (Independent Contractor or Employee?).* Well over 90 percent of all Realtor salespersons are classified as independent contractors, and that's probably typical of the entire industry. There are considerable advantages to both the company and to you in such an arrangement. For the company it means a simpler accounting and tax procedure, and it is much less costly because they don't have to contribute to things such as Social Security. For you, it means that you basically operate your own business within the framework of the company, and under the supervision of the broker. The advice I give my licensing students is this: As you are getting started in the business take all the assistance the brokerage provides. Get to the office early, attend all training sessions, volunteer for open houses, floor duty, and other activities that will put you in contact with potential customers. In other words, act like an employee until you attain the skill levels to operate as an independent contractor.

Wherever you work, and whatever your status, you will sign a contract (ordinarily a standard form) that specifies your legal classification and your obligations, as well as those of your broker. Ask for a copy to read over and study in advance.

■ *Training Programs.* These vary markedly among companies. In some agencies, training consists of giving you work space, a telephone, and a pat on the back (pat optional). In others, you must attend company seminars on listing, selling, and related matters before you can face a prospect alone. There could even be a fee associated with the training. If you join a national franchise or a very large independent, you can count on attending a structured, standardized orientation program, probably at some type of training center. Some time ago, I reviewed a product developed by one of the nation's largest franchise companies for training their new agents. They put their entire training program on one dinky little CD-ROM! Even with such a convenient format, there's still need for personal interaction, but you are likely to encounter more and more of these high-tech training products that puts the primary responsibility on you—the newcomer. If the company has some type of formal training course, consider it an asset. You might not wish to use all of the material you encounter, but it is good to have as many choices as possible. There is also a possibility that there may be a charge for the initial training program, depending on how complex and extensive it is. A student of mine, who interviewed with a national franchise brokerage that ostensibly charged for their training, was informed that in her case it would be "waived" if she decided to come to work with them.

■ *Support Facilities.* There will likely be written office procedures that describe what the broker provides and what you provide. Typically, you will get a work space, a telephone, and some secretarial support, although polices vary widely. For the most part, you will be required to pay for all expenses that relate to your specific activities, such as long distance telephone calls, postage, business cards, and other personal promotional material.

Several philosophies prevail relative to office planning. One is that agents' desks should be grouped together in large open spaces. The rationale is that this arrangement enhances the communicative process. Another view is that private offices are the most desirable. A third holds that having individual desks in a common area, with private rooms available for special occasional use, is the best. Don't be disappointed if you are given less than an executive suite when you start. You may even be required to share a desk with another agent. In my own case, I was given a small desk near the rear exit, next to the Coke machine. That didn't do much to boost my ego, but then again, there was nowhere to go but up (or out the back door). Be patient. If there is a particular office or desk you have your eye on, you may inherit it— if you stay around long enough and prove your mettle. Yes, I eventually got a much nicer office (as a matter of fact, the nicest one).

■ *Multiple Listing Service (MLS) Membership.* MLS is a cooperative arrangement in which member agencies make their listings available to all subscriber companies in their area. It is a well-developed, tightly controlled marketing system. As a member agent, you have use of the lockbox system most MLSs employ, thereby assuring you of convenient entry to most listed properties. I don't know of any MLS that is not now computerized. That means you have convenient access to all listing information. Generally, up-dates are provided on a daily basis. It is hard to conceive of any circumstance in which you would be better off working in an office that was not a sub-scriber to MLS, or a comparable service. You will need all the help you can get, and having ready-made access to hundreds of listings is about as helpful as anything you could devise. It also gets your own listings immediate, max-imum exposure.

■ *Realtor Affiliation.* As I pointed out in the preface, slightly less than half of all real estate licensees in the United States are Realtors. They are, however, the dominant organizational force in the real estate profession. Some seg-ments of the public erroneously think that "Realtor" is synonymous with "real estate agent," much to the understandable dismay of Realtors. An office may not use the logo or the term in advertising unless all those in the organi-zation have some form of Realtor membership. The association has a compre-hensive code of ethics that all members agree to follow, and a procedure for arbitrating disputes between members. It also conducts extensive educational programs, which I cover in more detail in the next chapter, and a well-funded national advertising program. Its official publication, *Realtor Magazine* (www.realtormag.com) is provided to all members, and is clearly one of the best periodicals of its kind in the nation. For more information visit www. re-altor.com. When you become a member there will be an incredible amount of additional information available to you on www.realtor.org. I've also at-tended several national Realtor conventions over the years and have always been impressed by the incredible amount of outstanding educational semi-nars and the very impressive and enjoyable social events.

I have been a member of NAR for many years, and I've participated ex-tensively in their educational programs and other activities. I have found the quality of the entire organization to be exceptional.

For all these reasons, plus the fact that it will provide you with an ideal way to develop your critically important personal business network, I strongly recommend that, if at all possible, you join an office with a Realtor affiliation, and that you become an active and contributing member.

■ *Office Ethics.* The office should have an internal set of rules and courtesies that govern business conduct among its sales agents. It is important that everyone understands and follows standards of conduct necessary to foster a feeling of cooperation and mutual respect. If a group of physicians were in business together in the same office, each would establish a practice composed of specific clientele. One physician would not think of attempting to entice a patient away from an associate. Attorneys observe similar ethical standards, as do accountants and all other professions of standing. In the best-run real estate offices, agents adhere to the same strict courtesies. In others, it is "catch as catch can," and whoever gets the name on the dotted line wins. The broker's philosophy will prevail, so find out what it is. If it's a survival-of-the-pushiest office, or the broker can't understand why you are concerned about such a subject, I would strongly suggest you keep looking— unless you feel comfortable swimming with sharks.

■ *Commission Splits.* Each broker has written instructions on how commissions are divided within the firm. There will be differences among companies, but the broker who takes a larger share of the commission dollar might provide more support in terms of advertising and facilities, so consider the whole picture. The general rule is that new agents earn a smaller percentage than experienced agents because they require a greater investment of supervisory time and effort. While this is valid, remember that as you become more successful, you can legitimately expect to retain more of each dollar you bring to the company. Even though the office might have a standard, published structure detailing percentages, bonuses, and incentives, you can negotiate directly and individually for yourself. It's to your broker's distinct advantage to keep high-volume producers and reward them appropriately. Early in your career, you will not be in a strong bargaining position, but keep these thoughts tucked away in the back of your mind for future use.

■ *Errors and Omissions (E&O) Insurance.* This form of liability insurance protects you from claims made against you as a result of your activities as a real estate professional. An increasing number of states make E&O insurance mandatory. Many observers feel that is the trend for the future. However, at the present time, there are offices in the United States that self-insure, which is a fancy way of saying they have no E&O coverage.

If E&O insurance is mandated in your state, the procedure for obtaining it will be well developed. If not, you have a number of options. One approach is for the company to contract for it and pay for the coverage on an annual basis, with the premiums being determined by the number of sales agents and the sales volume. Each salesperson typically contributes a monthly amount toward the premium. Some brokers buy insurance on an individual transaction basis. Another option may be for individual agents to purchase his or her own coverage. It is not cheap.

Regardless of how conscientious and sincere you might be, you can be a prime target for a lawsuit. Quite often, after all the dust has settled in a controversy, the real estate agent is the only individual left in the locality where the problem occurred. The agent may also be the one with "deep pockets"— the only person really capable of paying a judgment.

Many agents happily go through their entire career with not even a hint of litigation, but the fact is that the frequency of lawsuits has been increasing at an alarming rate over the past few years. In today's (and tomorrow's) environment, I simply would not sell real estate without E&O insurance. Not one transaction. None. Ever.

■ *Your Obligations to the Firm.* No matter how the office is organized, you will be expected to contribute in various ways to the operation. For example, there will be "floor" days when you will be the agent on call in the office to handle real estate inquiries. As an independent contractor, you technically must volunteer, but floor duty is one you should enthusiastically perform. It can be an excellent source of income. Not all duties, however, are so eagerly anticipated. In your discussions with the broker, make certain you are clear as to what will be expected of you. You will want to do your fair share, but the mark of a well-managed company is that licensed agents perform duties that only they can perform by virtue of holding that license. If it is clear that you will be expected to do a lot of routine clerical chores that anyone, licensed or not, can do, then you are probably dealing with a poorly run firm. You *will* be expected to do the basic clerical tasks in matters related to your own real estate transactions; in fact, you will probably have to do most of them.

■ *Special Functions.* Some real estate brokers are also builders and market their homes through their own company. This will offer an interesting dimension to your activities—the opportunity to sell new houses. However, you may be expected to give these homes preferential treatment in your sales efforts. Be certain you are clear on the ground rules.

It is also not unusual for real estate companies to have a property management department. This is an advantage, since renters often turn into buyers and the more buyers the better. One of the most enjoyable transactions I had was working with a young fellow who was renting an apartment through our company's property management operation. Almost all renters wish to become home owners, so if you have access to that type of a pool, there's great potential. There are also some companies with affiliated insurance, title and escrow, mortgage lending, and appraisal activities. Although having all these functions available within a single organization can be convenient for consumers (and profitable for the company), care must be exercised to ensure that a genuine freedom of choice exists, and that full disclosure is made. There are those who would say that all these functions would be best left in completely independent hands.

FRANCHISE VERSUS UNAFFILIATED BROKER

National real estate franchises have become very powerful components of the country's real estate makeup, currently making up about 44 percent of all Realtor affiliated real estate brokerages. Of those, approximately 33 percent are independently owned offices within the national franchise. Roughly 40 percent of all Realtor salespersons belong to a franchise office. It is difficult to find a city of any size that does not have them. Is working in a franchise office different from working in an unaffiliated office? The answer is a qualified yes. Franchises have the advantage of national recognition and ordinarily have standardized training programs in which all new agents are expected to participate. You are also less likely to be left to fend for yourself, at least initially. Remember, however, that most of these companies are independent operations within the franchise structure. It is possible to have a wide difference in philosophies of operation between different offices in the same franchise.

It is probable that you will feel more pressure within some franchises to follow standardized procedures such as wearing distinctive clothing and displaying ad signs on your car. If these things bother you, find out in advance how much latitude you will have to operate as you see fit.

SMALL CAN BE BEAUTIFUL

Small offices, those having ten or fewer agents, can have some advantages. For example, you will likely have closer contact with your broker and the rest of the sales staff. It also generally takes less time to get things done in a small organization and ideas are translated into programs and policies more quickly. Although formal training may be of the homegrown variety, and more independent study might be required of you, there is no reason it cannot be effective.

Size is not the sole determinant of quality. Tremendous opportunities can be found in larger firms, particularly in the area of initial training. On the other hand, a concerned and knowledgeable broker on one side of the desk and you on the other may be equally effective.

DISORGANIZED MAY NOT BE ALL BAD

Conventional wisdom would advise you to steer clear of any office that appears disorganized and confused. For most people, and for most offices, that is sound advice. However, it is possible to find some real potential for success in this type of environment. If the company is basically solvent (that is, has been around for a while), and you are the type of person who thrives on taking advantage of opportunities unrecognized by others, you might prosper in an organization where rules and procedures are not clearly defined. I should advise you that this particular bit of advice has not been enthusiastically endorsed by other members of the real estate community.

HOME IS WHERE YOU HANG YOUR LICENSE

By the time you finish your investigation and interviews, you will have a reasonably clear idea where you would like to go to work. Identify your top three or four selections and make yourself available to the first broker on your list. What happens if that broker does not offer you a position? If you need to start immediately, you simply progress through the list until you are successful. If your first choice is far above your second, check out the possibility of future placement. If the broker is encouraging about bringing you on board within two or three months, it could be worth the wait.

Take heart—your hard work will pay off. The strong likelihood is that you will have several offers. Your task will be to choose from among them and then to start what will hopefully be a long and prosperous career in real estate.

4

Getting Started on the Job

Getting Organized and Beating the Drums

If you are like most new agents, you will have mixed feelings as you begin work. On the one hand, you will be eager to begin doing the things that will earn you some money. On the other hand, you will feel the natural anxiety that comes with anything as important in life as starting a new career. It is essential that you clearly understand the nature of the challenge and that you be aware of what you can do to prepare.

WHAT YOU NEED TO KNOW UP FRONT

Your first year in real estate will likely be your toughest. That's how it was for most of us. Consider the story of Dorcas T. Helfant, past president of NAR and the first woman to hold that post. In an interview with a Realtor trade magazine shortly after she took office as NAR president, Helfant revealed that she entered real estate sales when she was twenty-one years old, facing a divorce, and raising an infant. A year went by with no business, which prompted her to apply for a job selling appliances for Sears. By the time Sears called, Helfant had put together five sales, and "from there I never looked back." She is still not looking back as the Managing Broker of the Virginia Beach, Virginia office of Coldwell-Banker Professional, Realtors. I'll provide guidance in this chapter that is designed to get you some early paydays, but be prepared to hang in there. You will very likely face serious emotional and financial challenges.

KINDS OF ON-THE-JOB TRAINING

Initial on-the-job training is designed to ease your transition from student to practitioner. It may be very formal or extremely casual, depending on where you work. If it is highly structured, you can expect to spend your early days mastering the basics of the trade. While licensing courses deal mainly with factual information, company sessions devote substantial time to traditional real estate sales and listing techniques. You can also expect a healthy amount of motivational material. You will be exposed to an array of ideas, techniques, and suggestions, most of which will be time-tested and valuable.

My strong recommendation is that you be open minded and receptive. Some of the material may be difficult for you and some of it uncomfortable, but withhold judgment. Your broker will be satisfied if you master the techniques and modify them to accommodate your own individual style and philosophy. Even if that were not her basic inclination, successful brokers are practical enough not to try to make you into something you are not.

THAT'S RIGHT: TODAY YOU DEFINITELY GET ORGANIZED

If you have been a successful businessperson, particularly in a commissioned sales job in which you worked with the general public, you know what it takes to do the job. One of the most immediately successful of my former students was an intelligent, personable, hard-working woman who made the transition from Avon Lady to real estate sales. If you've had sales experience, whatever worked for you before will likely work again. However, real estate is just different enough to make it worth your while to consider some of these ideas. If you have had little or no previous work experience, or none in sales, you will want to pay particular attention.

Pick a Partner

In every office there seems to be at least one agent who is exceptionally well organized. She always has the latest information on interest rates and loan programs, better property files than the local multiple listing service, and a personal data card for every person with whom she has ever done business. Her closed-deal files are masterpieces of organization, showing who said what to whom, and when. Find out early who this is in your office, and ask if you can look over her system.

Generally, someone like this takes a great deal of justifiable pride in how her work is organized, and she will probably be happy to share the information.

Even if your office does not have quite the paragon of virtue I have described, *any* established agent will know more about the practical aspects of administration than you will, so pick the person who seems to be the best qualified and with whom you are the most compatible. Some offices have a formal buddy or mentor system that pairs off each newcomer with an experienced agent, so the contact might be made for you. Others might have a structured coaching program in which you agree to pay for the personalized tutoring. Naturally, that's one of the things you'll make certain you're clear on before you sign on. No matter what the system, make sure that you find out how the official office files are maintained and learn how to locate things for yourself. You will become popular if you can find what you need without always asking for help.

Fishing for a Mentor

Let me relate a quick personal story to illustrate my suggestions for finding a model agent whom you may emulate. As a youth my first experience at fishing with my dad was a disaster. He neglected to tell me that when you take a catfish off your hook there is a specific procedure you need to follow to prevent getting a serious injury. After that I only went fishing when required to as a family event, and never developed the slightest skill as a fisherman. Fast forward a few decades and I'm taking my son fishing for the first time. We're on the riverbank and he's next to me as we both cast our lines. I'm getting nothing. He's getting nothing. Down the bank about twenty yards was an older man who was pulling a fish about as fast as he could bait his hook. I left the bank for a quick trip back to my car for some water. When I returned my son was about ten yards from the man, observing his every move. It worked. He started catching fish. Fortunately, the gentleman seemed honored (and slightly amused) that he was chosen as a model. Moral to the story: choose your mentors wisely. Make it someone who has clearly excelled in meeting the same challenges you are about to face, and someone whose business philosophy and ethics are compatible.

Organize Your Work Space

Whether you have a private office, a cubicle, or simply a desk in a common area, you should arrange your space to be efficient and to reflect your personality. Often you will need to locate something in a hurry while someone waits on the telephone. You'll become frantic if you need to sort through piles of unrelated information in the classic paper shuffle. The familiar, "I'll have to get back to you on that one," is the inevitable result. As a start, set up three or four desktop file baskets, each reserved for specific types of material. When your "action pending" basket starts to exceed the volume of all others combined (it will happen—it's a rule), you need to discipline yourself to act on items immediately. The file drawer in your desk (or a file cabinet, if you are lucky enough to have one) should be used for folders of individual clients, customers, prospects, and closed transactions, arranged alphabetically. Be optimistic: Reserve a big drawer for "closed deals." Of course, there are computer software programs now that incorporate much of what we're discussing and make it much more convenient to organize your affairs. Bottom line is, do what works best for you and watch carefully how the successful "old heads" do it.

If you have walls on which you can post personal material, the display of city and county maps will be useful to you and to those who visit your office, many of whom will be new to the area. After you close several transactions, you might wish to indicate each property with a pin on the map along with a small card to identify the people involved and the type of property. With different colored pins, you could show your current listings. After a while, it will be impressive. I developed this kind of display (after I moved up to an office with a non portable wall), and when prospects visited for our initial interview, that was inevitably the major focus of their attention. If you can locate a relief map of your state (the kind showing actual topography), your out-of-state visitors will find that particularly interesting.

On a professional note, frame documents showing your Realtor affiliation, membership in other professional organizations, and your diplomas from major real estate courses. If you receive any special awards, don't be bashful, display them. The first year you qualify, hang your Million Dollar Club emblem on the wall. One of my survey correspondents had "Three Million Dollar Agent" on his business card. There is no point in being modest.

Organize Your Information

One of the greatest practical problems of organization that new agents traditionally face is keeping all the information about one transaction or one person in one place. If you make separate notes on different pieces of paper for each telephone call or contact, you will invariably misplace one or more of them, and you will spend many panicky moments searching. One solution is to prepare an all-purpose form for each client, customer, or prospect on which you make a chronological record of all contacts and all pertinent actions. Again, this can be done on a computer with appropriate software or your own design. This type of organization accomplishes several things, in addition to giving you a single-source reference. There are times when disputes arise as to who took what action, when. Unfortunately, these disagreements sometimes result in litigation. If you have a formal record of your actions made at the time they occurred, you will be in an infinitely stronger position than would be the case if you simply assert, "To the very best of my recollection . . ." You will also find that months or even years might go by between contacts with a particular individual. It will be comforting to you, and impressive to others, to be able to recount past contacts accurately. Your office may have a form or software program for keeping these records, but the format you use is not important—the discipline to use a one-source system is.

Organize Your Time

It's easy to get carried away on this subject and you could spend most of your time organizing your time. But since 72 percent of the respondents in my survey indicated that an *inability to plan and manage time* was *very important* or *important* in causing real estate agents not to succeed (see Appendix A), it is apparent that time management is a serious matter.

There is general agreement on the basics. First, you need to organize your schedule each day in some fashion; second, you need to establish priorities. There are all sorts of calendars and planners on the market. You need to get one with which you are comfortable, have it with you all the time, and use it religiously. When the year is over save them. Never throw one away. Ever. Again, you can use the computer to aid you in this task, but I'm the old-fashioned type who carries my planning calendar everywhere I go.

Each evening, or *very* early in the morning, you need to formally plan your day *in writing* and identify those items that are the most important. My suggestion is to put at the top of your list tasks necessary to close a transaction (buyer and seller have agreed to terms, but things such as title check, removing contingencies, loan application and approval, pest inspection, and so on are yet to be done). These are paydays ready to happen, but Murphy's Law (whatever can go wrong, will go wrong) is alive and prospering in real estate. Approach each pending transaction with this question: "What could possibly go wrong with this deal today to keep it from closing, and how can I prevent that from happening?" (Quick note: I once used the word "deal" in an article I wrote for a Realtor publication and got a very indignant e-mail from a reader. I found that some in the profession consider the word beneath the dignity of a true professional. You've been alerted.) Your job will be to avert the dreaded "fall through"—a term with which I hope you will not become too familiar.

As you establish priorities on how to spend your time, keep in mind the way you earn money in real estate. Forgive the repetition, but the *only* way you are paid is for one of your listings to sell or for you to sell a property. It is remarkable how much time some real estate agents spend on fringe activities. The fact that I advocate a high degree of professionalism should not obscure the fact that I also believe passionately that the only really happy real estate agent is a well-paid one. That is not to say that you should not perform community service activities, help decorate the office for the Halloween party, keep your individual space looking impressive, or engage in enjoyable hobbies. Just remember how the bills are paid.

Set Goals for Yourself

Again you can spend an inordinate amount of time deciding what it is you want to accomplish. For most people, the first few months are best spent learning the profession and becoming aware of the various long-range opportunities. The more you know about what is available, the easier it will be to establish short-term and long-term career goals.

Some folks simply opt not to establish formal goals at all. If you don't really care where you're going in your career, then I suppose they are not necessary. Others may have goals but have rather unique methods of achieving them. Those with a more mystic bent put pictures of expensive cars, lavish mansions, and sleek yachts on their walls and have faith that positive thinking will make it so (although as far as I know, the young bachelor in my office who put a picture of a voluptuous young Hollywood starlet on his wall has yet to hear from her.)

LEARN THE NUTS AND BOLTS

It can be a frightening experience to realize that, after all the time you have spent getting your license, you wouldn't know how to write up an actual sales agreement should someone walk up to your desk and ask to buy a specific home. I didn't. The reason is that the offer to purchase form you studied for your license exam may bear little resemblance to the one that is used in the real world. Fortunately for me, there was about a twenty-four-hour period between the time the young couple decided they wanted the property and the time they made their formal offer. I spent that time frantically going over closed-deal files and preparing to write the actual offer to purchase. The amount of printed information on that form that I had not really read (or understood) before was astonishing. I also relied very heavily on the experienced salesperson on the staff who had agreed to be my "big sister." Most agents who have been in the business for a while remember the paralyzing experience of getting started and are more than willing to help you out. I strongly recommend that one of your first projects be to go over the offer to purchase form used in your area very, very carefully.

BECOME A PROFESSIONAL

Become active in your local chapter of the National Association of Realtors, and investigate its professional education offerings. The one with which you will be initially concerned is the Realtors Institute, which is composed of three individual courses. When you successfully complete all three of them all, you earn the right to use the term GRI (Graduate Realtors Institute). It is a designation that is recognized by others in the profession. Try to complete it sometime during your first two years. The course material will be helpful in your job, you will start to get a wider perspective of the profession, and you will meet energetic and career-minded professionals from other offices and other cities. The contacts will be invaluable in establishing your professional network, so cultivate and keep track of them.

While I was researching this subject I logged on to several state Realtor organization's websites to get an overview of their GRI offerings. Here's the GRI course descriptions I found at the Texas Association of Realtors web site (www.texasrealtors.com). GRI 1: Ethics and Liability (8 hours); Contract Forms (8 hours); Contract Procedures (8 hours); Finance (8 hours). GRI 2: Prospecting (8 hours); Seller Services (8 hours); Buyer Services (8 hours); New Homes (8 hours). GRI 3: Investment and Taxation (8 hours); Property Management (8 hours); Technology Tools (8 hours); Goals and Productivity (8 hours). Were I a new agent in the Lone Star State I would do my best to attend these sessions and earn my GRI.

You will also be inundated with offerings of real estate-oriented seminars and lectures. Most will be extremely well researched presentations given by individuals who are professional in every sense of the word. But beware, some are high-hype sessions given by people with monumental egos whose main goal seems to be to impress you with their superstar status. Until you have been around for a while, you might want to stick to the Realtors Institute offerings.

ORGANIZING FOR UNCLE SAM

There are at least two excellent reasons for knowing as much as possible about federal, state, and local income taxes and for arranging your business and personal affairs with taxes always in mind. First, a substantial portion of your income every year for as long as you live (and beyond) will be subject to taxes. Second, those to whom you provide professional services will expect you to know something about the subject. There are substantial income tax consequences involved with every real estate transaction. You need to understand basic concepts well enough to be able to discuss them intelligently, and to be able to recognize those questions you need to refer to a professional who specializes in taxes.

Tax time can be a genuinely mind-numbing nightmare if you have not planned ahead and kept informed. Here are some suggestions:

■ *Know who you are.* Although your initial license may say "salesperson" (or some sort of "broker" if you're in a single license state), you are really a self-employed entrepreneur who owns and runs a small business as a sole proprietor. Maybe it is only a one-person small business, but it is a small business nonetheless. You need to develop a total business plan with specific goals and strategies and a profit-oriented, no-nonsense philosophy in which you know your rights and obligations regarding taxes.

■ *Learn as much as you can on your own.* You can get a good basic overview by simply reading official IRS publications, which you can get free at your local IRS office. Better yet, log on to www.irs.gov. It's an incredibly helpful site, loaded with an abundance of information. The resource to start with is IRS publication 17, "Your Federal Income Tax". Next, get a copy of IRS publication 334, "Tax Guide for Small Business," which discusses a variety of tax issues that will be pertinent to you.

There are many other useful resources. Most likely your best resource for tax information as it relates to real estate is the web site of Vernon Hoven, CPA - www.hoven.com. His book *The Real Estate Investor's Tax Guide* would be an excellent addition to your library. It's updated frequently.

One final tip, relating to the IRS Web site I cited above: if you know how to navigate it, you can actually ask the IRS questions and get real answers! I've done it. In the past couple years, personal tax issues have arisen for which I was unable to find an answer. I sent e-mail inquiries through the IRS site and received clear answers signed by a real person. Just go past "frequently asked questions" to the "comments" section. "Comments" include questions, so fire away. In both instances, the answers I received saved me money.

■ *Work your business plan—and document your efforts.* The key to keeping good records is to establish a basic system and stick with it. Central to this is the maintenance of your daily planner. Jot down or log on the computer all appointments and meetings, thereby substantiating your general level of activity. Take the planner with you when you use your car and record all your mileage and transportation activity. An envelope in the glove compartment for gas credit card receipts will reduce the clutter. Another large envelope that you keep in your desk drawer marked *Business Receipts—Year XXXX* will also be useful. As you expand your activities, you will need several large envelopes, each to contain receipts for specific functions. My wife and I bought a software program last year to put our taxes on and I'm now transitioning from my "envelope" strategy to giving her all of my receipts to enter into a tax file on the computer. Be advised, however, that no matter how sophisticated your computer software, keep the written documents.

Pay for everything by check or credit card so that you will automatically have a receipt. If you pay cash, ask for a receipt, and make a note on the back of it indicating what the item was for. If it is not possible to get a receipt or if you forgot, jot down the amount, the date, and the purpose in your planner or on a piece of paper and put it in your business receipts envelope.

■ *Know your legitimate business expenses.* As the sole proprietor of your own business, you will be filing a "Profit or Loss From Business" schedule with your federal tax return. The critical thing to remember here is that your business expenses are deducted from income. I admit this is oversimplifying a very complex subject, but basically if you have an annual gross income of $65,000, and you incur expenses necessary to conduct your business in the amount of $10,000, you will pay taxes (including state and local income taxes as well as Social Security and Medicare) on the net—$55,000. The key is that your business expenses must be legitimate and you must be able to prove them.

Let's say that, through ignorance or faulty record keeping, you fail one year to claim legitimate deductions in the amount of $2,000 and your tax bracket is 28 percent. You will pay Uncle Sam $560 more in federal taxes out of your own pocket than he deserves or expects—but there is no case on record where he has turned it down. But wait . . . What about Social Security and the other taxes I mentioned? Together they could easily add another 20 to 30 percent. That means that the $2,000 in deductions you forgot to take could cost you $1,000 or more! As they say, a thousand here and a thousand there adds up in a hurry.

The checklist shown in Figure 4-1 provides a general guide to expenses commonly incurred by real estate professionals. As in all information pertaining to incomes taxes, you need to verify everything for yourself by referring to current IRS material. The checklist is simply designed to help you set up an accounting system of your own and to aid you in recognizing those areas in which deductions might be permissible.

■ *Get professional help.* If you develop the uneasy feeling that you are about to get in over your head, seek professional assistance. I did that my first year in real estate and never regretted it. As you generate more activity, your business affairs become more complicated. An old war horse (his term for himself) in my office put it this way: "Doing your own taxes makes about as much sense as doing your own surgery. Get a pro." My personal preference is a certified public accountant (CPA) who has extensive experience in working with real estate agents and real estate investors. Scout around before you choose, ask for referrals from other successful agents, and discuss fees ahead of time. When a CPA quotes you an hourly rate, it could result in a mild case of cardiac arrest; but with computers, they can get a lot done in a short period of time, particularly if you present them with well-organized basic information. The idea is that they will actually save you money and, equally as important, keep you out of trouble. Understand also that (as is the case with

Figure 4-1. Checklist of potential income tax deductions.

Advertising
    Business cards   Picture will cost extra—count it.
    Telephone listing   To identify yourself as real estate
                               agent. Block type possible.
    Career apparel   If it has company logo.
    Car signs (door)
    Client follow-up   Files, greeting cards, and so on.

Automobile expenses   All expenses deductible to the extent
                               (percentage) your auto is used for business
                               purposes.
    Gas and oil   Mileage to and from office not deductible. If
                               you use standard mileage deduction, make
                               certain you're up to date. It changes.
    Repairs
    Driver's license
    Parking and tolls   Don't forget parking meters. They can add
                               up.
    Wash and polish
    Motor club dues   Get emergency start/tow service.
    Insurance   Get adequate liability coverage.
    Depreciation   Special rules—investigate.

Dues
    Realtor dues
    Multiple listing service
    Chamber of Commerce   Clear/documented business purpose.
    Rotary, Elks, etc.   See above. Athletic, social and sporting clubs
                               do not qualify under any circumstance.

Education   Seminars/convention registration.
                               Continuing education only. Expenses to get
                               real estate license not deductible.

Entertainment   Special restrictive rules apply. Area of abuse,
                               hence special IRS interest. Review IRS
                               entertainment publication.

Gifts to clients   Permissible and advisable, but IRS has strict
                               rules.

Office supplies   The cost of pencils, paper, pens, staples, clips
                               and so on adds up over a year. Keep track.

Postage   The post office will provide a receipt upon
                               request. UPS and Federal Express

Legal/professional consultation	When related to business.
Laundry and dry cleaning	For career apparel only. All when out of town overnight on business.
Publications	
Business/real estate	The *Wall Street Journal, Business Week,* and so on.
Books	
Real estate license	Renewal only. Original not deductible.
Business travel expenses	
Transportation	IRS has strict rules.
Meals	Specific limits—check.
Lodging	
Taxis	
Tips	Add to credit card when practical.
Insurance	Errors and omission. Auto.
Telephone	
Business use	Log each call and verify when monthly bill arrives.
Special features	Call waiting, call forwarding, and so on.
Fax	Business use only.
Depreciation	Large, high-cost, capital expenditure items.
"Expensing"	Certain items (depending upon cost) may be written off (expensed) in year of purchase.
Wages to assistants	If business gets really good. (You can even hire relatives—but be careful.)
Rent	If you rent your office space from broker. (Most do not.)
In-home office expenses	Perodically a "red flag" item with the IRS. Check the rules carefully to see if you qualify. Very unlikely that you do.
Personal property taxes	For business equipment.

attorneys) when you call your CPA with a question, you will likely get a bill for the advice.

Even if you hire a CPA, you will still need to be an active participant in the process. In his words, here is how Albert J. Aiello, a nationally recognized CPA who specializes in real estate taxation issues, suggested I make the point to you: "Would you leave all your health concerns up to your doctor? Of course not! It's your health and your taxes and it is up to *you* to take care of it. Professionals such as doctors and CPAs are there for periodic review and the more difficult problems. You have to take care of everyday matters." As an added note, Albert at one time was a licensed real estate professional.

■ *Be scrupulously honest.* The tax authorities are fond of saying that they don't want you to pay any more tax than necessary. Be assured, however, that they will not tolerate it if you pay anything less—either through ignorance or intent. Even if honesty were not the best policy (and it is), it is incredibly foolish to incur the wrath of the federal (and/or state) government. Don't complicate the issue by using your own style of creative tax accounting. There's an old military adage that goes: "choose your enemies wisely". You do not want the IRS as an enemy. If it's creativity you want, secure professional counsel and then decide upon a course of action that suits your tolerance for uncertainty.

DRESS APPROPRIATELY

You have probably been getting dressed without much help for several years now, but since this subject has received so much attention, I'd like to discuss it. How you dress probably will not be the determining factor in whether you succeed or not. An *inability to dress acceptably* didn't even make the final list in my survey asking why people fail in real estate (see Appendix A). That doesn't mean it isn't important, but it does suggest that all you need to follow are some common-sense guidelines. Here are a few from my experience.

First, you should not dress to be noticed. If what people remember about you is the tight skirt or the lime green leisure suit, you made the wrong kind of impression. Second, dress for the occasion, keeping in mind the standards of the community. If you are going to talk to the president of the local bank about listing her home, naturally you would not show up in jeans—but jeans might be exactly right for talking to the local dairy farmer about selling his place. For your everyday attire, consider what those in your town who are successful in real estate wear. In some places, it will be jackets and ties for men and dresses for women—but not everywhere. As one survey respondent said about his locale: "This is a blue jeans society. A coat and tie arouse suspicion." Finally, don't feel compelled to rush out and buy a new wardrobe—unless you are looking for an excuse to do that. (And if you do, men, *please* don't buy a loud and tasteless plaid sports coat, the stereotypical trademark of the pushy salesman).

ARRANGE FOR WHEELS

Having dependable transportation is a necessity. Ideally, you should have a car that is comfortable, clean, and, above all, safe. Late-model, four-door, midsize sedans seems to be what many agents drive, but you'll see everything from VW Bugs (rare, I admit) to the hot new sports utility vehicles. If I lived in an area where it snowed frequently in the winter (I do), I would own a vehicle with four-wheel drive (we do). The cost of gasoline makes it imperative that you use a reasonably fuel-efficient car. Whatever you use, be a fanatic on safety, for you can leave yourself open to a lawsuit if someone is injured because of your negligence. Make certain your auto insurance company knows your are in the real estate business and that you do have adequate liability coverage.

When children come along, you will be faced with a special challenge, for most youngsters would rather go to the dentist for a root canal than look at houses. You may wish to keep a "kids' kit" in your car and stock it with reading material to occupy them for at least part of the time. (Do not provide crayons and a coloring book, or you may find purple marks on your beige upholstery, and do not leave anything within reach that could be ingested by a curious and hungry toddler.)

THINK SUCCESS AND RATE YOUR PROGRESS

How does a successful and professional real estate agent act? It will be hard for you to know before you even start, but you probably will have formed some kind of mental image. Sharpen that perception as you gain experience and through observation of others whom you admire. Here is a suggestion: Establish a rating guide for yourself in which you list factors you conclude are important for success. Periodically evaluate your own progress, since it is unlikely that anyone else ever will in a formal way.

To help you, I have prepared a hypothetical evaluation on a fictitious agent who has been in the business for two years (see Figure 4-2). It contains rating factors that most real estate professionals would agree are critical, and the comments are descriptive of an agent who has done a superior job. It is based on both my own personal observations and discussions with brokers

Figure 4-2. Job evaluation: Priscilla Perfect.

Job Title: Real estate salesperson.

Job Description: Specializes in residential sales and listings, with occasional transactions in related general real estate.

Time in Profession: 24 months.

Attitude: Has a positive, enthusiastic attitude. Is not a complainer and does not make excuses. Constructively critical of programs and ideas with which she does not agree. Not a "yes person."

Work Habits: She is a self-starter and a hard worker. Has day planned before she arrives. Has assigned a priority to all tasks. Spends only enough time at her desk to handle administration; spends the remainder in productive activities out of the office.

Judgment: Directs her efforts to areas that have the largest potential payoff for herself and the firm. Wastes little time in nonessential fringe activities.

Appearance: Keeps physically fit and trim. Dresses to the standards of other successful professionals in the community.

Professionalism: Observes highest ethical standards in working with her clients, customers, and associates. Member of National Association of Realtors and very active in the local chapter.

Job Knowledge: Keeps current on all trends relating to her profession. Completed Realtors Institute (GRI). Thoroughly familiar with the community and its resources. Keeps up-to-date on total housing inventory and office listings.

Creative Ability: Able to devise innovative ways of solving problems. Respects tradition, but not bound by obsolete concepts.

Human Relations: Gets along well with individuals of every background. Genuinely committed to equal opportunity for all. Enjoys solving "people problems." Associates appreciate her willingness to help when needed. Able to maintain professional objectivity in dealing with problems; does not overidentify.

Communicative Ability: Speaks and writes in a clear, concise, and personalized manner. Has mastered the important art of listening.

Growth Potential: She has the leadership ability to be an outstanding broker and the technical skills to excel in any specialized field she may select. Will be well prepared to achieve future goals because of diversity of activities in which she has engaged as a residential sales agent.

Bottom-Line Record		*(Last 12 Months)*	
Total listings	11	Total listings sold	10
Other closed sales	7	Fall-throughs	0
Outgoing referrals	7	Gross income	$87,600

Sarah Success
Broker/Owner, Professional Realty Inc.

who have had extensive experience supervising new salespeople, and it may be useful to you in establishing your goals and grading yourself.

SPREAD THE WORD

Now you are finally licensed, trained, organized, well dressed, and motivated. You have established realistic goals, have become a Realtor, and have a well-running car purring in the parking lot ready to take off. You lack only one thing: people willing to do business with you. The cupboard may not be quite as bare as you think. Here are some suggestions:

■ *Personally let people know you are in the business.* Being a professional in real estate does not mean that you sit and wait for people to beat a path to your door. That may happen after you are established, but you won't be able to depend on it immediately. They say the fellow who built the better mousetrap and waited for people to beat a path to *his* door is surviving on stale cheese in an isolated hovel somewhere in Vermont. Start by making a list of friends and associates. Prepare a brief letter in which you inform them that you are in the business, indicate where you are located, and invite them to call upon you if you can be of service. A form letter may be the only practical alternative, but computer-generated products can make form letters look very personalized, and always include a brief personal note. Enclose your business card. If you have your picture on the card, make certain the photograph is professionally done and it is recognizable as you. A former student of mine let me know she was in the business with a very well prepared e-mail news letter complete with her picture and biographical information. I get a new one each month, which now contains her new listings.

■ *Announce your entry into the field in the local newspaper.* This will probably mean taking out a paid advertisement. Even physicians and attorneys use this procedure, so don't feel shy. The most appropriate method is for the broker to announce your affiliation with the company. Some newspapers have "New Faces in Business," or some such related column. If so, make sure you take advantage of any free coverage.

■ *Have your listing in the telephone white pages changed.* It will cost some money, but use whatever options the phone company has available to make your name stand out and to identify you as a real estate agent. In some areas, your name can be printed in slightly bolder type than that used for regular listings.

■ *Give your individual listing on your broker's Web site a great deal of thought.* I'll have more to say on this in the chapter on technology. At this point, simply let me encourage you to appreciate the fact that people will be judging you by what they see and read here.

■ *Let your old classmates know.* If you're a college graduate, send a note to your college alumni magazine. Some of your former classmates may know someone moving to your area. Some old friends may even turn out to be prosperous and influential and be in a position to refer substantial business to you. In any event, it is good to make it a matter of public record that you are in real estate and plan to be in it for a while.

THE NEWBIE BLUES

In a military combat assignment overseas, people who have been at the station a while are respectfully called the "old heads," while the new arrivals are much less respectfully known as the "newbies." A newbie is not hard to spot: His combat fatigues will not have been washed yet and will be several shades darker than everyone else's. The newly issued boots will not have been broken in, causing him to walk with a gait called the "newbie shuffle."

As a new real estate agent, you may feel that you are being treated like a newbie and that you are not getting the respect you deserve. You may believe that people, particularly those in managerial positions, should pay more attention to you. A new agent in our office, frustrated at not being able to get in to see the sales manager as quickly as he thought he should, commented, "Man, you have to stand in line around here just to get ignored."

Here are my suggestions for curing the real estate newbie blues. First, make certain that you really need advice and guidance when you ask for it. There are some new agents (and a few old ones who should know better) who have to run to the boss at every turn, ostensibly for help in making the crucial decision that will permit further progress on that megabuck transaction. In reality, what is often being said is, "Look at how good I'm doing, chief. Aren't I just about the best little old rookie real estate agent you ever did see?" Develop the reputation as someone who needs constant head-patting and stroking, and it will be hard to find anyone to talk to when you really have something important to discuss.

Second, close a few deals. I assure you that nothing will get you respect and admiration more quickly than starting to pay part of your broker's overhead. After you have brought in a few commission checks, try this little experiment to see how far your respect quotient has risen. Gather together a stack of papers that looks like an offer to purchase. Stroll casually by your broker's office. Hesitate. Make sure he sees the papers. Study them. Look puzzled. Chances are he will strike like a catfish after a worm and rush to your side to offer guidance.

Eventually, you will even start to notice that he is beginning to visit you at your desk more often with questions like: "Hey, how's it going this morning? Got anything I can help you with?" At that point, people will accurately say of you, "When Sarah Smith speaks, people listen." Your boots will be broken in, your fatigues faded, and you will have achieved the revered old head status.

5

In the Beginning There Was . . . Agency

The Real Estate Profession's Identity Crises

I served tours in two combat zones while in the U.S. Air Force. One was in Vietnam and the other was at the University of California at Berkeley, where I commanded the Air Force ROTC unit. One day in the spring of 1970, in the wake of the Cambodian invasion and the tragedy at Kent State, the campus erupted. Rampaging crowds of students and street people, pursued by police, were everywhere, torching vehicles and generally wreaking havoc. I watched—from a safe distance and in civilian clothes—as U.C. Berkeley's riot de jour got really out of hand. At the epicenter in the middle of Sproul Plaza, apparently oblivious to what was going on around him, I noticed a lonely, solitary figure, sitting in a Ghandi-like pose and clothed only in cutoff jeans. His hands were stretched skyward and he was plaintively wailing, "Who am I? Who am I?" That's the question now being asked by many people in the real estate business. I'll do my best to answer it for you, since you need to know before you can fully appreciate your role as a real estate professional, and before we launch into our discussion of the specifics of listing and selling real estate.

AGENCY: WHERE WE'VE BEEN

In legal terminology, an agent is someone who represents another person in a business transaction. There are different types of agents, ranging from a "universal agent," in which the agent has the power to act in any and all matters, to a "special agent," in which the agent is authorized to act for the principal in a limited set of clearly prescribed activities. The agent assumes a fiduciary responsibility to the principal. Textbooks typically define the list of obligations that go into making up that responsibility as confidentiality, obedience, accountability, loyalty, and disclosure. In essence, it simply means that the agent puts the client's interests ahead of everyone else's in the transaction—including the agent's. If you grasp nothing else about agency, remember that. You put your client's interests above everyone else's—including yours. While teaching my real estate licensing class we role play. I am the Principal Broker and all my students are salespersons licensed under me. The company name: Golden Rule Realty. Simply another way of illustrating our guiding principle in doing business. Practical application—you're showing a property and you ask yourself: "should I disclose this fact about the house?" Your practical answer at Golden Rule Realty: "Would you want that fact disclosed to you if you were the buyer?" It's not an infallible guide line, but combined with common sense it works great almost all the time.

I can best illustrate the concept of agency as it relates to real estate if we fast-forward a bit and assume that you now have your license. Your first real shot at actually earning some money occurs when you list the home of Ed and Mary Johnson. They are highly motivated to sell, since they are relocating the family business and want to move into their new home in New Jersey to get their children in school for the fall term. That listing agreement between you and the Johnsons is a legally binding contract, in which you pledge your best efforts to secure a ready, willing, and able buyer. If you do that, the Johnsons agree to compensate you with a brokerage fee, typically 5, 6, or 7 percent of the eventual selling price. It's really an employment contract that creates an agency relationship in which the Johnsons actually hire your broker, for you are an agent of your broker. The listing you secure is called an "exclusive right to sell" listing, which means that no matter who sells the property you earn a commission. There are other types of listings about which you will learn in your real estate licensing classes, but that's the most common.

Your broker is the Johnsons' special agent, who is authorized to act for them in this limited set of circumstances. The contract typically gives the agent the authority to advertise the property, put a lockbox on it, submit it to the local multiple listing service, and cooperate with other real estate brokers in finding a buyer. You are a subagent to the Johnsons. The agent (your broker) and the subagent (you) owe that fiduciary duty to the Johnsons. Again, in its basic terms, it means placing their interests above everyone else's in any matter. The Johnsons are your *clients*. Your legal duty to third parties—buyers—is to deal honestly and reveal material facts. They are referred to as *customers*.

In the past, the standard procedure was for the home sellers to authorize the listing broker to submit the listing to the MLS, along with a unilateral offer of subagency, which meant that anyone who accepted that offer would represent the seller. The typical split on the brokerage fee would be 50 percent to the listing office and 50 percent to the selling office. The practical implication was that legally everyone represented the seller and no one legally represented the buyer. Your broker submitted the listing to the local MLS, and in the information describing the listing, included the phrase: "Sellers highly motivated—must be in New Jersey in time for school this fall."

Here's the problem that developed. Let's say Sam Snerdly, the broker at Sunset Realty and a member of the local MLS, noticed the Johnson listing and concluded it was just right for the Browns, a young couple with whom he had been working on finding a home for several months. He accepted that unilateral offer of subagency. Snerdly has never met the Johnsons. He has become very good friends with the Browns. He met them at the airport when they came to town for a house-hunting trip. He made hotel reservations for them. He got them preapproved for a mortgage loan. He took them to dinner. He offered advice on how to negotiate when buying a home. He gave them a six-month gift subscription to the local paper. He shows the Browns the Johnson house. They love it. He shares with them the fact that the sellers are really anxious to move. Because of Snerdly's advice, they offer $4,000 less than full price. Even though that's substantially less than comparable homes are selling for, the Johnsons accept, since they are so anxious to wrap it up and move on. The deal is done.

Question: Whom did Snerdly legally represent in this transaction? Answer: the Johnsons. He was required to put their interests first. They were his clients. He was their subagent, by virtue of accepting that unilateral offer of subagency. Question: Did he do that when he counseled the buyers to offer substantially less than full price, because he knew the Johnsons were "highly motivated?" Answer: Absolutely not. Question: Whom do you think the Browns thought Snerdly represented? Answer: Them, of course. What Snerdly did was enter into an undisclosed dual agency, since by his actions it was obvious that he was, in fact, representing the Browns, while legally and contractually obligated to represent the Johnsons. Acting as an undisclosed dual agent is illegal.

If everyone was happy with the outcome, then there was typically no adverse reaction. But let's suppose that after the Browns move in, they discover that the road bordering their home is going to be widened dramatically, which will substantially increase traffic noise. That information was not disclosed to them. They want out. They consult an attorney wise in the ways of agency. He asks the Browns to describe Snerdly's actions in the transaction. It's clear there has been a violation of the laws of agency, so that's what the attorney focuses on. All sorts of interesting things could result, including a revocation of the contract and perhaps even damages being levied against the sellers and the real estate agents involved. In an interesting sidelight, it became apparent that although agency violations were not typically the reasons that buyers were unhappy (generally it was nondisclosure of material facts), it became the focal point of the majority of lawsuits.

On the national level, how serious a problem was this? In 1984, the Federal Trade Commission conducted a study revealing that:

1. Of buyers (the Browns) who worked with cooperating agents (Snerdly, the subagent), 71 percent believed that agent represented them.

2. Of the buyers who worked with the listing agent (if the Browns came directly to you and bought the Johnson listing), 31 percent felt that the agent (you) represented them (the Browns).

3. Seventy-four percent of the sellers (the Johnsons) thought that the selling agent (Snerdly) represented the buyers.

This was the landmark study that forever changed the agency landscape in real estate. As a result, states started passing laws that made agency disclosure mandatory. When you take your licensing class, your state's requirements will be a major topic of discussion, so pay very close attention. If you log on to your state real estate agency web site, it's likely you will find pertinent state regulatory guidance.

AGENCY: WHERE WE ARE

There is not nearly the unanimity of practice now that there once was, but here's how things are sorting out in most parts of the country. The unilateral offer of subagency is essentially a thing of the past. Increasingly, selling agents are now representing buyers as buyers' agents. In not all instances are they entering into a formal agreement but are simply using an agency disclosure form as the basis for the buyer's agency role. There's real doubt that this is legally sufficient for establishing a legitimate agency relationship, but, for the most part, that's how it's being done. By working as a buyer's broker, the selling agent owes the fiduciary duty to the client buyer and the duty of fair dealing and disclosure to the customer seller. This is evolving rapidly, so stay tuned.

Traditionally, licensees who work with buyers have not secured the same type of contractual agreement with them to represent them exclusively in house hunting that licensees who secure listings have. Buyers have been completely free to work with anyone whom they chose and change agents as often as they wish. You can see that if you were a buyer's broker you would like that to change.

Who pays the commission to the buyer's agent? In the vast majority of instances it "comes from the transaction," which simply means that it's done the way it always was—out of the commission the seller agrees to pay the listing broker. Why would a seller agree to pay a broker to represent the buyer?

Because in the long run that increases the chances that they will sell their property by giving it the widest exposure, and besides the listing broker is representing their best interests. And in actual practice, that is essentially what was being done under the old system.

What happens if you list a property and then find a buyer for it yourself? Can you still sell your own listing and satisfy the agency laws? In most instances, yes, if you enter into an agreement in which you disclose to both parties that you are acting as a "disclosed dual agent." You obviously could not put either party's interests first, since you would be representing both. In Oregon the term used is: "disclosed limited agent".

As you might suspect, when the old order (everyone representing the seller with the unilateral offer of subagency) broke down, there was (and still is) some degree of turmoil in the ranks of the real estate profession. The concept of buyer agency was initially not warmly embraced by many in the business, based upon what was perceived by some as unwarranted attacks on the business practices of traditional brokerages. Several national-level buyers' brokerage organizations were formed that recruit real estate agents to act exclusively as buyers' agents. One of the most informative sources of information regarding the emergence of the buyer's agent movement can be found on the Web site of the National Association of Exclusive Buyer Agents (NAEBA). This is a professional organization devoted to the exclusive buyer's agent movement—in other words, agents who do not represent sellers—only buyers. Check it out at www.naeba.org.

AGENCY: THE FUTURE

As lawmakers wrestle with this problem, one of the alternatives to the traditional concept of agency that has developed is that of "transaction broker" or "facilitator." The idea here is that agency as it exists in common law is not really appropriate for the real estate profession, since the goal of the real estate licensee is to bring parties together and negotiate a mutually satisfactory solution—not to represent one party in a formal agency relationship. There's resistance to the idea, some of it based on philosophical convictions, and some based on vested interests.

AGENCY: THE BOTTOM LINE

Now let's take a step back and focus on the essentials. How do you get paid in real estate? Although there is a strong "fee-for-service" movement that we'll discuss in Chapter 17, most real estate agents are paid when the transaction closes—and only if the transaction closes. The transaction will close when all parties are satisfied. You are not likely to reach that kind of an agreement if there is an adversarial relationship between the real estate licensees involved. How much do you get paid? You typically receive a percentage of the sales price. That's great for the listing agent, since interests are compatible. The more you get for the home the more you make. But how about the buyer's agent? The more his client (the buyer) pays, the more he makes. That's a little inconsistency that hasn't been fully sorted out yet. If you are working with a buyer as a buyer's agent, I believe it would be wise to address this openly and honestly and counsel her to come up with an offering price that is within her means and fair to all parties. As with all other matters, the final decision is hers.

Here are my recommendations:

1. As you participate in your licensing training, pay close attention to the subject of agency as it is practiced in your state and your local area. There will be coverage of the subject in your basic text material, but you will need to integrate that into what the rules are in your state.

2. Make absolutely certain that if your state does have mandatory agency disclosure that you understand completely the formal requirements and that you make the necessary agency disclosures when called for—typically at the first substantive contact with a potential client. This can become burdensome, since the technical requirements of many agency disclosure laws mean that the typical house hunter, for example, could end up signing several disclosure forms.

3. Try to convince everyone that unless the transaction is fair to everyone, it's fair to no one. Be aware that this is not an opinion shared by all. Those who are proponents of a more adversarial form of agency don't agree with me on this one. They maintain you represent your client in the best manner possible, strike the best deal, and it's up to the other side to watch out for their interests. If they make a bad deal, that's their problem.

4. Understand that in some circles in the profession the depth of feeling runs deep on this issue. Most of the troops in the field have rolled with the flow and continue to try to do business legally and ethically while continuing to earn a living, but passions among some are intense—particularly those with vested interests. Do a lot of listening, studying, and asking questions before you become too generous with your personal opinions.

5. Don't be disappointed if, after you've completed your licensing training, you have the nagging feeling that you don't fully understand the subject of agency completely. A member of my network is one of the leading national authorities on this subject. I occasionally call him when I need guidance. His reaction the last time I called was, "The more I learn about agency, the less I know." Another associate of mine, who teaches real estate licensing

in an eastern state, said that when he's explaining agency, he can't help but be reminded of the old Abbott and Costello routine, "Who's on First?" As a matter of fact, he said one of his students suggested the similarity.

REAL WORLD AGENCY

I once overheard a conversation between two real estate agents. They were discussing a pending transaction and the question arose as to what home inspection company to recommend to the buyers. "Don't have them use Home Pro, they'll find everything that's wrong with the house!" said one agent. Why wouldn't you want an inspector to find everything that's wrong, particularly if you're representing them? Because if they do, it's possible that the buyers will become unhappy and back out. That means you don't get paid. Of course, if you are putting their interests first, above everyone else's— including yours, you would want the inspector to find everything that is wrong. Easily said, but when a really nice payday is hanging in the balance, it clearly presents a challenge to some agents. By the way, guess which inspection company I used when my wife and I were buying an investment property? Right—Home Pro.

MORE REAL WORLD AGENCY

Here is another quick personal example to illustrate how the agency issue relates to the real world. One of my former students, Ali Sarlak, runs a landscaping company in our city. He took my courses to learn more about investing. Recently my wife and I were ready to take off on a month-long automobile trip. I needed someone to water the yard, mow a couple of times, and generally look after things. I thought about hiring a youngster who lives nearby, but concluded it would be too big a job. I then started considering landscape companies. I got no further than Sarlak. I immediately realized that he would treat my yard as he would his own. (I've seen his.) I further realized that he would even do a better job than I, because he has the knowledge and experience I lack. When people think about hiring a real estate professional as their agent wouldn't it be great for them to reach the same conclusions about you?

WHEN THE DEAL IS DONE

You've listed the Johnsons' home. What is the best possible outcome for them? They get a fair price from a qualified buyer, with no unpleasant aftertaste (like a lawsuit). They get their check at close and move happily on to their new life in New Jersey. What is the best possible outcome for the buyers, the Browns? They pay a fair price and get a home that meets their needs. All material facts about the property are disclosed to them before they buy. What's the best possible outcome for you? In addition to that nice commission check, the Johnsons and the Browns are *both* so impressed by your consummate professionalism, hard work, creative problem solving ability, and integrity that they say nice things about you to all their friends and associates and vow that in the future they would never work with anyone but you. Don't become so involved in fighting the agency alligators that you forget that your primary job is to tidy up the swamp.

To assist you in focusing on your primary task in any real estate transaction in which you're involved, I'll share with you my TOUCH system of selling real estate. It has proved very popular with my students over the years. Of course, their grades were in the balance.

The TOUCH System of Selling Real Estate
(*Transaction Of Ultimate Cosmic Harmony*)
By Guru Ken

In the TOUCH system of selling real estate, my devoted and beloved followers, we implore you to seek an outcome wherein everyone involved in the transaction is supremely and serenely content with the outcome.

You should labor to ensure that your sellers are excruciatingly ecstatic and in complete and total harmony with the cosmos because they will have sold their little cottage by the babbling brook for a handsome monetary gain, although we know they will be less interested in the money than in serving the needs of humankind.

You should also strive to guarantee that your buyers be deliriously delighted because they will have finally realized their dream of a lifetime and can anticipate spending an eternity of blissful contemplation and tranquility in their new home.

Further, you must work hard to see that your broker is not aggravated by unhappy customers and clients and that he is so thoroughly thrilled with his brokerage fee that he will donate 20 percent of it to the Mother Teresa Memorial Trust and 30 percent to the Guru Ken Living Trust.

Yes, my loyal and faithful disciples, in the TOUCH system of selling real estate, we must all labor righteously to reach a state of existence wherein all elements of the universe are truly synchronous and each participant in the transaction is incredibly in touch with his inner being. Or, if we fail to reach Nirvana, my devout and worshipful grasshoppers, at least no one will be mad enough to sue your sorry butt.

Yours in perpetual interplanetary infinity—Guru Ken

6

Real Estate and the Technology Revolution

Technology has changed, is changing, and will change the way real estate professionals do business. Virtual tours of homes from the comfort of the real estate office or the home computer, computers that permit cross-country teleconferencing, entire training programs on one dinky little CD-ROM, software programs with bells and whistles for virtually every real estate need are all part of the landscape. The future possibilities boggle the imagination. Keep an open mind and try out all the new stuff. Approach it all with a spirit of adventure. For those of you (like me) who have been around the block a few times, don't try to understand it. Just accept on faith that it's a miracle and develop the ability to sort out the useful from the merely glitzy.

MANDATORY DISCLOSURE

One minor disclaimer before we get into the details. If you are not computer literate, stop. Do not pass "go." Get thee to a training facility immediately and master the basics. Local community colleges typically have a wide variety of programs. If you are a fellow member of AARP and qualify for senior discounts, your local senior center will likely have some special nonthreatening offerings for you. It's not an option. Do it. Your grandchildren can help you with your homework. And a bit of advice when you're doing any research on the Internet. If you simply type a key phrase into the search engine you will be absolutely amazed at the amount and variety of information you'll be provided. My biggest challenge is to stay focused on the information I was looking for, since there are so many other great sources on an almost limitless array of topics.

WELCOME ABOARD!

Here's the really good news. When you get your license and affiliate with a broker, you will be entering a functioning business. It will be your job to fit in and learn the ropes, but the system will be there. Real estate brokerages need to compete. They must stay up-to-date. Even if they came into the computer age dragging their feet, they must adapt if they want to survive. That's good for you as a newcomer. As you gain experience, you can build on and exploit any technological expertise you might attain, but in the beginning, you'll simply be expected to pay attention and learn how to operate the current systems and programs. If there is a formal training program, it will constitute a major segment of the curriculum. Pay particular attention to those agents in your office who are generating substantial leads and income from their web sites. I'm guessing one of your first exposures to formal computer training will be your indoctrination into your local Multiple Listing Service, since that's an indispensable tool for your day to day business. It's a great place to start.

THROUGH THE CONSUMERS' EYES

Clearly, one of the most visible public manifestations of a real estate brokerage's mastery of modern technology is its Web site. As I counseled in Chapter 3, when we were discussing your approach to choosing a company with which to affiliate, one of your best tools for judging brokerages is how they come across on their Web page. If they don't have a Web page, loan them a copy of this book. Check out all your local real estate companies, even if you've already made your decision as to where you want to hang your license. You'll notice a marked degree of similarity and differences. My preference would be one that has a link from their main page to their agents, including you. Typically that would include a picture and some biographical information that you would be asked to compose. When one of my former students affiliates with a real estate company, I log on to their Web page and check out my student's biographical information. Most of the time they do a good job. On occasion, however, I'm disappointed. In one instance, for example, I knew what an incredibly impressive background one of my students had, but her bio on the Web page was, to be charitable, inadequate. Yes, I sent her an e-mail. And have your photo done by a professional. Many successful agents also have individual Web sites with specific addresses, such as www.bestrealestateagentintheuniverse.com (check for current availability). I also prefer company sites that give consumers useful information, as opposed to just enough to motivate them to contact the company. This is not an opinion shared by all.

WEB SITES: BEST OF SHOW

Several years ago the editors of *Realtor Magazine* evaluated the Web sites of hundreds of Realtors. From those they picked their top ten. I thought it would be instructive to see if they are still up and running. Eight of them are still operating. I've referenced them below. Here is what I suggest: Assume you are contemplating a move to one of the communities in which these agents operate. What did you like about the Web site? What did you not like? While several of these agents have changed companies, each still has their original web site address.

- www.wynnea.com (Wynne Achatz, ABR, CRS, GRI, LTG, Westrick Associates, Inc. Marine City, Michigan)
- www.michaelgreenwald.com (Michael Greenwald, Sotheby's International Realty, Brentwood, California). Incidentally, when I visited this web site, there was a modest little 20 acre listing in the Santa Monica Hills for a cool eleven million five. Let's see, that commission would be . . .
- www.judysells.com (Judy Niemeyer, CRS, GRI, RE/MAX By the Bay, Fairhope, Alabama)
- www.dallashomes.com (Judy McCutchin, ABR, CRS, RE/MAX Premier, Preston Road, Dallas, Texas)
- www.arizonagolfproperties.com (Dean Benigno, Realty Executives, Scottsdale, Arizona)
- www.come2az.com (Alice Held, CRS, GRI, RE/MAX Excaliber, Scottsdale, Arizona)
- www.munsteragent.com (John Reipsa, GRI, and Pam Reipsa, McColly Real Estate Brokerage, Schereville, Indiana)
- www.maryjanedeering.com (Mary Jane Deering, LTC, Alain Pinel Realtors, Pleasanton, California)

READING ASSIGNMENT

Here's a handy little book you will want to add to your library early in your career. It's *Real Estate Technology Guide—Winning With Technology* by Saul Klein, John Reilly, and Mike Barnett and published by Dearborn publishers. My recommendation is that you simply review the contents while you're getting settled into your company operation. It will give you a good long term overview of the technological challenges and opportunities you will be encountering in your real estate career, and will assist you in deciding how to best proceed to accomplish your objectives.

An NAR professional designation program you will find described in the book is that of e-Pro. The authors operate the program and also maintain an online real estate discussion community know as RealTalk. You can check it out at www.realtalk.internetcrusade.com. While you are there, click the e-Pro link and it will take you to the NAR Web site that describes the e-Pro curriculum in detail. As an overview, here are the four major modules: Understanding the Miracle of the Internet; Becoming an E-Mail Powerhouse; World Wide Web - Marketing, Publishing, Service and Support; and Tying it All Together - Tools of the Trade; Virtual Community, and Technology Plan of Action. The authors travel around the country presenting e-Pro seminars. If they offer one in your area it would be time well spent to attend.

READING ASSIGNMENT NUMBER TWO

As you will see in later chapters, I highly recommend the real estate career book *Make Millions Selling Real Estate* by Oregonian Jim Remley. As it relates to our current discussion, let me point you to the chapter in his book titled "Building A Technology Plan". Here are the specific topics he covers: contact management systems, personal digital assistants (PDA's), presentation tools, wireless technology, Internet safety, building profitable websites, and developing effective e-mail systems.

YOUR PERSONAL COACH

Allen Hainge, CRS, is a former top producing real estate professional who has been teaching real estate technology seminars for over a decade. He has been a featured speaker at a number of NAR national conventions and was a Senior Instructor for the Council of Residential Specialists technology course for eleven years. I attended a seminar he presented at an Oregon Association of Realtors convention and was impressed with his ability to make the complex comprehensible and even entertaining. I reviewed his books *Dominate! Capturing Your Market With Today's Technology* and *Secrets of the Cyberstars—Making Money With Today's Technology* for *The Real Estate Professional* magazine. I highly recommend both books as solid sources on the topic of technology as it relates to the real estate professional. To order the books log on to his web site at www.afhseminars.com.

In his *Dominate!* book Hainge outlines a technology action plan for real estate professionals at the beginner, intermediate, and advanced levels. Since you're probably looking beyond the beginning stage, I'll include all three levels. If you're just starting to explore the wonders of technology you may need to do some additional research to understand all his guidance, but it will be worth your efforts. Regarding the number one step of hiring a coach, you'll want to do a lot of research before you implement that one.

Beginner

- Hire a technology coach, one who also knows real estate.
- Get a good notebook computer.
- Connect to the Internet using an ISP (Internet Service Provider).
- Acquire your own domain name. Incorporate if into your e-mail address and begin publicizing that address.
- Learn to use the major components of e-mail: attachments, filters, signatures, and mailboxes.
- Make sure you know the principal functions of Windows.
- Spend one to two hours a day looking at agent sites nationwide and learning new technology.
- Get a good template website.

Intermediate

- Create multiple "signatures" for your e-mail, one for every routine request you receive and several for use at the end of your e-mail messages.
- Intensify your campaign to gather e-mail address of both consumers and other top agents.
- Start your custom e-mail newsletter, personalizing it though the use of your real estate database or WordMerge.
- Learn Microsoft Publisher and begin creating custom marketing pieces for your seller and buyer presentations.
- Begin to check out major real estate websites on a regular basis, specifically Realty Times.
- Create and implement a plan for adding more content to your website.
- Formulate your plan to publicize your website.
- Get VisualTour.com software. Learn how to create your own multimedia tours, how to put them on your site, how to save them to disk and how to e-mail them.
- Get eNeighborhoods. Learn how to do reports and how to e-mail them to prospects.
- If you don't have one, get a good real estate database and move your business into it.

Advanced

- Hire a technically literate Personal Assistant.
- Create VisualTour.com tours for your overall market area and move

each specific area of subdivision within that area. Post them to your website and copy them to disks for distribution

- Get the e-mail addresses of the top 10% of the agents in your local association. Begin e-mailing them multimedia tours of your new listings, after having obtained their permission to do so.
- Analyze your printed mailing expenses for the previous twelve months. Create and implement a plan for reducing that expense by at least 40% through the use of e-mail, HotSend and PDF files on your site.
- Hire a site designer to create personalized site.
- Formulate major campaign to brand your website in your area.
- If your site designer does not do so, get the services of a good graphic artist to create original artwork for your site and all your promotional materials.
- Create an extranet on your site for updating all current buyers, sellers and anyone involved in your current transactions.
- Spend one hour a day looking at nationwide agent sites. When you find a good one, e-mail the agent asking for a link to his or her site. Add the agent to your e-mail newsletter database.
- Attend every real estate convention you can: local association, state association, NAR and franchise. Network with other top agents at the convention.

In the event you haven't burned yourself out checking out real estate websites, I've got another project for you. Log on to www.cyberstars.net. This is the Allen Hainge website. You will find easy to navigate links to a group he founded, the CyberStars, a nationwide group of over 150 top real estate sales professionals who use technology to dominate their marketplace. It will be quite a learning experience for you. Not only are the websites models of cutting edge technology, but there are a number of articles on the individual websites written by various CyberStars. Many are aimed at newcomers to the profession. Check them out.

ONE LAST WEBSITE (I PROMISE)

While researching another writing project I ran across a resource that I think will be of particular interest to you. It's the website of Team Rothenberg Pacific Union, located in the San Francisco East Bay community of Lafayette, California. Log on to www.teamrothenberg.com. While I was stationed with the Air Force at Cal Berkeley 1966-70 my family and I lived in Walnut Creek, which is just a few miles from Lafayette. I drove through it each day on my commute to Berkeley. It's an incredibly lovely area with homes that are, to say the least, somewhat pricey.

Here is what impressed me about this site. There are a number of cities in the immediate area, all of which would be legitimate markets for a company headquartered in Lafayette. I clicked on my old stomping grounds of Walnut Creek. What popped up was what appears to be the entire inventory of all listings (not just the Rothenberg's) in Walnut Creek, starting with the most expensive at a cool $2,499,000. There were 193 listings in all. Each had a link to the individual property, many with photos and contact information for the listing brokerage. I didn't need to type in the kind of property I was looking for or the price range. There were search engines on the web site you could do this, but here you just scrolled down and checked them all out. You also did not have to log in, give your name, rank, and serial number to get information.

There was an e-mail update feature for new listings if you wished to be contacted, but you could do the whole thing in complete anonymity. There was another feature that really impressed me. For most listings you could map out the location. I typed in the address of our old home and it showed me exactly how to get from there to the listed property. Here's my point: It gave me what I wanted to know. Not just enough information to hook me into contacting the real estate company. Trust me, if I were heading back to the East Bay I would contact team Rothenberg.

Incidentally, if you're looking for a "real estate is a great investment" story, consider this. When we bought our nice, brand new three bedroom two bath home in a great little Walnut Creek neighborhood in 1966 we paid $30,000 (no down, federal VA loan.) One of the listings on the Rothenberg website was a four bedroom, three bath home just down the street from ours. It was built by the same builder in the same year. As I recall it was priced in the mid thirty thousands. The listing price: $1,299,000! My ears are still ringing from my wife screaming: "I told you we should have kept that house!" as she was looking over my shoulder as I was writing this.

TECHNOLOGY: TOOLS OF THE TRADE

One of the most memorable of the computer related TV ads I recall showed a young fellow who had just purchased the latest computer package, the Whiz Banger Ultimo Model 101. It had all the bells and whistles. As he was happily driving home to set up his new playmate he passed a billboard. Workers were putting up a huge ad touting the brand new, completely revolutionary, blow everything before it out of the water, Whiz Banger Ultimo Model 102. Relax. The important thing is to know what basic tools you need, get them, and learn how to use them. Then when something new comes along you'll be able to make an informed decision as to whether you need to upgrade or not.

Speaking of tools, *Realtor Magazine* recently ran a *Technology Buyer's Guide* supplement to their regular magazine. They included their suggestions for a "Budget Toolbox," a "Midrange Toolbox," and a "Deluxe Toolbox." In each category they suggested specific products, but the categories are what are informative. Here are the basics they recommended for each toolbox: a cell phone, a digital camera, a Palmtop, and a Laptop. Naturally you'll wish to stay tuned, since I recently saw a news release discussing a product under development that will combine many functions into one instrument.

Each time I run across an article in a real estate magazine or on the Internet which deals with "Top Real Estate Tech Tools" I take note. One item that has appeared in each piece is the REDTablet PC. It's a flat, portable tablet computer designed specifically for real estate agents. It works in conjunction with the Real Estate Dashboard software to offer a mobile and paperless business tool for agents. It lets them take notes in their own handwriting, convert them to a Word file, collect e-signatures, manage documents digitally, and access transaction files wirelessly. Of course, by the time you read this you may be saying: "How quaint and old fashioned. My REDTablet is in my antique cabinet along with my IBM Selectric typewriter."

WHAT MATTERS MOST

A couple of years ago I was working with an associate in my office in locating a home for our daughter and grandson. She was an experienced real estate professional with a complete grasp of all the technological innovations as they relate to real estate. Her husband is a computer engineer at the local Hewlett-Packard plant. I'm not sure whether they have a computer in every room, but close. All that was noteworthy, but here's what really impressed me. Several years before she had worked with a home inspection company in an administrative capacity. When we located the home we wanted to buy and made an offer on it we naturally made it subject to a full home inspection. She was a virtual fountain of useful information before, during, and after the inspection. Is it important to your real estate career to be able to use the tools of technology productively? Of course. Just remember what really matters most to your customers and clients.

My experience is borne out by highly successful professionals. For example, Margaret Vierra, a top producing agent in Morgan Hills, California (www.mvierra.com) was posed this question for in an interview for a *Realtor Magazine* article in their *Technology Buyer's Guide:* "How do you use technology?" Her answer: "Gingerly. I capture the attention of prospective clients with Internet advertising and stay connected with my cell phone. But once I establish a relationship with a client, personal attention is essential to success." Should we follow her guidance? Here was her "tech tip" for readers: "The bottom line for success is to take good care of your customers. Stay connected but don't rely too much on technology. By striking a balance, I grossed more than $12 million last year."

SPELLING "BEA"

I know it can be intimidating when you are faced with technological challenges and when you encounter someone who seems to know all there is to know about, let's say, computers. But to put things in perspective and to emphasize that there are many skills you probably already possess that matter just as much, consider this: When my wife and I were setting up our first computer in our home, we were having difficulty getting all the systems integrated. At the time, my wife worked at a local educational institution. It had a huge array of computers for the staff. We hired the young man in charge of the whole system to come out and get everything set up for us. He did a magnificent job. When he finished, he asked me for a key word he could type in to see if a particular program was working properly. I said, "Type in real estate." He typed, "reel estate."

7
Listing Residential Property

Finding the Sellers and Moving the Merchandise

"If you list, you last" sums up the sentiment of most brokers. It's not hard to appreciate why they feel that way. Listings are the basic inventory of the real estate business. They are what's for sale up on the shelf. It's been said: "When your last listing is gone, you've had your going-out-of-business sale." That's not much of an overstatement. Even though there are now brokerages that specialize in working exclusively with buyers, it's clear that unless there is something to sell, everything grinds to a halt.

Lots of positive things happen when a good listing comes into the office. First, everyone, including all those using the local multiple listing service, can start to look for a buyer. In most cases, no matter who finally sells a listing, the listing agent and broker collect their fees. Second, the listing can be advertised, which generates activity that benefits the entire staff. Finally, a "For Sale" sign can be placed in the yard—and having those in front of dozens of prime properties (with a rider with your name prominently displayed on many of them as the listing agent) is one of the best forms of advertising possible.

Your broker will also want you to have a success experience early on—a desire you will share passionately. It's generally easier to get a listing than to make a sale because there are typically more people who want to sell than there are qualified buyers who want to purchase. For all these reasons expect to be encouraged to develop your listing skills as your first order of business.

FINDING THE SELLERS

If, as they say, "old salespeople never die, they just become listless," then here are some suggested sources of listings to keep you alive and perky. In the discussion that follows, I am assuming a traditional relationship between the licensee (you) and seller in which the owner who lists a property is the client, pays the commission, and is owed a fiduciary responsibility.

■ *Former Clients of Agents No Longer in the Office.* All offices have some turnover of agents, and not every broker does what would be in his best interests-that is, assign someone to take over abandoned accounts. For example, the Pearsons bought a home through your brokerage eight years ago from an agent long since gone. No one is keeping in touch with them. Research the situation. You would do that by reviewing the "deal files" that all brokerages maintain. When you locate these cases, ask to handle them, for legally they are your broker's listing, not that previous agent's. If you get the go-ahead, send the prospects a letter with your card and any other appropriate promotional material, and follow up with a phone call or a personal visit. I did this when I was getting started (with my broker's blessing) and came up with several leads that eventually resulted in a couple of listings - and sales.

■ *Builders and Remodelers.* Be very selective in cultivating this source. Builders differ greatly in their perception of how business should be conducted. Naturally, you want to list the homes of builders who share your philosophy. If you are fortunate to establish rapport with one who does quality work and who will market his homes through you, it will add an interesting and profitable dimension to your activities. Of course, you could really strike it rich if you happen to land the account of a large-scale builder who is developing subdivisions of homes. I was fortunate. My primary broker was also a large-scale builder (we're talking subdivisions), and I also represented two young, enthusiastic, incredibly ethical young men who had their own company. They built one quality home at a time and I sold it for them.

■ *Absentee Owners.* People who own real estate in your community but live out of the area are excellent prospects. This is especially true if they are absentee rental property owners, since the aggravation associated with that arrangement can provide a terrific motivation to sell. The first step is to pick an area and research a manageable number of properties. There are public records in the assessor's or tax collector's office that you can use, and there is probably a reverse directory for your community, published annually, which lists residences by address and indicates the occupants' names, along with a notation as to whether they are owners or renters. The Internet is also a great source of information.

After you obtain the addresses of the owners, prepare a letter in which you introduce yourself and your company and offer your marketing assistance to them, should they wish to sell. Personalize it with a handwritten note and call the particularly promising prospects. It is remarkable how positively most people react to long-distance business calls that are properly handled.

Don't call before 9 A.M. or after 10 P.M. (*their* time, not yours). It is hard to establish rapport with someone you have just awakened.

■ *For Sale by Owner (FSBO).* Every new real estate agent has probably been advised or required to call people who are attempting to sell their homes themselves. The reason for pursuing homes for sale by owner (FSBO—or "fizzbos," as they are fondly known) is simple. History shows that a large percentage of them find the whole process so daunting that they eventually list with a broker. If you can convince them that you can do a better job than they can and net them as much money (or more), they are likely to list with you.

Calling fizzbos gets mixed reviews from agents. Some very successful ones do it as a matter of routine and develop a real knack for it. Others abandon the effort after they secure other sources. Some never do it at all. No matter what course you select, there is one instance when you should definitely call. If you are working with a buyer for whom a particular fizzbo listing looks promising, call and ask for a one-party listing. This is a listing that would be valid for only the person to whom you showed the property.

Be prepared for skepticism when you call, however, for one of the gimmicks some unethical agents use is to call and indicate they have a buyer and would like to preview the property. The buyer is fictitious, but, for some agents, the chance to get their foot in the door seems to justify the dishonesty. Once they've been taken (or hear from someone who has), sellers understandably become wary, so when you approach them with the genuine article they are hard to convince. However, if you have a legitimate prospect, it is definitely worth your effort. *The For Sale By Owner Kit* by Robert Irwin (see "Real Estate Marketing," Appendix C) is an excellent source of information. It's written for the consumer—the potential fizzbo—and will give you a good insight on how you might tap into the market. *Home Selling For Dummies* by Ray Brown is another excellent basic reference, and there's even a website, www.myfsbo.com you might want to visit to see how the fizzbo market is being targeted.

My experience in working with fizzbo's is that they are frequently uninformed on one critical item—how to price their home. It's a sensitive area, but one in which you need to develop expertise so that you may offer sound guidance.

■ *Expired Listings.* If a property has been on the open market for an extended period and has not sold, ask yourself why. If it was because the listing agent did not handle the marketing properly or did not try to get price reductions when it did not sell, there is a good chance that a fresh, more professional approach will get better results. If it was because the sellers were not motivated or some other factor you cannot change, it probably will not be worth your time. The fact of the matter is that the number one reason listings don't sell is price, so you need to factor that into your approach.

Whether you work expired listings or not, keep track of them. You may encounter a buyer who is looking for exactly the kind of property that was previously on the market. Very unique listings, especially extremely high-priced ones, may go unsold, so it is worth keeping tabs on them. In working expired listings, be circumspect in dealing with the owners, for they have had an unsuccessful experience with another real estate agent. Out of professional courtesy, resist any temptation (no matter how well justified) to criticize your predecessor's efforts. Never, under any circumstances, contact a seller *before* a listing has expired, in anticipation of being able to secure the listing later. That is unethical and could get you in serious difficulty.

■ *Ads Generated by Buyer Contacts.* Some buyers are in no hurry. They will describe an ideal property to you, whether it is a home, a small acreage, or a business. If you can find what they are looking for, fine. Otherwise, they will stay put. If you occasionally run short newspaper ads indicating that you have a potential buyer for a specific type of property, you may be able to generate some excellent listings. Again, you will probably encounter skepticism, for an advertisement for a prospective buyer is a ploy used by those few who are willing to bend the truth to make the phone ring.

■ *Farming.* The prospecting technique known as *farming* is covered in almost all real estate training programs. In its classic form, it involves an agent deciding on a specific area of town (typically a section with 200 to 300 homes in a homogeneous, contiguous neighborhood) and "farming it" for listings. The tactic most usually advocated is a series of personal visits to each home on the farm, spaced throughout the year. The objective is to become so well known to the home owners that they will automatically think of you when it is time to sell.

Suggested farming procedures include leaving gifts (calendars, pens, pot holders, memo pads—all with your name and phone number on them), writing a newsletter (including neighborhood information, such as who baby-sits, who is moving out or in, and so on), and organizing neighborhood activities (get-togethers for newcomers, block parties). The recommended initial contact is through a door-to-door "cold call" (no previous contact), using a rehearsed, introductory speech.

Some agents have gotten rich farming and stay rich by doing it faithfully. Others are not comfortable with the door-to-door solicitation approach (in some places there are laws against it) and remain unconvinced that it is a wise expenditure of time. Others farm, but use techniques such as phone calls, printed newsletters, and e-mail contacts.

If you decide to farm, do your homework. We've owned a modest condominium that we've rented out for a decade or so. Several years ago, an eager real estate agent decided to farm that neighborhood. He never bothered to check to see who owned the property. Our tenant was delighted to keep receiving the gifts, but the potential payoff for the agent was nonexistent.

Let's assume you do decide to homestead a nice little farm. What information do you think would be of most interest to those in your area? Hands down, it's the price of homes that have sold. A college friend of my wife's lived with her husband in Austin, Texas, for many years. She informed me that for the entire time they were there the agent who sold them their home originally sent out a monthly newsletter to all the neighbors. In addition to general real estate information, the selling price of every home that ever sold in the area was always included. When they moved from Austin to Dripping Springs, Texas, (really, there is such a place) they listed with that agent.

■ *Focused Fandango Farming.* Here's a suggestion. When you get your first listing (after the celebration party is over) use that as a vehicle to develop a well defined, focused farm. You will have printed flyers promoting the property, there will be a For Sale sign in the front yard (hopefully with your name on it), and you'll schedule an open house early in the listing. What better justification for knocking on every door in the neighborhood and introducing yourself? Your first step will be to define the geographic area precisely and get information on each household, including naturally the names of the owners. Make it a manageable farm. Believe me, they will all be interested in how much their neighbors are asking for their property. They will also be paying close attention to how you handle the listing. And when that "sold" sign appears on the sign what do you think their reaction will be? Right, in addition to being impressed with you, they will really want to know how much it sold for. In this situation every time you contact the people in your nice little focused farm, you'll have a legitimate reason. From that point on you'll keep in contact with printed or e-mail newsletters and perhaps an occasional phone call and maybe even a personal visit. Let's move down the path a couple of years. You've had a dozen or so sold listings. Think of the incredible number of contacts you will have. You know them. They know you. Keep it personal and keep it informative. As with all your projects, you'll want to coordinate with this one with your broker.

Here's a variation of Focused Fandango Farming. As soon as you license is activated, get a list of names and addresses of all your neighbors. Send them personalized letters announcing your entry into the profession. Include your business card. Also include information on sales within the neighborhood (you'll need to define the territory you want to cover) for the past year or so. Let them know that as soon as any other sales occur in your neighborhood you will keep them informed. Don't be shy. Ask for their business and their referrals. A monthly newsletter would be a good vehicle to get this done.

And why Focused "Fandango" Farming? Because you will be dancing all the way to the bank.

■ *Cold-Call Telephone Canvassing.* This is another traditional prospecting device. Homeowners are called (sometimes at random, other times with a plan) and asked if they are considering selling their home or if they know anyone who might be. Specific scripts are generally used, with recommended answers to just about any conceivable home owner question or objection. As is the case with farming, cold-call canvassing has its share of both converts and detractors. Some swear by it, others at it.

■ *Whatever Works for You.* It will be impossible for you to follow completely all the suggestions for getting listings that will be given in your training program (or, for that matter, in this discussion). Much will be dictated by local circumstances and by your personality. Simply become familiar with all the potential sources and concentrate your efforts on those that appear to have the greatest potential. It is entirely possible that you may end up spending most of your time on one specific program that turns out to be particularly productive.

When you are considering the alternatives, don't be too quick to write off procedures because you react adversely to the basic concept. For example, you might conclude that a traditional prospecting program does not suit you, but with some adaptation and refinement, it might have real possibilities. Whatever system you decide on, give it some time before you expect it to start paying dividends. Finally, don't be discouraged. Remember, getting started is the hardest part, and almost any organized approach that is followed diligently is almost certain to be better than no system at all.

BE READY!

Here is a quick story about one of my former students who was well known in the local business community. Shortly after he was licensed, he called and invited me to meet for a free cup of coffee. He nervously informed me that he had anticipated his first listing might be a nice modestly priced little bungalow in the suburbs. Much to his utter amazement, the owner of a huge motel-restaurant complex (with an individual home thrown in for good measure) learned that he was in real estate and wanted to list the property with him. My advice was to talk to his broker and get help from a more experienced agent in the company. He did and the story has a happy ending; but don't assume you'll start with a nice, easy introductory real estate project.

Working with Sellers

After you become well established, people will often simply call and tell you they want to sell their property and they want you to handle it for them. It might be a family you sold a house to or sold a house for, or it might be someone who was referred to you. That is when real estate becomes really satisfying and profitable. In these cases, you merely prepare ahead of time by coming up with pricing information and a marketing plan and meet with the people to take the listing. It won't be quite that easy in the beginning.

Most people, when they decide they want to list, call several different real estate companies. That way they get three or four estimates of an asking price and they have a chance to evaluate the real estate agent who would handle the listing. To be competitive in such an environment, you need to convince the owners that you are a highly competent practitioner who is capable of selling the property.

Preparing for the Listing Appointment

Let's assume you have secured an appointment to discuss listing a residential home. Here are some of the steps you can take to ensure that you do a professional job in making your presentation, taking the listing, marketing it, and seeing the transaction through to a successful close. I should disclose to you that the approach I advocate is a somewhat more lengthy listing process than other approaches. There is a school of thought that says, "Get it all done in one visit and move on out." You can choose. Here's my recommendation:

1. Research the property thoroughly. The first step is to secure a listing packet. In some areas, the local title company will provide you with one for free that includes things such as the legal description, a plat map (showing property boundaries), assessor's tax information, and ownership data. If you have to do the research yourself, all the information will generally be available in public records. Increasingly such information is available via computer, but however you get it, the information is essential. There will be a formalized system in place in the brokerage with which you affiliate, so learn the details early.

2. Visit the residence. Remember, this is *before* the formal listing appointment. At this point, you are gathering information. Inspect the neighborhood and the home, take measurements, become familiar with the amenities, ask questions about how things work, and get a feel for the general area. The listing form your office uses will provide guidelines. When you visit the home, take along one or two other agents from your office. It is always good to get a balanced input. Each agent should give you suggestions

on pricing. You will do the same for them on their listings, so don't feel you are imposing.

Be sure to become fully aware of all immediate neighborhood properties currently or recently on the market, whether they're for sale by owners or are listed. Homeowners are generally familiar with what is going on around them. If you do not include this information in your market analysis, you will lose credibility.

3. Complete a market analysis. A competitive market analysis (CMA) is simply a process in which you do research to determine your estimate of the market value of a property. Your office will have forms to help you prepare yours, but you may eventually want to adapt these to meet your needs. Your first few will take some time, but soon you will perform them quickly, as a matter of routine. With the advent of computers, it's now more a matter of knowing the right buttons to push and being able to interpret the results.

Your goal is to present the home owners with information upon which they may make their pricing decision—how much they will ask for their home. To do this you will compare their home to similar properties in the same area that sold recently. You will also include information on unsold homes currently on the market and homes that were on the market but did not sell. It's basically the process an appraiser uses in arriving at an estimate of value for residential properties. It will be tempting to suggest a specific asking price, and many agents do just that (I will admit I did). However, it is probably wiser to present the information and let the home owner make the decision on a specific asking price. It won't be a big secret what you think a reasonable figure should be.

4. Bring your listing folder up-to-date. You need to make certain that you have all the forms that the sellers need to review, descriptive material about you and your office, and information (including pictures and flyers) about other listings you have. A display binder with plastic inserts is often used. Many agents also now carry along laptop computers that can plug in to the local MLS to display pictures and information on other current listings. You can also do incredible things now with a digital camera, which allows you to take pictures of the property and display them immediately.

You wouldn't stand before an audience to deliver a thirty-minute speech without having prepared an outline ahead of time. Neither should you go to a listing appointment without some idea as to how you would like to proceed when you get there. I do not, however, recommend reciting canned presentations, for the same reason that speech instructors do not recommend presenting memorized speeches. If you forget your lines, you'll come across as a mumbling, incompetent novice. Work out an approach you are comfortable with, make sure you cover the major items that any seller needs to know, and be flexible.

Before you arrive, confirm that all the decision makers will be on hand for the appointment. Also, suggest as tactfully as possible that non-decision makers not be there. Friends and relatives kibitzing from the sidelines can complicate the situation for everyone.

During the Listing Appointment

Here are some things to consider during the listing appointment. Make sure you have all the information and forms handy.

1. Go over the market analysis. The logical order of events suggests itself if you understand what is uppermost in the minds of the sellers. They want to know how much you think their home is worth. They also want to judge you.

Most training programs advocate going through a long ritual before you share pricing information with the poor folks. That always seemed artificial and self-defeating to me, but do what works for you. The first figures I discussed with them was the price range I thought their home was in, based upon *closed sales* of comparable properties. Emphasize that where in that range *they* decide to establish the asking price will be determined largely by their motivation to sell. As you would suspect, the lower in the price range, the more likely the home will move quickly, although determining real estate value is an art, not a science, so be very conservative in how you phrase your statements.

The second item on the agenda is for the home owners to decide on a suggested asking price, which is almost always somewhat higher than the anticipated selling price (in recognition of the universal procedure among buyers to offer less than full price). It's at this point you need to suggest that your sellers look at the transaction through the eyes of potential buyers. It's quite likely that if the asking price is inflated well beyond what the owners would actually sell for, many excellent prospects will never even bother to look at the home, assuming that it's out of their price range.

Be sensitive to feedback. You should be able to tell whether you are gaining the sellers' confidence or not, but do not be afraid to ask questions. Not even the most experienced real estate agent is infallible, so if it is apparent that they think their home is worth a lot more than your analysis seems to indicate (rarely do they think it's worth less), agree to review it and seek another agent's opinion.

2. Provide information about yourself and your company. You can use your listing folder for this and maybe some snappy computer graphics. Some agents even have a short promotional video. You want the sellers to see you for what you are—a skilled professional. After you've been in the business a few years you can impress them with the number of listings you've sold and provide them with names of past clients as referrals. You also want your com-

pany to come across as an aggressive, wide-awake organization that is respected within the community. If you have letters of appreciation and diplomas from educational programs such as GRI, have copies displayed in the plastic inserts. Modesty will dictate a low-key approach when extolling your own virtues, but people do want to know something about you.

Explain how the multiple listing service works, and describe in detail any special marketing techniques you use, such as advertisements, flyers, the Internet, and contacts with special groups of buyers. Describe your company. If there are successful agents who work there, that fact will enhance the likelihood that a listed property will be sold.

3. Show them the actual forms they will sign. Use the listing form itself to explain the various ramifications of listing a property, including the formal agency relationship, the role of your broker, the obligations they incur, and the actions you pledge. Leave the forms with them to review and study, unless they want to proceed with the listing immediately.

4. Go over a "net proceeds to seller" computation. Sellers are interested in the bottom-line amount they will get from the sale. It is what they walk away with at closing that concerns them. At this time, you can give only a rough idea, because there are as yet many unknown factors. Despite the limitations, you can provide a fairly good estimate, with the major variable being the final sales price. After outstanding mortgage and other financial encumbrances are paid, the largest single cost is generally the commission (be ready to describe all the things you do to earn those big bucks). The simplest way of presenting the net-proceeds-to-seller information is as part of the market analysis, on the same form, although some offices use separate forms. When the actual offer is presented, you will do a more detailed "seller's net" sheet.

In most cases, property owners will thank you for your time and tell you that they will think it over and give you their decision later. There is a series of techniques designed to forestall that and to convince them to list immediately. Chances are they will have encountered this approach if they have talked to other agents. There are those who believe a low-key, no-pressure approach actually works better. They realize that it is probably a good idea for the sellers to take a little time; after all, the home owner is making a very important decision. Those agents maintain that sellers are generally so relieved not to be hassled that they become very receptive to doing business.

Taking the Listing

You call to follow up (no, you don't wait for them to call you) and are informed you've got the listing. You will then return for another appointment to get the signed contract.

1. Complete the listing agreement. The home owners have had the documents to review and you have gone over it with them, but this time it's for the record, and they will have questions. Make certain that you fill in all the items (don't skip something and say, "We'll fill that in later") and ensure the listing has an expiration date.

Almost all listing forms contain an item about "known defects." Most states now have mandatory property condition disclosure forms. No home is perfect, not even a new one, and if there are defects that the owners know of, they must disclose them.

2. Discuss hidden defects. Selling real estate is more complicated and much riskier than it once was. The concept of *caveat emptor* (let the buyer beware) is rapidly changing. Courts are ruling that sellers and agents are liable to buyers for defects they should have known about but did not. Even in the states where there are no mandatory disclosure laws, many brokers will not take a listing without a formal written property disclosure. That's a very sound practice.

An independent inspection will help. It would be better for the sellers to have the inspection done and to correct any deficiencies before putting the property on the market, but it's not always easy to convince them of that. If the sellers decide to order an inspection, advise them to hire a company that does not also do structural repair (in some places that's not permitted by law), because they have a disconcerting habit of finding a lot of work that needs to be done. Sellers may be reluctant to get an early inspection, but if there is bad news, it is better for them to know about it up front than to wait for the issue to surface later.

3. Agree on the asking price. What happens if the sellers inform you that they have decided to list their home for substantially more than the highest range you documented? Should you take the listing? You will quickly learn that there are few things more frustrating and time-consuming than servicing an overpriced listing. However, if you make the sellers aware of the dangers inherent in listing above the market and if the price is not flagrantly excessive, you will probably want to take the listing. During your first year or so in the business, you will probably take a listing at almost any price. Be sensitive to market conditions, however, and recommend a price reduction if the listing has not generated interest after a reasonable period of time.

4. Avoid the temptation to "buy a listing". Here's what I mean. If a home owner has interviewed several agents and has received an estimate of market value from each, it may be tempting, assuming the owner shares the results with you, to offer an estimate higher than anyone else just to motivate the owner to list with you. Yes, it's done in the real world.

For example, I'm very familiar with a townhouse development in the local area. All the homes were built in the same time frame by the same builder and were all the same design and size. A rigorous Homeowner's Association keeps the development impeccably groomed and maintained. All of this results in property values that are very similar, as past sales clearly indicate. I recently saw a "For Sale" sign in front of one of the town homes with brochures available. The listing price was clearly well above market. It stayed on the market unsold for over three months (average days on market were much shorter at that point). It eventually sold after two price reductions. Did the agent "buy" the listing? You decide.

5. Provide a checklist for the home owners. The final step is to give the owners a standardized checklist on how to prepare their home to show. In many localities, the multiple listing service provides a checklist. If it's not available from MLS, someone in your office may have one, or you can make one up yourself with just a little thought. There are even videos on the market that present the information in an entertaining way.

The advantage of giving your clients a preprinted form or a video suggesting steps such as cleaning, painting, and keeping the house neat is that you will not be perceived as criticizing their house or yard—you are simply providing generalized guidance. Be prepared, however, to diplomatically bring up any specific problems that may detract from showing the home. The family dog often poses a particular difficulty, especially if, like most dogs, he is very unreceptive to strangers tromping around on his turf. If the owners are not home, the dog should be left in a secure area so the showing can take place with a minimum of disruption to Rover's tranquility and your prospects' nerves.

If you would like further information on products to assist you in working with sellers in prepping their properties, visit the Web site of Barb Schwarz at www.stagedhomes.com. Schwarz is the pioneer in this activity within the real estate profession. A DVD she markets is designed to be presented to home sellers. It's titled "How to Stage Your Home to Sell for Top Dollar". It's described and is available from her Web site. Schwarz has also founded the International Association of Home Staging Professionals (www.iahsp.com) which awards the professional designation of Accredited Staging Professional (ASP). Incidentally, it's a real estate career option that some folks find exciting and profitable.

After Getting the Listing

To "move the merchandise," you need to be aggressive and creative in developing a marketing plan for each of your listings, and you must follow up to keep your clients informed. Perhaps the most common complaint among home owners who have listed is that "after all the sweet talk, we never heard from the agent again." You can help forestall that by enlisting their efforts in calling you each time the home is shown by an agent. Here are some specific things you need to do when carrying out your marketing strategy.

1. Prepare the multiple listing entry. Review listings as they appear in your multiple listing. You will find that many are sparse. Make yours complete. Although MLS formatting requirements have standardized most entries, there is still typically room for a few comments. Remember that the users are other real estate agents, so answer the questions that they will have. Include measurements of major rooms, indicate the size of the lot, describe unique features, and by all means, outline the terms upon which the house may be purchased. If there is an assumable loan, verify with the lender in writing under what conditions it may be assumed. If the seller will help with financing, point that out. In a tough market, terms often sell houses.

2. Place signs on the property. In many locales, "For Sale" signs sell more property than any other marketing device. In some exceptional instances, your client may not permit a sign, but most relent when they learn how effective they are. A rider on the sign that says, "Ask for Sarah Smith" will give you good exposure. As you service the listing, drive by periodically to make sure the sign is still up and visible. There are also "talking house" signs that work well for some agents. These permit a drive-by prospect to tune in to a local radio frequency and pick up information on the property (see Appendix C, under "Real Estate Promotionals"). As a minimum it's essential to have a supply of printed brochures in a box in the front yard so folks who pass by can pick up information. More details about those later.

3. Arrange for access to the property. Lock boxes are effective and convenient, but using them can pose problems. Real estate agents are busy and the easier a home is to show the more likely they are to show it. A lockbox contains a key to a home and members of the local multiple listing service are the only people who have access to the lock boxes, so you would think that security would be pretty effective. Unfortunately, carelessness and downright dishonesty have resulted in some home owners being wary of relying on the lockbox technique. If a lockbox is not used and if the key is left in your office, it is crucial that a foolproof and responsive system be implemented that will permit the property to be shown easily and at the same time provide owners the safety and security they deserve.

4. Advertise the property. All advertising must be done under your broker's supervision. If you are asked to prepare copy on your listings, keep it simple, honest, and interesting. We mentioned "Talking House" as a possibility previously, but here are some things you can do on your own that are very effective.

First, prepare a one-page flyer for each of your listings. You can do it on your computer or have it done by a printer. Secure a picture of the property for the flyer and then simply list features that prospective purchasers will probably be interested in, including price and terms. Place your business card at the bottom and clearly indicate your broker affiliation. Include a disclaimer on the bottom making it clear that, although you believe the information is correct, you cannot guarantee it. However it's prepared, make the flyer look professional. There are a number of standard formats you can access on the Internet.

Place copies in a prominent place at the home itself for agents and prospects who are looking at the property. A box next to the "For Sale" sign is the standard procedure. Give your sellers a large number of extra copies to put in the box if the supply is exhausted. If you are working any type of marketing program in which you correspond with prospects, send some copies along. You will want to put one up on your office wall for visitors to see, and you should give other agents in your office as many as they require.

Should you include the asking price of the property on your flyer that you place in a box in the front yard? OK, whom are you representing? Whose interests are you putting above everyone else? Who gave you the authority to put the sign in the front yard? Of course, the answer to "all of the above" is the home owner who listed the property with you. People interested in that house want to know the asking price and if it's not there they could simply move on out of frustration and look elsewhere.. Some training programs counsel not including the price on the brochure, which will require the prospect to call the agent. That means it's a good potential marketing tool for the agent (perhaps for other listings that might be in the buyer's price range), but does it best serve the listing client? I report. You decide. If I'm your supervising broker you know the answer.

Get the information, including pictures, to your company's Web site as quickly as possible. Believe me, the home owner will be following that closely. Virtual tours are becoming more and more common and can be an extremely effective marketing device. Incredibly, some people make offers on homes as a result of seeing a virtual tour, subject to actually visiting the property.

5. Hold an open house. Although it is rare for an open house to result in a sale for that specific listing, it does happen. Even if it doesn't, the exposure you get from conducting an open house is beneficial. Most home owners will probably want you to hold one so it is a good idea to establish a routine that will allow you to achieve maximum results. Maintain a log of who visits, both as a record for the home owner and for you, and as a way of maintaining security. If you indicate to your visitors that the owners have asked for the information, most will comply willingly. Pay attention to each individual. Introduce yourself and attempt to fix name and face. Invite them to look at the home and give them a flyer. Many will be browsers, but some will likely be immediate prospects for a purchase—perhaps not for that home, but for another. The more you know about the visitors and their motivations, the better you can meet their needs. If they are non communicative, don't push. Be friendly, businesslike, and unobtrusive. If any appear suspi-

cious, keep an attentive eye on them and be particularly wary if two people arrive and one of them occupies you in conversation while the other disappears.

After the open house, send all visitors a note thanking them for stopping by, along with your card. Try to prepare the notes right after the open house and mail them from the post office so that they will be delivered the next day. If you judged anyone to be strong potential prospects (buyers or sellers), prepare a card on each one for your prospect file, and follow up.

6. Follow up on visits by real estate agents. Agents who either preview or show a listing are obligated to leave their business cards as a record of their visit. You will want to follow up with each agent personally. Get each one's reaction to the home, and secure feedback on pricing. If an agent noticed things that detract from the listing, discuss it with the owners.

Handling the Offer

Unless you sell your own listing to a prospect you are working with, the ball will typically get rolling by a telephone call from another agent, informing you: "I've got an offer on the Jones listing."

1. Present the offer. Procedures vary around the country as to what is good form in presenting offers, so local custom and courtesies will prevail. In many instances, agents will want to be with you when you meet with the Joneses. Some might not want to go over the offer with you before it is formally presented, but unless you preview everything, there is no way you can do your job properly. For example, verify that the other agent has made certain the prospective buyers are qualified. Sellers are concerned about both the motivation of the buyers and their financial capability.

2. Compute a net-proceeds sheet. One of the most important documents that sellers consider when they make their decision is the net proceeds to seller form. Because all the costs of the sale can now be accurately estimated based on a proposed sale price and exact terms (including a projected closing date), you can give your sellers a reasonably precise breakdown.

The first few forms you complete will be tough and you will need help. Prorating expenses can be tricky and time consuming. I received a lot of patient tutoring from a bright young escrow agent in a local title company. Computer programs are also now available that offer a convenient and helpful format.

It is always best to estimate potential expenditures on the high side, so that the sellers will end up getting no less than they expect. If you overlook or underestimate an expense and actual net proceeds are less than projected, you will have disgruntled sellers. They might even suspect you of inflating their expectations intentionally to get them to accept the offer so that you could earn a quick commission.

3. Let the sellers decide. After the offer has been presented, you should discuss it with the sellers privately and they should be given time to consider their decision. However, there are some advantages to accepting a good offer from highly qualified buyers when it's presented. Until an offer is accepted and the buyers are informed, they are under no obligation to consummate the transaction.

Following Up to Close

After the sellers accept and that is officially communicated to the buyers, the whole transaction enters its most crucial stage, and you need to stay on top of it to make sure that the things that need to be done, get done, and on time.

1. Make a list. Write down every task that needs to be accomplished, who must do it, and when it needs to be done. Some offices have a prepared checklist. Do not *assume* that something will be done. Make sure it *has* been done. Check on it yourself. Put it on the top of your daily schedule under number one priority. Do not accept evasive answers such as, "To the best of my knowledge the loan application has been submitted," or, "I am reasonably sure the credit check has been ordered." Your clients do not get their money until the transaction closes and neither do you. Be tough. Eliminate fall-throughs.

2. Give advice judiciously. Your sellers might ask for your advice in choosing other professionals, such as CPAs, attorneys, and title companies, to handle specialized phases of the transaction. It is wise to suggest two or three possibilities, particularly in the case of attorneys and CPAs, and let people make their own choices. If you steer a client toward someone specific and it does not work out, there could be repercussions. I would never recommend anyone with whom I had not had a personal, positive experience.

3. Follow up doggedly. It is very important to establish a personal working relationship with all other professionals involved in the transaction. At times, they will need prodding to get a job done expeditiously, because they are paid whether the transaction closes or not. Tact and good-natured persistence will be your best tools. Never recommend any company or individual who may have a vested interest in the outcome of the transaction without making that interest clear to all parties. Real estate brokers, for example, sometimes have partial ownership of title, escrow, and insurance companies.

"PLEASE LADY, DON'T INTERRUPT"

About a year after I joined the agency, our broker decided to affiliate with a national franchise. That meant all the agents had to go to a regional center for a week long training session on listing and selling. The facility, the staff, and the training techniques were all impressive. The center had the latest in instructional aids, including a videotaping device that allowed us to tape our listing presentations and play them back for critique. Instructors strongly believed in a structured, practiced approach to selling real estate and had little use for the more casual "do what the situation demands" method that had been my style.

Although my listing appointments had always seemed to work out well, I decided that I should be open minded and learn their system. That meant using charts and graphs to accompany a step-by-step rehearsed presentation that included answers for every possible objection. Depending on how many of those answers you had to use, the entire script was designed to last about forty-five to fifty minutes and to ensure that you walk out of the house with a signed listing agreement.

My first chance to use it in the field came when a woman called the office one day while I was on floor duty. She wanted someone to "come and tell me how much I can get for my house." The next day I went by to look at it and to take measurements to prepare for the actual listing appointment. The owner, Bonnie, was a young, single parent who worked to support herself and her little boy. She wanted to move to a larger town where job opportunities were better.

I spent almost an hour looking at the house and the grounds and asking questions. It was a lovely home. I was particularly impressed with the number of fruit-bearing trees and the ornamental shrubs she had, so I made a diagram of the yard with her help. We talked at length, but I was careful to save the "good stuff" for my upcoming presentation. An associate of mine went by later for a quick look of her own to help me arrive at a suggested price range.

The next day I returned for the listing appointment, bringing my entire arsenal of paraphernalia and ready to deliver a sales pitch that could have convinced King Tut to list his pyramid with me. I was dazzling as I tripped lightly and confidently from one point to the next, pausing only long enough to get her to answer setup questions (called minor closes).

After about fifteen minutes, I noticed a shift in mood. She became a bit less attentive and that pained "Lord, will this ever end?" look became evident in her face. (I recognized it from the days when I used to practice my school assignment speeches in front of my wife.) Maybe she needs to go to the bathroom, I thought, so I stopped momentarily to ask if everything was all right. "Oh yes, Mr. Edwards, but would it be OK with you if I went ahead and signed those papers now?" Sign now?! But I have charts I haven't shown you, accomplishments I haven't bragged about, and marketing programs I haven't explained. Worst of all, you have not come up with a *single* objection for me to counter! Sign now?! "Sure, Bonnie, that would be great. Right here. Press hard."

It was a fine listing. We sold it quickly and Bonnie moved to a larger city. She still calls when she visits. She later confided to me that she really wanted to sign that first day I came out, but that I seemed so intent on doing things my way that she didn't want to bring it up.

The training I received at the listing seminar was excellent. It was logical, orderly, and convincing. I used much of it later on during other listing appointments. I still have the padded simulated-leather listing folder that opens up for use as a visual aid on a table. The obvious point is that any training you receive must be adapted to your style and to the situation, and that nothing replaces common sense and good judgment. You will also find that if you show a genuine and knowledgeable interest in the property and the people, the personal rapport you achieve will overcome shortcomings in other areas.

IS IT WORTH ALL THE EFFORT?

It may occur to you that there is a lot of hard work involved in listing and marketing residential property. There is, if you do it right. There is also a great deal of satisfaction to be gained from it and excellent money to be made. Remember, when you secure a listing and put it on the MLS, every other agent in town immediately starts trying to find a buyer. If you have several realistically priced properties on the market at any one time, you will have a lot of help in making a living.

8

Selling Residential Property

Finding the Buyers, Listening to Them, and Satisfying Their Needs

If hitting a home run is the magic moment in baseball, then selling a house is the glamour event in residential real estate. Just find qualified buyers, match them with the home they want, and touch all the bases on your way to the bank. It's little wonder that new agents are chomping at the bit to go out there and sell houses.

Of course, selling real estate isn't that easy, but it does have special appeal. First, it can be extremely profitable. For what is often a comparatively short investment of your time, there is the potential for a very substantial commission. Second, working with motivated, qualified buyers can be a pure joy—for them, when they move into the home of their choice; for the sellers, when they collect their check at closing; and for you, when you get paid in satisfaction and money.

"Motivated" and "qualified" are the critical words when applied to buyers. If an agent can continually come face-to-face with people who are ready to buy and who have the means (called "belly-button-to-belly-button contact" in less genteel circles), it would be hard not to succeed. Although you will have plenty of competition in your quest for these prizes, you can win more than your fair share if you approach your task systematically and creatively.

As you consider this material, keep in mind our discussion of agency in Chapter 5. In keeping with what seems to be the trend, we will assume that in working with buyers you are representing them as their agent and that you owe them a fiduciary duty. We will also assume, however, that you do not have an exclusive contract with them and that they remain free to work with whomever they wish. Although there is a strong movement among buyer's agent groups to reach the point where buyers sign exclusive contracts with buyer's agents, we're not there yet. Even if you had such an agreement, most permit termination without much difficulty.

ARE BUYERS LIARS?

So, under our scenario, your potential buyers likely have no legal obligation to any agent. They can work with whomever they choose, whenever they choose. Some salespeople are devastated when they learn that buyers with whom they were in contact bought through someone else. If you are doing things correctly that will not happen often, but it will happen. When it does, you should analyze what you did wrong, or someone else did better, but there is nothing to gain by feeling betrayed. Buyers are concerned with their best interests, not yours, and that is perfectly understandable. You will thoroughly enjoy working with almost all of them, and most will display a remarkable loyalty to you—but there will be losses. Most buyers are not liars, although they may sometimes tell you what they think you want to hear to avoid hurting your feelings or to take the pressure off themselves. Reverse the roles and we would likely do the same.

CATEGORIES OF HOME BUYERS

Home buyers fall into rather broad, identifiable groups, each with somewhat different motivations and capabilities. What follows are the major segments of the buying public as they are most often classified. Some agents become so adept at working with certain types of buyers that they spend most of their time doing just that.

■ *First-Time Buyers.* Whether they're single or married with a small family or DINKS (double income, no kids), first-time buyers generally have less money for a down payment and a smaller monthly income. By necessity, they are more likely to accept small homes and attached homes. Those who are handy look for older, cheaper homes to buy and repair, but financing on such projects can be tricky. Be prepared to work with parents and older friends who are often called in to inspect potential purchases. Relatives often chip in for a portion of the down payments.

■ *Move-Up Buyers.* Most buyers in this category are married with children. They can come up with a hefty down payment because they have typically sold a home and are looking for something larger in which to raise the family. They tend to see detached housing as essential, and are often drawn to homes in the suburbs with large yards or small acreage.

■ *Empty Nesters.* Generally, empty nesters have a substantial amount to put down, because they have sold a house that became too large for them once their children left. They are experienced buyers. Listen carefully when they describe what they want, because they know. Depending on individual circumstances and preference, they will accept attached or detached housing.

■ *Retirees.* Like empty nesters, retirees probably have a sizable down payment, but monthly cost will be important if they are on a fixed income. They most often prefer a single-level house, because climbing stairs can pose a problem. Having lived through the golden years of the American dream of home ownership, they look upon owning a home as a solid financial invest-ment as well as a fulfilling emotional experience. Most seniors with whom I worked responded best to unhurried, uncomplicated house hunting and viewed with suspicion gimmicky financing. In some cases, you will work with children who want to look at the parents' choice before a final commit-ment is made. I'll expand somewhat on this topic in Chapter 17.

The following suggestions are intended to help you keep your "prospects" file full of one of the most coveted of all assets—ready, willing, and able buyers. You can never have too many of them.

MAKING THE MOST OF FLOOR DUTY

In most real estate offices, each day (or portion of it) one agent is desig-nated the "floor agent" and is required to be in the office to handle telephone inquiries and walk-ins. In some offices, the person on the floor also handles that day's correspondence in which someone requests information. If you are new, most brokers will require that you complete all the training programs before you perform floor duty.

Take floor duty as often as you can. In an active office, it could result in several excellent contacts each day. Almost 20 percent of my total income while I was actively selling came as a direct result of days on the floor. There's an adage among the troops in the military to "never volunteer for anything!" This is definitely an exception to that rule. You will most commonly deal with two types of inquires when you are on floor duty—call-ins and walk-ins. Here are some tips for handling these prospects.

Call-Ins

If an individual calls on a home-for-sale advertisement, he generally wants only one piece of information: the location of the property (assuming the price is stated in the ad). What he wants to do is what you would probably want to do under similar circumstances—drive by to see if it looks interesting.

No training program or text on real estate with which I am familiar advocates giving out the addresses in such instances. Some brokers absolutely refuse to let their agents do so. The fear is that the caller will drive by and, if he likes it, contact some other real estate company and buy through it.

There is an alternative approach that works well for some agents. Unless the home owners have specifically requested that the address of their home not be given out for drive-bys (rare, but possible), give the callers the information they want. Proponents of this approach maintain that callers are so relieved that they don't have to agree to an appointment to get the information that they become easy to work with. In addition, there can be no argument that it certainly gets exposure for the seller's home, and that is your primary duty.

With any call, your basic objective is to get to know the caller and sound like what you are: an informed real estate professional. You also need information, so try to finish each telephone conversation with the person's name, address, phone number, the type of home they are looking for, and a good idea of the caller's financial status. That may seem ambitious and even pushy, but you can't effectively solve housing problems unless you know the capabilities and limitations of the people involved. If they do not wish to immediately share such information, do not persist. Never antagonize a caller—it's mighty easy for them to hang up and deal with someone who is more congenial. At some point, ask whether it would be acceptable for you to call later if you encounter a listing that seems particularly well suited for them. With just a little experience and confidence, you can expect a high percentage of yes answers. If that doesn't happen, you're doing something wrong.

When you get names and addresses (including e-mail), immediately send a note with your card thanking the person for calling. If your conversation progresses beyond a simple exchange of information, inquire as to whether the caller has been working with anyone else in your office. If so, professional courtesy dictates that you inform that salesperson and turn the follow-up over to them. In some offices, if the listing agent is available, all incoming calls will be directed to that person.

It is not unusual for someone who calls on one of your broker's advertisements to be calling several other real estate companies about their advertisements at the same time. The person may be in town on a house-hunting trip, sitting in a motel room with the real estate section of your local newspaper spread out. Ask whether there is any other advertisement that they would like information about. Information on most properties is in multiple listings and thus immediately available to you; if the house is not multiple listed, you can get the information with a quick phone call to the listing broker. Assure the caller that you can show any house in which she has an interest, or you can put her in touch with someone who can.

Further, tell her that if she passes a house with any real estate company's "For Sale" sign in front of it and wants to know the price, she can call you. Many people think that the only company that can show or sell a house is the one whose sign is in front of it. (OK, I admit it. That's what I thought before I got my real estate license.) If a caller judges you to be honest and you are responsive, it is likely that you will turn out to be her sole real estate contact. The ultimate compliment will occur when one of your prospects calls and wants you to check on a "For Sale by Owner" for her, because you may be able to get a one-party listing in such an instance.

Walk-Ins

As the name implies, walk-ins are people who visit your office unannounced, wanting real estate information. When you talk to them, your goal is to gain their confidence and gather as much information as possible. Occasionally, however, walk-ins come in to look at a specific property with the intention of buying it if they like it or to list a piece of property they own. If that's the case, naturally you will not waste time with a lot of formalities.

PREPARING FOR FLOOR DUTY

Given the importance of floor duty, there are several things you should do to prepare for it. Make sure that you know well in advance when it is to be your turn "up." Mark the date on your calendar and make no other commitments for that day. Arrange for a backup to be on call if you have to leave the office for an extended period. Most agents have slipped up once, arriving at work unaware that they have floor duty. The ensuing panic is generally adequate to ensure that it does not happen again.

On the day you are actually on duty, get to your desk even earlier than usual so that you will be prepared if you get a call or a walk-in right at the opening of business. Some house hunters are early starters. Because many of the inquiries you receive will be in response to advertisements, make certain you are thoroughly familiar with those of your company, both the current ones and those from the immediate past. There is no substitute for firsthand knowledge, so try to personally visit each of the properties advertised.

Most companies discuss upcoming advertisements during staff meetings, with the listing agents presiding. Current advertisements represent only a portion of your brokerage's total listings, so it is essential that you bring yourself completely up-to-date on all the listings. Try to visit each property with the listing salesperson when the home is listed. Otherwise, you will need to hustle to catch up by looking at the ones you have missed, because it is crucial that you know the total inventory. If there are "listing caravans" in your locality where specific days are set aside to visit new listings, try hard to take advantage of them.

It is also important to read the advertisements of the other real estate companies in the area so that you can respond intelligently if you are asked about their listings. Using all the information you have from all sources, prepare a short list of select properties, similar to the ones in your advertisement. You will then be prepared to suggest alternatives if the advertised property does not meet the buyer's needs.

Have a form ready on which to record each call-in and walk-in. Your office will likely have a log for this. When you answer the telephone, a simple and confident, "Professional Realty, Sally Smith" gives the caller all the information needed to proceed. Some agents insist on answering with a minifilibuster ("Good morning! Thanks for calling Professional Realty, where service makes the difference. This is Sally Smith. How may I help you solve your housing problems?"), but that technique seems a little contrived. An effective way of handling calls you receive at home is to answer with just your name. Simply saying "hello" doesn't really help.

RECOGNIZING SPECIAL TARGETS

Certain groups of home buyers have exceptional potential. The better you understand them, the better the possibility of doing business with them.

Incoming Job Transfers.

People moving to your area because of a company transfer will probably have sold homes elsewhere, have sizable amounts of money to put down, and be motivated buyers.

Identify the companies, businesses, federal and state agencies, hospitals, universities, and other schools that have large numbers of employees. Those that are expanding or have high turnover rates have the greatest potential for generating customers for you. If you live near a military installation, you have the ingredients for sustained activity, because the military rotates its personnel every few years as a matter of policy. Be aware when you sell to a military family, however, that they will, in all likelihood, be moving in three or four years. Make sure the home is one you think you can resell for the family later.

Some agents work exclusively in corporate or organizational relocation and do very well, once they have established their procedures and contacts. Check with your broker to see if there is a program in your agency. Chances are there will be some gaps. Identify those and determine the best way to fill them. If your broker is established within the community, he may be able to arrange a meeting with personnel directors, but don't depend upon this, and be prepared to do the legwork yourself.

You are interested in the names of people who are coming in for either jobs or job interviews. You would like to send them material, refer them to your home page on the Internet, contact them by telephone, and meet with them when they are in town. If you have prepared a professional-looking information packet that includes maps and information about real estate, weather, schools, shopping, medical facilities, transportation, churches, and recreation, there is a chance that the personnel director might be willing to work with you. Done properly, your efforts could save the company time and expense, for this is the kind of service they would normally provide.

Do not, however, discount the importance of informal contacts. Department heads, managers, and supervisors provide the kinds of grassroots sources that are generally built up over a period of time as a result of personal referrals.

The potential of working with a corporate program can be impressive. In our local community, for example, there is a division of an internationally successful electronics company. As a result of various programs and referrals, I sold homes to sixteen of their employees (mostly engineers). Without exception, they knew what they wanted, knew what they could afford, recognized it when they saw it, and acted decisively. If you can locate and cultivate a similar source, I can assure you that you will enjoy real estate sales.

Buyers Who Qualify for Specialized Programs.

Any agent who has worked with a veteran in processing a Veterans Administration (VA) loan knows that it takes both specialized knowledge and a general appreciation of how large bureaucracies work. There are a variety of federal and state programs; some have been around for years, while others come and go. All have precise eligibility requirements. If you become expert in who qualifies for what, you can develop a reputation that will attract potential participants to you. Some agents announce their expertise on their business cards, such as "Specialist in Veterans' Affairs."

Knowing the eligibility requirements, however, is only part of the equation—and not the hardest part at that. You must appreciate how things are done in a bureaucracy (and at what pace) and what motivates program administrators and what does not.

First, there will be a series of specific steps that must be taken and an abundance of forms that must be filled out in an explicit manner. There is no point in fussing about the foolishness or redundancy of any task or any part of the paperwork. It is written in stone. Do the drudgework cheerfully and exactly the way that it's asked for.

Second, bureaucrats are not excited by the profit motive. They are paid the same amount whether your loan application is processed or not. The finest among them are dedicated public servants trying to do the best job they can with an often overwhelming workload. The worst defy rational analysis. Bad-tempered badgering will get you nowhere, except perhaps to have your loan application end up at the bottom of the pile. Make everyone's job as easy as possible by doing things the way they need to be done. (Not everyone is temperamentally able to follow this advice. One of my survey participants seemed thoroughly convinced that his local VA representative was an operative of an unfriendly government planted there to sabotage our capitalistic system.)

If you can master the intricacies of any specialized program and know how to work within the system, it will provide you with a valuable source of income. But you will earn every penny you make.

BEING CREATIVE

Your local situation and your imagination will dictate what possibilities exist. Let me describe how my wife and I turned our company's arrangement with the Chamber of Commerce into a program that resulted in ten to twelve home sales a year.

When people are considering moving into a new community, they often write to the Chamber of Commerce for information. Our chamber maintained a file of those letters and shared them with local real estate agents who were members. That file turned out to be a gold mine of prospects. Once each week my wife reviewed incoming letters. During some weeks, there might be thirty or forty (and ours is a community of only about forty thousand). She read each letter and jotted down the essential information, such as name and address, along with any pertinent statements from the letters, such as, "We hope to be able to move to your city as soon as our home here sells." We would then prepare a cover letter and a packet of information that showed samples of listings currently on the market. Primarily, we used flyers from listings in our office (mostly my own). I wrote a personal note at the bottom of each letter, included a housing questionnaire, a stamped, self-addressed envelope, and my business card, and promptly mailed the entire package out to the prospect. If I were operating that system today, of course, I would be doing a lot of e-mailing also.

We mailed all the packets out by Tuesday of each week and Saturday morning I followed up with phone calls to the most promising prospects. Although the same information was available to every other real estate office in town, ours was the only one with a centralized program handled by a single agent. The result was that we accounted for the majority of all sales in the community from this source.

If your Chamber of Commerce does not have a program of this kind, start one. If they do, do not be afraid of the competition, because you will be going after a lucrative market. People who write ahead to a community in advance of their move are often well-organized problem solvers. They gather all the information available before making a decision. Chances are good that they have used these same skills in solving other problems, such as how to amass enough money to afford the home of their choice.

QUALIFYING BUYERS

Qualifying a buyer simply means finding out how much he can afford. It is your most critical immediate task. If you don't do this correctly, you do not pass "go," and you do not collect any money. Qualifying buyers is a step that is awkward for some real estate agents, even experienced ones. It should not be, because it will be impossible for you to work productively with buyers if you do not have the information. You do not want to waste their time or yours by showing them properties out of their price range, or by showing them anything, if they can't afford to buy at all. If they do make an offer and need financing, a steely eyed, no-nonsense loan officer at a lending institution will ask the same hard questions in conjunction with a loan application, so why not get the information at the start? Of course, the ideal situation would be for the buyers to prequalify with a lending institution or a mortgage broker before they even start looking at homes, and this is becoming the standard in the profession.

Do not judge buyers without investigation, because looks can be deceiving. The couple who drives up in the clanking pickup truck dressed like refugees from Skunk Hollow may be cash customers for the costliest item in your inventory. On the other hand, I once spent almost a week showing the most expensive homes in town to a couple who dazzled me with their big talk, wardrobe, car, and $100 hairdo (his). To be charitable, let's just say it turned out that their tastes exceeded their financial capabilities—by a very wide margin. The key is to ask the right questions and do some discreet checking of your own.

ARE PURCHASERS PREVARICATORS?

Buyers generally have a good idea of what they want. It is wise to ask them, take notes, and show them the kind of property they say they are after.

All of this assumes, of course, that they can afford what they say they want. For some reason I do not yet fully understand, it is hard for many agents to listen to buyers. They seem almost compelled to dominate the conversation and tell folks what they *should* want. This is not to say that you should not be flexible, because everyone who has sold real estate has a story about people who say they are interested in one type of home and end up falling in love with and buying something quite different (in a worst case scenario from another agent, after you have spent untold hours showing them what they *said* they wanted). It would be dangerous to conclude, however, that buyers do not know their own minds, or are somehow being less than honest with you. In the normal course of events, they typically select something very close to what they indicated they prefer, assuming it is available.

It is particularly bad form to try to manipulate buyers toward specific listings in which you, your broker, or some other agent in your office has a vested interest. This does not mean you should not show your own listings, but it does mean that you will lose a lot of sales if your judgment is clouded by any factor other than selecting properties that best meet the buyers' expressed interests and qualifications. There are plenty of competent real estate agents who have the good sense to show buyers what they want, not what the agent or broker wants to sell them.

"WHAT A BEAUTIFUL VIEW!"

Something that was very difficult for me was to put my own tastes on the shelf. For example, I was once showing a young couple a home that bordered a huge wrecking yard. I would have never considered buying it myself, but it was a new home and in their price range. We went to the backyard and the three of us peered over the fence into the sea of rusting Edsels. They didn't mind at all. They bought the house. The phrase that occurred to me at the time was "not my will, but thine."

GETTING IT FINANCED

When mortgage money is plentiful, and when it can be borrowed at reasonable interest rates, financing is a comparatively easy step in the home-buying process. When interest rates soar, as they have an aggravating habit of doing periodically, lenders become nervous and buyers have trouble qualifying. When that happens, the type of financing available on a particular property often becomes the most important factor in the whole process. To ensure your long-term success, you must continually stay on top of what is going on in the home-financing market. These are the basic options:

■ *Fixed-Rate Loans.* Long-term fixed-rate loans will continue to be available, but they command the premium interest rate. Because this is the type of financing that most consumers understand and have experience with, it is by far their first choice. Know what the current rates are and use them as your standard of comparison for other options.

■ *Adjustable-Rate Mortgages (ARMs).* In the past, lenders were badly burned when changing economic circumstances forced them to start paying more for their money while their assets were tied up in long-term, low-yielding real estate loans. To protect themselves, they have searched for alternative forms of home financing. The problem has been to find a solution that lenders like and that consumers will accept.

The program that has emerged as the leading contender is the ARM. In this loan, the interest rate is adjusted periodically (up and down) using as a basis some objective "cost of funds" standard. There will typically be a limit on how much a loan can go up during a year or over the life of the loan (called "caps"). The main problem with the ARM is that people do not as a rule consider worst-case scenarios and realistically assess their capability of making ends meet if their ARM goes to the limit. Lenders like ARMs, since the rate fluctuation risk is passed on to the borrower, so they offer ARMs at an attractive rate. Just make sure your buyers are fully educated.

■ *Federal Housing Administration (FHA) and Veterans Administration (VA).* These two programs have been in existence through good times and bad and have provided sorely needed stability to the home financing industry. Each will likely continue to offer traditional fixed-rate loans as well as many of the newer options. Because of their widespread familiarity, and because of their built-in consumer protection features, buyers like to know what is available through the FHA and VA, so you need to be well informed.

■ *Creative Financing.* When traditional ways of solving problems no longer work, and where large sums of money are involved, ingenious solutions emerge. In home buying, these solutions are called creative financing. Although it is a term that covers a broad range of techniques, owner-assisted financing is one of the most common. Let's say a seller has $100,000 of equity in a $300,000 home, along with an attractive, low-interest, assumable loan of $200,000. For $20,000 down and a promissory note for $80,000 (secured by a second mortgage) at "interest only" payments of 10 percent with a three-year balloon, he will sell the home. The buyer assumes the underlying loan. The idea is that this will make the home affordable to the buyer, and during the three-year period, it can be refinanced. There will be no problem if the buyer can find affordable refinancing. If he cannot, he may be in trouble.

Owner-assisted financing is a legitimate and accepted means of facilitating a real estate transaction, but great care must be exercised to ensure that it is fair to all parties, and particularly to the buyer, whom you represent. All too often, creative financing has simply meant that buyers end up getting in over their heads because a transaction was made too easy for them, or they buy a piece of property that could not have qualified for financing through standard methods.

You see here a practical application of the principal of agency and real-world ethics. You are legally and ethically required to put your client buyer's interests first, certainly above your own. If you arrange shaky creative financing that gets the deal done and earns you a payday, that's in your best interests. But if down the road it comes back to bite your buyer, then you've obviously violated your fiduciary responsibility. It's also very bad business. Word gets around.

As noted in the previous example, an element of creative financing may involve assuming a loan that already exists on the property. The only safe way to determine whether a loan can be assumed or not, and on what terms, is to contact the lending institution in writing. A lot of innocent (and some not so innocent) buyers have been led to believe by unscrupulous sellers (and, regrettably, by real estate agents) that a loan was assumable when that was not the case. If the buyers do not plan to openly contact the lender and follow their instructions about assuming the loan, urge them to consult a real estate attorney for advice before proceeding. Make your recommendation in writing so it will be a matter of record.

SHOWING PROPERTIES

Although you will be current on the general inventory, you need to revisit properties you have selected to show a specific prospect. You also need to review your files on expired listings and fizzbos to see if there are any possibilities for a one-party listing. When looking at the material on the multiple listing service, read the information carefully. If it says to show only in the afternoons, that is when you need to make the appointment. If it says not to let the cat out of the garage or not to pet Fang the Doberman, take notes.

It is unrealistic to show more than five or six properties in one outing, unless the buyers have limited time and must work at an accelerated pace. To make the job easier, provide them with a form on which they can make notes about the houses they see. After a while, even the most veteran house hunters start to confuse properties. It is also wise to give them a copy of the sales agreement they will use when they make an offer, so they can study it.

Geographic convenience will likely dictate the order in which you show homes. I do not advocate showing less desirable houses first to "set up" the remainder so they look good by comparison. That technique, although still used, is so transparent that it will cost you in credibility. At the close of (or during) each house-hunting session, ask for feedback to see if you are on the right track.

HORROR STORY (PG-13)

Let me tell you a brief little horror story, designed to convince you to do your homework thoroughly before you show a property. It is embarrassingly true.

I was working with a couple from Los Angeles with whom I had made contact as a result of our Chamber of Commerce prospecting program. Both were executives in a large company. They were articulate, affluent, and an absolute delight to work with. Their daughter, who was a nurse, was moving to our city to work in the local hospital. They were interested in locating a duplex or fourplex for her to live in and as an investment for them.

The choices in our small town were limited, but there were four properties I thought might have potential. Far and away my first choice was a beautiful duplex that had recently come out on multiple listing. I had visited it when it was brand-new a year or so earlier, and it was classy—just like the people from Los Angeles.

The showing instructions said that no appointment was necessary and that the keys were in the mailbox. The three of us arrived and I looked in the mailbox. No keys. "Maybe they put them under the doormat," my resourceful prospect volunteered. He was right.

I let us in and it was apparent I had made the right choice. They were dazzled. It was exactly what they were looking for. You just love moments like that, when it all comes together.

"Oh, it even has a wood stove!" the wife says. Wood stove? I didn't recall the listing saying anything about a wood stove. I got nervous and start checking other features against my listing book. "We may have a little trouble here folks," I announced as I ran out to the front door to check the house number. "We are in the wrong duplex. The one across the street is for sale."

When I saw the blurry picture with the familiar street name in the multiple listing entry, I incorrectly assumed the duplex was the nifty one I had visited earlier. (The one across the street was not nifty.)

The story does have a happy ending, because we found another property that fit my prospects' needs. They never even told my broker about my shortcomings as an address finder—but if the tenant had been home and had suffered cardiac arrest when three well-dressed intruders burst in on her, I would just about now be qualifying for a work-release program.

CLOSING A SALE

In sales terminology, a sale is "closed" when customers sign their names to whatever documents are necessary to approve the transaction. In real estate it happens when a buyer signs the offer to purchase. (Do not confuse this with the "closing" that takes place later when all legal documents are signed and the ownership of property is formally transferred.) There can be no argument as to the importance of the closing step in the initial sales process, because without it, the commissioned salesperson never makes any money. There are, however, basic philosophical differences among those in the profession about how salespeople should conduct themselves in working with customers in reaching the critical buying decision.

The most prevalent theory, encountered in almost all sales training programs, is that folks need to be helped along in the decision-making process. To do this, a whole series of closing techniques have been devised, named, cataloged, and taught. Each is designed to facilitate the process as you guide your prospects smoothly and efficiently toward the major close by achieving a series of "minor closes" (less important decisions the client makes along the way).

Here is one overly simplified technique, but using a setting outside of real estate. It is called the alternative-of-choice close. Assume you are in a store looking at suits. After some time the clerk asks, "Do you want the blue suit or the brown?" Either choice is acceptable to him, when in fact you may not want either one, or for that matter, anything he has in the store. Books on real estate and training programs routinely cover closing techniques as though there was no argument about whether they fulfill the spirit of the agency relationship, or whether they are ethical.

Those who question the appropriateness of procedures such as this do so on the grounds that they are manipulative and hence unprofessional. They maintain that the only acceptable closing technique is to provide people all the information they need to make an informed choice, and then permit them the courtesy of reaching their decision in their own time.

HANDLING OFFERS

One of the most exciting moments in real estate occurs when prospective purchasers do, in fact, decide to buy. How you handle the offer influences greatly whether it will be accepted or not.

■ *The Offering Price.* Since we are assuming that you are representing the buyers as a buyer's agent, your fiduciary responsibility is to them. That means you should attempt to negotiate the best possible price. "How much do you think they will take?" is the inevitable question.

Even the least sophisticated first-time buyers seem to have been told never to offer full price for a home. All parties ordinarily expect some give and take, and that's generally what happens, but the buyers must ultimately determine what their offering price will be. How much can they afford? How much do they want the house? Is it a buyer's market or a seller's market? Is the home priced competitively with other similar properties on the market? Let your buyers know that they are not operating in a vacuum, and that as long as the owners have not accepted an offer, the house is on the market. You will also recall that in our discussion of listings, we mentioned the competitive market analysis, in which sellers are provided a synopsis of similar homes that have sold recently. The same type of approach works well with buyers, and I strongly recommend them.

■ *The Amount of Earnest Money.* "Earnest money" is a deposit made by the buyer as evidence of good faith. It is customary for the buyer to give the seller earnest money when the offer is made. Some buyers do not seem very earnest. It they want to put up $100 earnest money on a $200,000 house, counsel them to reconsider. I know it's hard to believe, but some buyers do not realize that their earnest money is applied against the expenses of their purchase. They think it is an extra charge, so make it clear.

■ *Preparation of Estimated Buyer Costs.* Before buyers actually sign an offer to purchase, they should be given a written estimate of the total costs involved, including their one-time expenses incident to closing and their recurrent monthly payments. In some jurisdictions, the form you use is prescribed for you. Whatever the case, the objective is to inform the buyers before they make a commitment. Some brokers think that introducing a form such as this just when the buyers have reached the decision to sign takes the bloom off an otherwise rapturous moment, but it is best if cool and objective heads prevail throughout.

■ *Presenting the Offer.* Once buyers have signed the offer and delivered an earnest money check, the operative term becomes "time is of the essence!" In other words, *hustle!* "You snooze, you lose" is the term those in the trade use. Contact the listing broker immediately, tell her you have an offer, and ask for the earliest opportunity to present it. Rest assured that the sellers are intensely interested in seeing all offers as soon as possible. If you get an offer at 6 P.M., try to get together with the sellers at 7 P.M. or 8 P.M. Try to secure permission to present the offer yourself (with the listing agent present), local rules and courtesies permitting. Remember that you have buyers who have emotionally committed to a house and who are anxiously awaiting a decision. Get the ball out of your court immediately. The first time you lose a sale because you dawdled, it will make a believer out of you. There are times in real estate when you need to push, and this is one of them.

■ *Negotiating the Offer.* The more complex the transaction, the more likely it is that some negotiation will be required. In residential sales, negotiations are ordinarily straightforward and relate mainly to price. If the sellers want to counter the offer, there is a simple form that permits that, listing their specific counterproposal. The important thing to remember in any negotiation process is to keep it as businesslike and unemotional as possible. Isolate areas of disagreement and quantify them, if possible. It is amazing how excited people often become over matters that may amount to a comparatively few dollars. Put in the proper context (how much does it cost?) such issues often evaporate.

As a reminder, the strongest asset you will have in any transaction is the "ready, willing, and able buyer". Just do the best job you can of packaging your prospects to insure they score high in every one of those categories.

■ *Using Your Commission to Resolve Conflicts.* Two generally accepted rules regarding the brokerage fee are: (1) do not give away any part of your fee to hold a transaction together until and unless absolutely necessary, and (2) something is better than nothing. If, early in the negotiation process, you volunteer to pay for certain items out of your brokerage fee, it is amazing how the participants will then look to you to resolve future conflicts in the same way. Remember also that you need your broker's approval to commit any portion of the commission, but if it means kicking in $100 to solve a problem and save a $5,000 fee, you know what her answer will be.

COUNTDOWN TO PAYDAY

After you have an accepted offer the painstaking, unglamorous work begins. Whether you eventually are paid or not for all your efforts depends on your ability and willingness to follow through.

■ *The Loan Application.* Go with your buyers to make a formal loan application. Let them know exactly the kind of information the loan officer will need, such as savings account numbers, credit references, and so on. As a matter of policy, give them a copy of the loan application itself ahead of time to prepare them for their meeting. Actually, I would do this when you first start looking at homes. It provides really good focus. When the appointment takes place, remember that this is the loan officer's moment, not yours. Volunteer information, if needed, but generally keep an amiable low profile.

The buyers will want to know how long it will take for loan approval and so will you, so ask if they do not. Make notes about any items the buyers might need to research and produce later, and follow up to make sure they do. As part of the loan application process, the lender is required by federal law to give the applicants a good faith estimate of the settlement charges that they are likely to incur. The information should be essentially the same as the estimate you prepared when the earnest money was signed. If there are significant differences, determine why and explain the reasons to the buyers.

You will know by the conclusion of the meeting whether you can anticipate problems. Unless you have made a serious error in qualifying the buyers, the loan application meeting is ordinarily short, businesslike, and cordial. Every four or five days after the meeting call the loan officer and see if everything is progressing well. If something needs to be done, volunteer your services, if appropriate. Keep in constant contact with the buyers and let them know everything you know. "Buyer's remorse" (when buyers are unhappy with their decision) seems mainly to afflict buyers who were hustled through the buying process and then left to fend for themselves.

■ *Closing.* Procedures vary around the country as to who chooses the title company or attorney who will do the title research and the closing itself. No matter who chooses and who pays, you need to establish immediate contact with the "action officer"—the person who will do the actual work. Provide anything needed and follow up every few days.

At the closing itself (in most areas there's a formal meeting), you will again be a guest, but if you have done your job properly, you will know more about the entire transaction than anyone at the table. (In most states, sellers and buyers have separate closings, although in some states, it is combined.) Because closing is the time when all final documents are signed and money changes hands, it can be tense and small misunderstandings can escalate. It is a good policy to go over the official documents with the closing officer *well before* the buyers arrive to make sure you understand everything fully. If at all possible, have your buyers preview the basic closing documents ahead of time, as the law permits.

In most areas, buyers need to show up at the close with some kind of negotiable instrument, such as a certified check or bank draft in a specific amount. Be sure they know that amount and that they are aware that a personal check will not do. As a final action, some type of gift to the buyers is appropriate. If your local multiple listing service has taken a photo of the home, you can use that, or an enlargement of it, in a nice frame.

■ *After Closing.* If your buyers give you permission, send notices to their new neighbors that they are moving in. Most people think this is a great idea, but there are those who do not. Not only is it a good icebreaker for the newcomers, it is good exposure for you. You should also call a welcome wagon if the folks are new to the community.

IT IS WORK—BUT IT GETS EASIER

Your first exposure to the whole residential selling process could well make you want to sit down and have a good cry, because it sounds so hopelessly complex. It is work and there are details to be taken care of, but much of it will become a smooth-running routine after the first few sales. You will waste less time bogged down on dead-end missions with unqualified buyers (the terminal scourge of so many agents) and you will know who to contact to get things done and where to go to get straight answers to your questions. Remember, too, that only a small percentage of your competition will be working as hard and as smart as you. Finally, you will feel real personal satisfaction when you help people to solve one of the most important problems they will ever face—how to buy a home.

9
Listing and Selling Specialized Properties

Custom-Built Homes, Investment Properties,
Rural Properties, and More

Even as you are busily becoming established in residential real estate, it will become clear to you that there is more to the profession than just listing and selling homes. You might see another salesperson in your office list and market a $750,000 farm (it will make you giddy just to think about what your share of a commission like that would be). At the local Realtors' meeting, you might hear about a multimillion-dollar commercial deal put together by several agents you know (now we are talking *big* money). Or you could read about a forty-year-old ex-housewife in Indiana who, after only a year in the business, is earning a high six-figure annual income structuring real estate exchanges. Your interest will definitely be piqued.

BYPASSING "HARD KNOCKS U"

If you are accustomed to earning a $2,000 or $3,000 commission on your real estate transactions, and you suddenly see an opportunity to earn five to ten times that much, you'll be tempted to drop everything and concentrate on the big money. That's a fine idea—if you know what you are doing. The sad fact of the matter is that often the novice develops delusions of grandeur ("Good Lord, that would mean a $15,000 commission!"), gets in over his head, attempts to bluff and bluster his way through, and ends up with nothing but a costly lesson in the real estate facts of life. My purpose in this chapter is to look at some of the possibilities for career broadening that you will be exposed to merely as a result of being active in general real estate and to offer some counsel on how to best take advantage of them.

First, here are a few friendly suggestions:

1. Don't cut yourself off from other income. If you have developed a reasonably stable income from listing and selling residential real estate, it is a good idea to maintain at least a minimal level of activity in those functions. You should retain your residential sales expertise and stay in touch with previous contacts to take advantage of their follow-up business. You may also need the money. Before you burn any bridges behind you, make sure you won't have to go back over the river now and then.

2. Get help from professionals. A true professional knows the limits of his own knowledge and seeks assistance when he needs it. Just as some real estate agents have trouble listening, there are others, I am told, who consider it to be a sign of weakness to admit there are a few areas in which they are not expert. That could be a fatal flaw. It will be time and money well spent to get help when you need it.

Let's say, for example, that you are going to list a home on a large acreage that also has marketable trees on it. Chances are that it would be a hard property for you to price, but there are professionals you could consult who specialize in appraising the value of standing timber. Any prospective purchaser who is even slightly cautious would insist on some proof of estimated value. Ordinarily, the cost of professional service will be borne by either the sellers or buyers, although it is not always easy to convince them of that. Whoever pays, it is a wise investment. Be particularly wary when you enter the murky waters of law and tax accounting.

3. Get help from the home front. There may be an experienced agent within your office who concentrates her activities in some narrow segment of real estate, such as investments or rural properties. If so, you need to check with your broker on the ground rules, for some insist that only certain agents become involved in the specialized fields. Even if that is the case, it is not always easy to precisely categorize each potential transaction.

Let's say a former client of yours from a residential transaction comes to you and asks for your help in putting together a complex real estate investment venture. You immediately recognize two things: One, whoever puts the deal together will make a whole lot of money and two, you are in over your head. What you might want to do is secure your broker's permission to work with an agent in the office who has experience in such transactions. An agreed-upon split in the commission that recognizes the relative contribution of effort would be appropriate. You gain valuable experience, retain your client for the long term, and make some money. Your clients get the type of professional attention they deserve, and the other agent is compensated for her technical expertise.

4. Watch your backside. You should realize that when you first begin dealing in these specialized activities, you will encounter many buyers, sellers, and other real estate agents who will know a great deal more about what is going on than you do. It is an environment that demands caution. A prospective client, for example, can quickly find out how informed you are by asking you a question to which he already knows the answer. You may not think such a tactic is particularly nice, but it is very common and very effective. I admit I use it occasionally (OK, frequently). Some people will simply write you off and not do business with you if they judge you to be uniformed. Others (particularly those on the other side of the bargaining table) may relish the idea of working with someone whose zeal and ambition exceeds their skill and judgment, but it would be the type of relationship you should avoid.

TYPES OF SPECIALIZED PROPERTIES

Here is an overview of some specialized areas of real estate that may have an attraction for you, while you are still active in a general brokerage.

Speculation Homes

In a brisk, fast-moving real estate market, many professional home-builders construct what they call "spec" (speculation) homes. This simply means that they build the homes before they have a buyer and gamble that they will sell before costs associated with construction and financing eat away the potential profit. The ultimate example of this can be seen in large subdivisions, where a builder has several model homes constructed for purchasers to inspect, and replicas of these models in the subdivision to purchase. It is a pretty straightforward transaction to sell a home that is already completed or one that will be built to emulate a preexisting structure that the buyer can examine.

Some builders employ a sales staff of their own and do not work with other real estate brokerages. Others have a sales staff, but will "co-op" (split the commission with the selling agent). Still others have no sales staff and list their homes with a real estate broker. Those are typically put on multiple listing, making them available for sale by all members.

Custom-Built Homes

Another alternative is the custom-built home. In this arrangement, the buyer purchases a lot and then looks for a builder to construct his individualized home. Very frequently you may be involved in not only locating the lot but also in recommending a builder with whom to work. In those cases, you would collect a referral fee from the builder (it could be a flat fee or a small percentage of the sales price), and then let the buyers and builder proceed with the project.

Residential Multifamily Investment Properties

It is common for an agent specializing in residential sales to encounter a prospect who wishes to buy a small investment property such as a duplex, fourplex, or sixplex. With just a little research and practice, you should be able to handle these transactions with confidence.

There are straightforward and generally agreed upon guidelines that you can apply to any income-producing residential property for determining the quality of the investment for a particular individual. Standard forms are easily available in all states, and with just a moderate amount of training, you can complete them quickly and explain them to others. There are computer programs that let you perform the same type of analyses, only a lot faster.

Whether you do it manually or with a computer, the expenses of ownership are compared to rents received to come up with a before-tax monthly cash flow. The individual's specific tax status would determine the after tax position. This approach can be used whether you are considering an individual house that a buyer might wish to purchase as an investment property or a two-hundred-unit apartment complex.

A word of caution: Some owners of residential investment property have been known to inflate their income figures when trying to sell. No buyer should commit himself without verifying the information by reviewing the owner's latest federal income tax return, which lists each property separately. The owner's motivation when he fills out a tax return is to list all expenses and to not report income he did not receive. If you are working with an owner on a potential listing, diplomatically let him know that buyers are going to want to see basic documents. He may be inclined to be more conservative when he decides how much he is going to ask.

Businesses

Somewhere along the line, you are likely to encounter someone who has a yen to buy or establish a small business. It's the dream of many people.

The sobering fact about businesses, particularly the small ones, is that they fail at an alarming rate. My experience in dealing with people who are thinking of setting up their own reveals that there is often a startling amount of naiveté and innocence on their part. Your first chore in dealing with such prospects is to determine their depth of knowledge and their financial capability. If they are very experienced in business matters, you will probably learn from them. If they are not, recommend that they enlist the services of both an accountant and an attorney and that they talk with the business loan officer at the local bank before you begin a serious search for possible opportunities. You may need to take the initiative in arranging the meeting. Make certain everyone has a clear understanding of intentions, capabilities, and limitations. In my rookie year, I learned these lessons the hard way.

Investment Property Exchanges

As you become experienced in listing and selling investment property, you might find you have a flair for it. If so, you may wish to consider putting together exchange transactions.

People exchange investment properties for two major reasons. First, there are substantial income tax advantages. Rules have changed through the years, but the basic concept has remained intact: Taxes on a profit realized upon the disposition of investment real estate can be deferred if the property is exchanged for like property of higher value.

Let's say someone bought a duplex from you five years ago and has built up a huge equity in that property. If the investor were to sell the duplex now, she would face a tax on the profit. If she exchanges it, say for a sixplex, however, she can delay the tax payment (not avoid it). At the same time, your investor's continuing year-to-year tax advantage would almost certainly be improved by acquiring a larger property.

The second major reason for exchanging property is to use the built-up equity in much the same manner as cash. If owners sold the property to get at their money, not only will they trigger tax consequences, they may encounter substantial transaction fees and might have to carry back part of their equity in the form of a contract with the purchaser.

An agent who becomes really skilled in exchange techniques is rare. Those who do so are so sought after that they are among the best-paid agents in the industry. Because several properties are generally involved in an exchange, there is excellent income potential. It is possible to become well versed enough to handle comparatively simple exchanges and still conduct other real estate activities, but if you really get serious, you will be compelled to do it on a full-time basis.

Here are four Web sites for further research: www.1031exchange. com; www.1031it.com; www.1031tax.com; and www.1031properties.com. Why the repeated 1031 citation? That's the pertinent IRS code reference.

Investment Groups

Large, high-priced investments often present the best opportunities, but the small investor is generally not able to participate. However, if several small investors band together into an investment group, they would have the assets needed to go after more expensive properties; a group of, say, ten people with $30,000 each to invest has a lot of clout and staying power. If you can structure such a group, the potential is there for you to handle acquisition and disposition of properties for the group.

As you are becoming established, keep track of people with whom you have worked who might be logical candidates for an investment group, and keep in mind that compatibility of investment objectives is critical. You might not need a lot of cash to participate in the group yourself, because there will be a commission paid on the transactions, part of which will be yours to use as a portion of your contribution. No matter how successful you become, remember that you need to discuss forming an investment group with your broker before you proceed. Your activities could be subject to Securities and Exchange Commission rules as well as real estate laws.

Rural Properties

The desire for "five acres and independence in the country" is a bug that has bitten a lot of people. You could be dealing with buyers who want a place in the country or sellers *with* a place in the country who have tried it and desperately want something else instead. Before you lace up your boots and slip into your Levis, a few matters unique to rural property need to be mentioned.

Any acreage, whether small or large, should be surveyed and marked prior to a sale. Ideally, that will have been done by the owners when they listed the property, but since it can be expensive, it is not always done. The consequences of finding that the beautiful knoll on which the buyers want to build their dream house is actually on the neighbor's property are dire, so it is better to resolve the issue early. Don't rely on fences to accurately indicate property lines. Take it from someone who made that mistake—once.

You also need to be sure that you understand state and federal tax rules as they pertain to rural and farm property. In many states, tax advantages are given to those who use their land for certain agricultural purposes. To be eligible, the owners must meet specific qualifications. If they sell to someone and the property use changes, the land might not continue to qualify for the favored tax treatment. In fact, the new owners could be liable for deferred taxes from *before they owned the land!* Get the tax information from the owners, verify it with the county tax assessor, and ensure that the buyers (and you) know exactly what is going on. Include the information on the sales documents so that it is a matter of written agreement.

Zoning is another subject about which you need to be clear. In many areas, land use laws are restrictive. If you locate a beautiful twenty-acre parcel in the hills with a magnificent view and building site, don't automatically assume that a residence can be built on it, although that *might* be the case. There's a chance that the zoning laws may preclude it from being used for residential purposes. Even more restrictive are prohibitions against dividing large parcels of land. Many buyers are under the mistaken impression that they can partition their land any way they wish. In most places that is no longer true.

Building a house in the country is different from building one in the city. If you list or sell a residential lot in a subdivision inside the city limits, you can be reasonably confident that a house can be built on it. Even in those cases, it is a good idea to check with local authorities to determine the costs associated with hooking up city water and sewer services, and to find out whether any major improvement projects (such as road widening) are planned for which property owners would be financially liable.

Outside the city limits there are other things to think about. First and most important, determine what conditions must be met before a building permit can be issued. Generally, the owner must have a water source and a sewage disposal capability. Septic systems and wells will no doubt be used. There is a great deal to know about each, so educate yourself before you get too involved. City and county officials possess the most up-to-date, unbiased information. If you did not meet with these people as part of your office-training program, arrange with your broker to invite them to a staff training session.

I have listed two excellent references on this topic in Appendix C, "Real Estate Marketing," for further study. *Finding & Buying Your Place in the Country* by attorney Les Scher and his wife, consumer advocate Carol Scher, richly deserves its best-selling status. On a more academic level, *Farm and Ranch Marketing* by Johnnie Rosenauer, Michael Hennessey, and James Mullen provides an excellent road map if you want to develop a career in farm and land brokerage.

A Votre Sante!

If you're looking for a really unique niche in farm and ranch marketing how about wineries? If that has any interest to you, here's some research for you to accomplish. First, take a look at website www.springhillcellers.com. This is the website of a beautiful 20 acre winery in Albany, Oregon. The owner, with his wife Karen, is Realtor Mike McLain. Now go to the website www.oregonvineyardland.com. This is the website of Mike's real estate company, McLain and Associates, "the Willamette Valley's oldest brokerage specializing in vineyard and winery properties." Check out the current and past listings if you would like a glimpse of the lush state of Oregon at its beautiful best. I'm certain that you will also notice that the price tags for properties such as this are typically very impressive. I also like Mike's company motto: "If we wouldn't buy it and plant it in grapes ourselves, we won't show it to you. Period". It occurred to me that with just a slight modification in wording, that would be a great business philosophy for any type of real estate activity.

Movin' On Up

Did you know that the rush to million dollar plus homes is rising dramatically? Neither did I until I did some research on the topic. Why would you be interested? Well, it's obvious with that type of price, the brokerage fee would be rather impressive. Interestingly, there's now even an organization that trains agents who work in the upper tier of the market. It's the Institute for Luxury Home Marketing, founded by veteran real estate professional Laurie Moore-Moore. They offer the professional designation Certified Luxury Home Marketing Specialist (CLHMS). To earn it you need to complete educational requirements and sell a certain number of high level (really high level) properties. If you're interested in further information, check out www.luxuryhomemarketing.com and/or read Laurie's book *Rich Buyer, Rich Seller! The Real Estate Agent's Guide to Marketing Luxury Homes.* Another interesting and informative resource is the web site www.luxuryhomes.com.

Churches, Jails, and Gold Mines—Oh My!

A couple of years ago I reviewed a book for *The Real Estate Professional* magazine that relates well to this topic. It's *Churches, Jails, and Gold Mines* by Steven Good. Good is the Chairman and CEO of Sheldon Good & Company, the largest U.S. firm exclusively conducting real estate auctions. The book gives insights not only into transactions involving churches, jails, and gold mines, but also such unique properties as private islands, bowling alleys, police stations, airports, and night clubs. It's an interesting read and a fascinating topic. At this point it might be appropriate to recall the old phrase "fools rush in, etc.", so make certain you do adequate research before pursuing any of these exotic career paths.

WHEN YOU RUN INTO A CLOSED DOOR

If you like diversity in your job, you will love real estate. Your problem will be to restrain yourself from running off in all directions at once to take advantage of what are clearly great opportunities. As you are learning the basics of your trade and as you start to expand your activities, it is inevitable that you will get your nose bloodied occasionally. One response is to pull into a shell, become less adventurous, and avoid unfamiliar situations. In real estate, that is a formula for disaster. The preferred reaction is to shake it off and press on with a somewhat more seasoned brand of enthusiasm.

10

Avoiding Problems

Things to Watch Out For From Day One

Precautionary paralysis is a common affliction. You see it in the teenage driver who, after conscientiously studying his driver's manual and practicing diligently for months, freezes at the wheel during his driving test and is unable to get out of the parking lot. The primary symptom is an unwillingness or inability to act for fear of making a mistake—a mistake with consequences too dire to contemplate. In real estate, such paralysis is most prevalent among two groups of new agents: those who have been told so many things *not* to do that they are afraid to do anything and those who have tried something new and have been burned.

To combat the effects of this stupor-inducing ailment, the positive approach is best. First, make peace with yourself. Understand that you will make mistakes and that not everyone will always be happy with what you do. If you educate yourself, follow sound and ethical business practices, keep up-to-date about what is going on in the profession, and temper it all with a moderate amount of prudence, you will develop the confidence you need to relax and do your job. Of course, it's assumed that you will have adequate Errors and Omissions Insurance. If you missed that discussion in Chapter 3, now would be a particularly appropriate time to review it. Errors and Omissions Insurance is an absolute "must" as long as you are in the business.

WHERE THE ICE GETS THIN

It also helps if you know what specific things can cause you trouble. That way you can concentrate on avoiding the real pitfalls, rather than worrying about the imaginary ones. (That is, "Don't sweat the small stuff.") The trouble spots are reasonably easy to identify. Each state has a set of administrative rules and regulations that governs the conduct of those who have real estate licenses. Typically, a number of violations are cited that could result in some sort of disciplinary action. In most states, the list has grown over the years, largely in response to adverse public reaction to transgressions committed by those who sell real estate. When I teach my real estate licensing class in Oregon, I title my session on this topic: "33 Ways to Lose Your License (Or, Do It and You're in Deep Doo-Doo)." By the time you read this the list will have likely grown well beyond thirty three.

LESSONS FROM THE GOLDEN STATE

It's instructive to look at my old home state of California's rules. Because of the huge numbers involved, if a problem in putting together a real estate transaction can occur, it has happened in California, a lawsuit has been filed, it has gone to the Supreme Court, a TV miniseries has been produced, and it's all encapsulated into the next edition of the state publication, *Real Estate Law* (see "Real Estate Reference" in Appendix C). Their list of "no-no's" (more accurately, "Grounds for Disciplinary Action") varies in content and format with the publication of each new *Real Estate Law,* but the following list is representative. I'm including it not to intimidate you but to give you an excellent primer on prohibited activities. The information will be more meaningful to you after you've had some practical experience in the field, but at this point, it provides a helpful overview. I suggest you read each entry carefully and attempt to envision how it might play out in a real world transaction in which you may be involved. For those of us who have toiled in the fields for a few years, it is unfortunately very easy to see how each of these rules evolved and the necessity for each.

1. Knowingly making a substantial misrepresentation of the likely value of real property to:

   A. Its owner either for the purpose of securing a listing or for the purpose of acquiring an interest in the property for the licensee's own account.

   B. A prospective buyer for the purpose of inducing the buyer to make an offer to purchase the real property.

2. Representing to an owner of real property when seeking a listing that the licensee has obtained a bona fide written offer to purchase the property, unless at the time of the representation the licensee has possession of a bona fide written offer to purchase.

3. Stating or implying to an owner of real property during the listing negotiations that the licensee is precluded by law, by regulation, or by the rules of any organization, other than the broker firm seeking the listing, from charging less than the commission or fee quoted to the owner by the licensee.

4. Knowingly making substantial misrepresentations regarding the licensee's relationship with an individual broker, corporate broker, or franchised brokerage company or that entity's/person's responsibility for the licensee's activities.

5. Knowingly underestimating the probable closing costs in a communication to the prospective buyer or seller of real property to induce that person to make or to accept an offer to purchase the property.

6. Knowingly making a false or misleading representation to the seller of real property as to the form, amount, and/or treatment of a deposit toward the purchase of the property made by an offeror.

7. Knowingly making a false or misleading representation to a seller of real property, who has agreed to finance all or part of a purchase price by carrying back a loan, about a buyer's ability to repay the loan in accordance with its terms and conditions.

8. Making an addition to or modification of the terms of an instrument previously signed or initialed by a party to a transaction without the knowledge and consent of the party.

9. As a principal or agent, making representations to a prospective purchaser of a promissory note secured by real property about the market value of the securing property without a reasonable basis for believing the truth and accuracy of the representation.

10. Knowingly making a false or misleading representation or representing, without a reasonable basis for believing its truth, the nature and/or condition of the interior or exterior features of a property when soliciting an offer.

11. Knowingly making a false or misleading representation or representing, without a reasonable basis for believing its truth, the size of a parcel, square footage of improvements, or the location of the boundary lines of real property being offered for sale, lease, or exchange.

12. Knowingly making a false or misleading representation or representing to a prospective buyer or lessee of real property, without a reasonable basis to believe its truth, that the property can be used for certain purposes with the intent of inducing the prospective buyer or lessee to acquire an interest in the real property.

13. When acting in the capacity of an agent in a transaction for the sale, lease, or exchange of real property, failing to disclose to the prospective purchaser or lessee facts known to the licensee materially affecting the value or desirability of the property, when the licensee has reason to believe that such facts are not known to nor readily observable by a prospective purchaser or lessee.

14. Willfully failing, when acting as a listing agent, to present or cause to be presented to the owner of the property any written offer to purchase received prior to the closing of a sale, unless expressly instructed by the owner not to present such an offer, or unless the offer is patently frivolous.

15. When acting as the listing agent, presenting competing written offers to purchase real property to the owner in such a manner as to induce the owner to accept the offer that will provide the greatest compensation to the listing broker without regard to the benefits, advantages, and/or disadvantages to the owner.

16. Failing to explain to the parties or prospective parties to a real estate transaction for whom the licensee is acting as an agent the meaning and probable significance of a contingency in an offer or contract that the licensee knows or reasonably believes may affect the closing date of the transaction, or the timing of the vacating of the property by the seller or its occupancy by the buyer.

17. Failing to disclose to the seller of real property in a transaction in which the licensee is an agent for the seller the nature and extent of any direct or indirect interest that the licensee expects to acquire as a result of the sale. The prospective purchase of the property by an entity in which the licensee has an ownership interest, or purchase by any other person with whom the licensee occupies a special relationship where there is reasonable probability that the licensee could be indirectly acquiring an interest in the property, shall be disclosed to the seller.

18. Failing to disclose to the buyer of real property in a transaction in which the licensee is an agent of the buyer the nature and extent of a licensee's direct or indirect ownership interest in such real property. The direct or indirect ownership interest in the property by a person related to the licensee by blood or marriage, by an entity in which the licensee has an ownership interest, or by any person with whom the licensee occupies a special relationship shall be disclosed to the buyer.

19. Failing to disclose to a principal for whom the licensee is acting as an agent any significant interest the licensee has in a particular entity when the licensee recommends the use of services or products of such entity.

WAIT, THERE'S MORE!

As hard as it may be to believe, the foregoing list is far from inclusive. To round out the picture somewhat, and to expand upon a few areas that have traditionally caused licensees particular difficulties, here are a few more observations. In most instances, good business practice alone justifies observing these cautions, whether they are legally prohibited or not.

■ *Broker-Agent Relationship.* Loyalty, common sense, and law dictate that as a salesperson or associate broker you work under your broker's direct, personal, and continuing supervision. This is true whether you are an independent contractor or an employee. Keep your broker informed of all your plans, programs, and activities. Even though she will expect you to vigorously pursue your own personal goals, do not become careless about the special relationship that exists. There are some evolutionary regulatory changes taking place in single-license states regarding broker-agent relationship, but the essentials are likely to remain constant.

Regarding compensation: You are paid in one way, and one way only. The commission, when you earn it, is paid to your broker, who pays you in accordance with your contractual agreement. You may not accept compensation from anyone else for your services as a real estate agent. Does that mean you cannot accept a modest bonus directly from a satisfied client? Yes, it means just that. It must come through your broker. Again, double-check your state rules and regulations to see if there are any exceptions to this standard where you are to be licensed.

■ *Practicing Law.* It is always wise to recommend that principals seek legal counsel when the situation warrants. Never, ever, ever recommend that an attorney *not* be consulted. Each state has guidelines indicating what you can do as a licensed real estate agent, and what represents the unauthorized practice of law. In many cases, there is a fine line of distinction, but it is one you need to recognize and honor. The most common rule is that the real estate licensee can act as a "scrivener." That essentially means you can fill in the blanks of a legally binding contract by writing down what your client tells you to write. In most instances, standardized forms are used. I'm certain you can see the challenge and the perils involved here—and the necessity of proceeding with extreme caution.

■ *Guarantees.* Never use the word *guarantee* (or similar words, such as *promise*) when describing future profits from the sale of real estate. As a matter of fact, I recommend that you never use such words at all unless you are, in fact, willing to guarantee results. Even such seemingly innocent phrases as, "I guarantee this duplex will be a moneymaker for you" could cause difficulty.

■ *Prizes and Contests.* You will be on safe ground if you completely avoid any type of activity of this nature, designed to induce prospective clients to buy or sell real estate. Almost all states have restrictions, most of which were enacted to prevent past excesses from recurring.

■ *Fair Housing Laws.* Few things will get you on the griddle more quickly than failing to abide by both the letter and the spirit of the Fair Housing Laws. As you are aware, in your role as a real estate licensee, you have a legal obligation not to discriminate based upon race, color, religion, national origin, ethnic group, sex, familial status, or handicap. Some states and local communities have laws that are more restrictive than federal laws. Even if you are genuinely and honestly committed to equal treatment for all, you will have to work hard to implement that approach. Finally, it is an area where humor, no matter how well intentioned, is dangerous. Sensitivities are so keen that even the most innocently intended remark could offend. The National Association of Realtors has some excellent educational material on this subject so check in with your local Board on its availability.

■ *Representations to Lenders.* Make no verbal or written representations to any lender indicating anything but the true sales price and terms in any transaction. This is a matter of particular concern, as it seems to have become an accepted practice in some circles to present an inflated, erroneous sales price in order to secure a higher loan amount. Do not be misled by the "everyone does it" argument. Everyone doesn't do it.

■ *Advertising.* Misleading or untruthful advertising is specifically forbidden almost everywhere. As a salesperson, all your advertising must be done in the name of your broker. He will probably prepare his formal media advertising himself, or have a specialist on his staff do it. However, flyers you may prepare on your listings are also considered advertising, as would be information on the Internet. Even business cards and answering machine recordings qualify. The fact that there appears to be widespread tolerance of abuses in this activity is not likely to help if you become carried away with your descriptions or claims, and someone complains.

■ *Conflicts with Other Agents.* In the course of your real estate career, you will inevitably become involved in business disagreements with other real estate agents. Hopefully, they will be infrequent and rapidly resolved. Most are likely to be misunderstandings caused by breakdowns in communication, which can be cleared up by you or through your broker. If all parties to the dispute are Realtors, a binding arbitration apparatus is in place at the local level. No matter what else transpires, do not let any controversy jeopardize, delay, or interfere with any phase of a real estate transaction. Get the job done of satisfying the needs of the principals, and then fuss about the less important issues. It's inexcusable, but there have been cases in which arguments between agents over who is entitled to the commission have resulted in whole deals falling apart.

■ *Contracts.* Real estate is a competitive business, but the competition must take place *before* contracts are signed. Any action by you that could be construed as an attempt to induce a buyer or seller to break a contractual agreement will be viewed as grounds for disciplinary action. Eager agents who work expired listings often run afoul of this rule. They often contact sellers *before* the owner's listing with another broker actually expires. Some agents even present an offer directly to the sellers after contracts have been finalized but before the transaction closes. Give it your best shot before papers are signed—then back off and respect the legal relationship.

■ *Money.* As you might suspect, each state is very particular about how you handle money in any transaction. You and your broker can get into serious difficulties if you ignore or inadvertently overlook the rules. Know what is required, give written receipts in acceptable legal format, do no commingle money from business transactions with personal funds, and get all money to your broker immediately to be placed in an approved holding account.

GETTING NUMB?

The length of this "better not try it" and "do it and you're dead" discussion may have induced a mild numbness. That can be encouraging if it's a symptom of your increased sensitivity to potential problems and not a prelude to inertia. If you are looking for an excellent resource for further study on this subject, my number one recommendation is the book *The Digital Paper Trail In Real Estate Transactions* by Oliver Frascona and Katherine Reece. Frascona is an attorney who is also a licensed real estate broker in Colorado. His firm's website, www.frascona.com, has some excellent real world real estate law resource material. Katherine Reece is an experienced real estate broker who holds several advanced Realtor professional designations. The book starts with a thirteen item "Pledge of Allegiance to Members of the Public", which is a great blue print for professional conduct. For example, "I pledge to safeguard to the best of my abilities the trust that is placed in me to assist you with your housing needs", and "I will disclose to you all material facts associated with the property actually known to me". There's also a section titled "Profiles of a Plaintiff" that I always spend some time on with my real estate class. Here's my favorite: "Someone who tells you about the poor conduct of another real estate professional, lawyer, doctor, or lender. You may be next in line."

Finally, if you're looking for guidance on determining whether or not your real estate career might be encountering rough waters, I thought you might be interested in my list of the "Top Ten Ways to Tell When Your Real Estate Career Is In The Dumps." It has proved to be a popular feature in Realtor publications around the country, which proves that folks in the profession do have a healthy (or weird) sense of humor.

Real estate has no more dangers for its practitioners than any other profession—and it's a lot more enjoyable than most of them. What makes it so interesting are the diversity of the people you will meet and the challenging nature of the situations you face. You can appreciate it all more if you have a preview of what to expect, so that's the subject of Chapter 11.

Top Ten Ways to Tell When Your Real Estate Career Is in the Dumps

10. The Errors and Omissions insurance carrier will only issue you a policy with a million-dollar deductible.
9. When you ask your sales manager where your invitation to the company picnic is, she keeps replying, "It's in the mail."
8. The state Real Estate Commissioner continues to send you "Be All You Can Be" U.S. Army recruiting literature.
7. Your only listing has been on the market so long that it has qualified for the national roster of historic homes.
6. The President of the local Board of Realtors asks you not to wear your Realtor pin in public.
5. Your broker changes the locks on the office door and does not give you a key.
4. Your spouse buys a used bike and gets an early morning paper route as a second job.
3. The IRS sends you a sympathy card along with a credit voucher for a thousand dollars.
2. A family of vultures starts following your car as you are showing properties to clients.
1. Your mother lists her home with another agent.

11

Dealing with Difficult People and Difficult Situations

Challenges—Not Problems (Right)

If everyone with whom you worked each day shared essentially the same perception of reality, and if the business situations you faced all had a certain gray sameness, things would get very boring, wouldn't they? I personally guarantee that whatever else you may ever say about your real estate career, you will *never* say it's dull. Let's take a look at a few of the people and some of the situations that provide the stimulants.

DEALING WITH DIFFICULT PEOPLE

A couple of qualifiers are in order. First, there is absolutely no requirement that you become friends with everyone involved in every transaction. The best mortgage loan officer in town may not be the type of person with whom you would like to associate socially, but you would be foolish to steer people away because of that. You want the job done right, period. Second, because some of the people you must deal with may be pursuing an agenda somewhat different from your own or may be following slightly different business practices, don't cast them as bad guys who are out to make things difficult for you and scuttle your deals. I've seen agents who develop a real paranoia and find it essential to blame others for the inevitable problems that arise in every transaction. ("Well, *they* did it to me again!") So even though we discuss them under the heading of "difficult people," it might be more accurate to refer to the following as "real estate's most unforgettable characters."

The Deal Killers

Everyone involved in a real estate transaction is normally anxious for the details to be worked out and for it to close. Some, however, are more anxious than others. There are two categories of participants who have caused real estate agents particular anxiety: lawyers and relatives.

■ *Lawyers.* You may encounter an attorney at just about any stage of your transaction. In some jurisdictions, attorneys provide title services and act as settlement agents, while in others their main role may be to review offers and prepare contracts. If you understand their role, and learn how to work with them, there should seldom be any real problem.

Understand, first, that lawyers are representing their clients and, second, that they are searching for potential problems. If they find one, the process stops until it is resolved. If it cannot be resolved to their satisfaction, they will likely recommend that their client pull out. Their attitude is one of caution and conservatism. It's probably the attitude you would want in an attorney who represented you.

Real estate people generally have two major gripes about attorneys: They too often offer financial advice when that's not why they were retained ("You really think this is a fair price for your home?"), and they take much too long to do whatever it is that they do (the fact that they get paid by the hour fuels speculation in this area). As an agent, you need to make absolutely certain that price and terms have been agreed to by all parties and spelled out in writing before attorneys get involved. Then establish a reasonable time for attorney reviews to be completed and include those deadlines in your agreement.

I enjoyed working with lawyers. When all participants in a transaction knew one was going to be reviewing the proceedings, it seemed to keep everyone on their toes and on their best behavior. If a lawyer kills your deal, perhaps it deserved to die.

I should point out that my benevolent attitude concerning lawyers was shaped by my experience in selling mainly residential real estate in a small university town where everyone in the professions pretty much knew everyone else. If an attorney had the reputation as someone who intentionally prolonged negotiations simply to keep his high-price-meter running, it would have been, in the long run, bad for his business. An attorney member of my network in another part of the country (who, for obvious reasons, insisted that he remain anonymous), after reviewing my manuscript offered the opinion that "deal killer" was much too polite a term for attorneys who scuttle complex transactions simply because they don't fully understand them and are unwilling to admit it. Unfortunately, he observed, it is not an infrequent occurrence. You are now forewarned.

■ *Veto-Wielding Relatives.* I once worked with a young bachelor who was looking for a first home. We located a modest condominium that seemed to fit his needs. He made an offer to purchase contingent upon his father's inspection. Dad found fault not only with the condominium but also with the seller, the real estate agent (me), and the financing. I felt bad for the young fellow, because it seemed clear that dad was simply asserting control. I really doubt that anything the boy could afford would have passed inspection. On the other hand, I have worked successfully with children who passed on their parents' choice, and with parents who were concerned, but reasonable, participants in the process (and who often came up with a big chunk of the down payment). It is important to know early who all the decision makers are, and whether any out-of-town experts will be flown in. Get to know all the players early.

There are other types of difficult people you're sure to meet eventually. Let's consider them.

The Lowballers

Some buyers will, no matter what, offer significantly less than the asking price for a property. If you are dealing with sophisticated sellers who are accustomed to bargaining, there is really no problem; everyone understands what is going on, and enters into the spirit of negotiation. Most home owners, however, are generally so appalled at a lowball offer that they become insulted and make all sorts of creative suggestions as to what the buyer can do with his offer.

When working with a lowballer who is shopping for a home, try to (1) get him to make a decent offer that will not alienate the sellers (good luck!), (2) prepare the sellers for what to expect (good luck!), and (3) work hard for a counteroffer. If, by whatever fortuitous circumstance, a lowballer comes into contact with a seller who is asking 30 percent to 40 percent more for his property than it's worth or he really expects to get, you have the potential for a match made in heaven. Lowballers are not always astute buyers. Some incorrectly assume that any property they can get at a huge discount has to be a good deal.

The Boy Scout Rejects

Will Rogers may have never met a person he didn't like, but, as far as I know, Will never sold real estate for a living. You will meet at least a few unsavory characters, and on rare occasions, you will encounter buyers or sellers you judge to be flat-out dishonest. It is not always easy to just walk away.

In one of my several moves within our office, I shared a large room with my wife. Her desk was on the other side of a divider, and we could hear each other's conversations clearly. I was frequently critiqued at home (at my request, of course) about how I handled certain situations. In one instance, she was dumfounded at how difficult I made it for a prospect to make an offer on a house. "The poor man was almost begging you to write up the offer!" It wasn't that I didn't want the business, it was just that I was getting very disturbing signals and was having trouble believing everything I was being told.

Later events proved my intuition was correct (or I wouldn't be telling the story, right?), but we did end up doing business with no difficulty on that transaction, and a couple of years later listed and sold the home he bought. The point is to be on the lookout for indications of serious character flaws. When you spot them, document every step of the transaction in writing, check and double-check all information you are given, take absolutely nothing on its face value, and generally cover yourself. It's much better that you be overly cautious than end up trying to explain to a disgruntled broker why you were naive enough to get conned.

The Lookers

Some people like to look at houses as a hobby. Others do it just to keep harmony in the household. In one instance, over a span of three years, I spent untold hours each summer with a couple from out of state who said they wanted to locate a nice place with a mother-in-law setup in the house. The wife had an elderly mother who would move with them. They were lovely people, and I thoroughly enjoyed each visit. It became clear to me, however, after finding almost exactly what they said they were looking for, that the husband was going through the whole exercise just to pacify his mate. There was no way he was ever going to sell the place he was in and move. As he had it arranged, his mother-in-law had a separate, detached cottage on their property. ("Separate" and "detached" were the key words.)

When you are working with any prospect, it is good to ask these questions:

"How long have you been looking?"

"What is the closest thing you have found to what you are looking for?"

"Are you prepared to make an offer on the property when you find it?" (Judge for yourself the answer to this question: "Will you know it when you see it?")

In working with buyers, I did the best job I could of determining motivation and qualifications and of finding the type of property they said they wanted. If I found it, or as near to it as I judged reasonably possible, and if they didn't buy, I stopped spending a lot of time with them. You can remain cordial and keep in touch, and call them if something happens along that seems particularly promising. You will lose a few with this policy, but it is not a wise expenditure of your time to keep showing property to people who are either not motivated or not capable of making a buying decision.

The Seminar Attenders

I just hated it when a prospective buyer would call and say something like: "I just attended this great seminar on how to get rich in real estate without using any of my own money. I'm really anxious to get started buying houses. When can we meet?"

Some of these schemes are truly incredible, so it's best if you become familiar with the most popular ones for self-defense. Do any of these get-rich-quick schemes actually work? I suppose that under the right set of conditions some of them might, but it's very unlikely that you, as the real estate agent, would ever realize much out of the deal. You would have to spend most of your time searching for the perfect set of circumstances, and then you'd have to try to structure a transaction in which you are paid in a timely manner with readily negotiable instruments. You should know that a common element in these maneuvers is to make the real estate agent wait for her commission or to offer something in lieu of money-like a bale of cotton.

If you are dealing with otherwise reasonable people, you may sometimes be able to convert them into legitimate buyers. It generally becomes clear to them that, for the seminar's scheme to work, the moon has to be in its seventh high, Jupiter has to be aligned with Mars, and Halley's comet has to be clearly visible in the southern sky at high noon. Then they must locate sellers with IQs that would prohibit them from going outside unattended and bank loan officers gullible enough to loan money to an alligator. Of course, anything is possible. Early in your relationship, you might try to work in a reference to the old Russian proverb, "The only free cheese is in the mousetrap."

The Tenants

Now, renters, on the whole, are every bit as nice and honorable as home owners. But renters who occupy homes that are put on the market sometimes develop a nasty streak when their residence is about to be sold out from under them. They are not ordinarily the least bit motivated to make your job easy. If you sell the property, they need to move. If they happen to be present while prospects are being shown the home, it is not at all unusual for them to criticize the property, the neighbors, and the landlord, sometimes in very colorful language. I tried my best to be as considerate of renters as possible, and to show the property when they were not at home. Here's why:

Shock Therapy. Let's say you are previewing a cozy little bungalow rented by a young woman and her little boy. You call the tenant and make an appointment to inspect the house at 10 A.M. for a noon showing. The woman informs you that she and her child will be going shopping so that would work out fine. You arrive a few minutes before they are to leave, wait for them to come out of the house, introduce yourself, and thank her for her cooperation. They leave and you let yourself in with the key you had received from the listing agent. You hear water running upstairs, investigate, and find the shower has carelessly been left on. You reach in and turn the first knob you come to. At that point, you hear a bloodcurdling scream.

The lady's male houseguest is taking a shower, and you have just cut off his hot water. The renter later informs you that she thought Tyrone would sleep through the showing, and it wasn't any big deal anyway. You may correctly conclude that the foregoing illustration is based upon a personal experience.

Moral: It pays to be very cautious when working with renters. That sweet little lady to whom you were planning to show the house would have been shocked to bump into Tyrone, the wet male streaker.

DEALING WITH DIFFICULT SITUATIONS.

Look at it this way. If every real estate transaction were uncomplicated and trauma-free, there would be little demand for your services, right? Don't worry. Even the most routine situation has the potential to be complex and stressful enough to make the majority of people anxious to enlist your services and happy to pay your fee. The more difficult ones separate the journeymen from the real pros, for they will require not only your professional competence but unusual interpersonal skills as well. Here are a few that will enliven your career and enhance your bank account.

Where There's a Will, There Are Relatives

A death in the family brings out the best and the worst in people. Under ideal circumstances, the survivors are interested only in paying their respects to the deceased and comforting each other. When there is even a modest amount of property left behind, however, there is often a regrettable scramble for it, generating intensely bitter feelings. You may become the listing agent for a piece of real property for the estate, either through your contract with an attorney or with the executor of the will.

In such cases, your first and most important step is to know exactly for whom you are working and who has the legal authority to make decisions. Next, make arrangements for a professional appraiser to evaluate the property, because a routine market analysis won't be sufficient. Every relative who stands to collect a percentage of the net proceeds from the sale will be intensely interested and will be quick to criticize. Self-appointed experts on real property value will emerge from the woodwork in numbers you never thought possible.

Personal property can be a particular problem. Often there will be personal effects left in the house. Some items will have a monetary value and any item will no doubt have emotional value to someone. Establish clearly what personal property, if any, is to be included in the sale, and do your best to have the remainder removed by responsible parties before showing the home to prospective buyers. Otherwise, if the family Bible or the rare coin collection comes up missing, you will be in big trouble.

Finally, be prepared to deal with attorneys and courts and to document exhaustively what you've done. Your hard work can pay off, because if you do a professional job on an estate sale, it's quite probable that there will be others.

Divorce, American Style

A year after you sell that cute little Cape Cod in the suburbs to that nice young couple, you could get a call from one of them telling you they are splitting and want you to list the house. They both still like you; they just can't stand each other. If they are desperate, it is likely to be a quick (albeit unpleasant) transaction. They will frequently agree to almost anything to end the relationship. In more acrimonious situations, you might have to deal with attorneys almost exclusively. Sometimes no one trusts anyone enough to move faster than a snail's pace, and principals are often separated by a distance of several thousand miles. In any case, tact, diplomacy, compassion, and patience will be your best allies. Resist any temptation to take sides, for that's a no-win proposition.

Clutching at Straws—The Lease Option

In this arrangement, a potential buyer leases a home for a specific period of time (perhaps a year) with a portion of the monthly payment being credited toward an eventual down payment. During the period of the agreement, the person leasing the home has the option of buying it at a price that has been agreed upon up front. In theory it sounds fine, and in fairness I must admit that many mutually beneficial lease options have probably resulted in sales. I've just never seen one.

What you often have is a desperate owner who has already tried unsuccessfully to sell her property and is clutching at straws, and a buyer who doesn't have enough money for a down payment and might not be able to qualify for a loan. That is not a great combination.

Remember also that an option is a legal document with specific rights and obligations for all principals. Because lease options are fairly uncommon in many markets, people frequently enter into them without adequate legal counsel. Finally, if an option agreement is signed, money will change hands and you deserve to be compensated at that point, as well as when (and if) the option is exercised. Do your homework on this one before you become deeply involved.

Honeymoon First, Vows Later—Possession Prior to Close

In some instances, buyers are anxious to move into a home before the actual close of the transaction. Closing might be days or even weeks away, because things such as appraisals, employment verification, and credit checks take time. Normally, the buyer pays a daily rental fee based upon the new mortgage payment, or something slightly less. It's an arrangement that lets buyers get in and settled without having to worry about securing temporary housing, and it gives the seller some unanticipated income. I moved in early once when I was buying a home, and I have been involved in several other early move-ins, both as the listing and selling agent. If you are dealing with reasonable buyers and understanding sellers, it can work to everyone's advantage, but be advised that it does have explosive potential.

People who have closed the deal have a different attitude toward small household problems than "renters" do. If the faucet leaks or the window sticks, they fix the problem and go their happy way. But if they haven't yet made that final payment at the closing and everyone has not finally signed on dotted lines, they may not be as content. Perhaps a neighbor who fancies himself an expert on area property values reacts in shocked disbelief when he finds out how much they paid. "You paid what!? Too bad you didn't deal through my niece, 'Honest Angelica.' She could have saved you $10,000 easy. I know those people were desperate to sell." Or maybe the wind changes and they get a whiff of the onion-processing plant over the hill—and the wife becomes nauseated when she smells onions. (Never mind that you can't live anywhere in the county without smelling onions.) Then there is also the matter of liability and insurance and responsibility for potential loss. Finally, if the buyers make improvements on the property and then the transaction falls apart before it closes, the situation becomes even more muddled.

On the whole, it is best for the delights and privileges of home ownership to be reserved for that time when everyone has said "I do," and all the other legal niceties have been concluded.

Loathe to Leave—Possession After Close

A less frequent, but equally dangerous, practice involves the sellers staying in the house for a short period of time after the close of the transaction. For the buyers, this poses a couple of serious potential problems. First, they will not be able to inspect the home after the buyers have vacated and before the close. That's standard in some parts of the country. It really motivates sellers to leave things shipshape. Second, at the point the transaction closes and the house becomes theirs, they legally become landlords and the sellers become tenants. In a worst-case scenario, the sellers refuse to vacate on time. They then become "holdover tenants" and it could take formal eviction action to get them out. I admit this rarely happens, but the elements are there for some serious headaches.

"There May Be Another Buyer. Really. I'm Not Kidding!"

Absolutely nothing will cause people to buy more quickly than the belief that someone else is interested in the same property and may get it before they can.

The quickest reversal of field I ever saw occurred when I was working with a young engineer and his wife who were looking for a home. I showed them a wide variety, but they kept coming back to the same one, a brand-new home on a large wooded city lot. It was clear that it was their first choice. They loved it and it was within their price range, but they were hesitant because I had told them that the builder was adamant on price and she would accept nothing but a full-price offer. No negotiating. (I had sold several of her homes before. I knew she was a rock.)

As we concluded our third or fourth visit to the house, they said they would go back to the motel and consider it, but they also wanted to continue the search the next day. Just as we were leaving, another agent (a successful agent who looked the part) drove up in her shiny new car with the real estate sign on the door and out stepped two of the most affluent-looking people you would ever want to see. The man had a briefcase that easily could have been full of thousand-dollar bills. My prospects looked at each other, looked at me, and looked back at the smiling couple as they disappeared into the house. "Say, I think we've probably seen enough houses. What do you say we head back to your office and write up an offer? A full-price offer. Now." (I was kissed only once at a closing. It was when they gave the wife the keys to her new home.)

I often found it difficult to make it clear to buyers that we were not operating in a vacuum. They seemed to believe that they were the only ones looking and that the property would always be available to them. I always made my little speech before we looked at the first house. I pointed out that I took my work very seriously and that the homes I showed them represented what I thought were the very best on the market for what they said they wanted and what they could afford. I told them that all the other agents in town were doing the same thing for their prospects, and that the most desirable properties go the fastest. Maybe I was too low-key, but I rarely got the idea that buyers felt much of a sense of urgency. People have heard the there-may-be-another-buyer pitch so often that they tend to tune it out. You need to continue to make the effort, because there are other buyers and the more successful agents seem attracted to the same properties. I regularly crossed paths with a handful of the same salespeople.

Unfulfilled Dreams—The Unsold Listing

Of all the difficult situations you will face, the unsold listing has the potential to do the greatest harm to your mental health. Let me illustrate.

My wife and I were friendly with an older gentleman who owned one of the most beautiful homes in our city. It was more than 4,000 square feet, on a hill, in an exclusive neighborhood, with a magnificent view of the Cascade Mountains. When our friend decided he wanted to sell and move to a luxury apartment in the city, he called me to list his home. The only problem was that he wanted about $30,000 more than our estimate of market value. We took the listing at his price, after we informed him that we thought we were substantially above the market. We never worked harder on a listing, and although we generated a lot of traffic, four months went by without a sale.

I attempted to convince him that a price reduction was in order, but he was cordially insistent upon staying the course. Three months later, he took it off the market and said he would try again when conditions were better, and assured me he would list it with me again. A short time after that he died suddenly and unexpectedly.

In most respects my friend was an astute businessperson, and he had his overall estate in good order, but he went to his grave with one major unresolved financial problem: the sale of his house. Shortly after his death, the executor of his estate listed the home with another company at a realistic price. Within a month, it was sold to a family that had visited one of our many open houses when we had the listing.

Property owners have to make their own decisions when it comes to setting a price. You can only give advice based on your best professional judgment. But try hard not to let extraneous factors cloud your thinking, and remember that you always have the option of walking away from a potential listing, if you believe you should. You will end up with one or two fewer listings, but you will also have fewer haunting memories.

One Person's Meat, Another's Poison—Negotiating

I recall a rookie agent in our office who was working on one of his first transactions. He had written up an offer to purchase a home and had presented it the night before. He had just received the owner's counteroffer from the listing agent. After she left, and after he had a chance to go over the documents, he came slowly out of his office, visibly shaken. Our broker, who was in the lobby, spotted him and asked what was wrong. "Awful news," he whispered through an obviously tight throat. "The Smedleys just countered the Whimpsters' offer. They'll be devastated. It looks like the whole thing is dead in the water."

Naturally, our broker (who, like most brokers, was an eternal optimist) had a different perspective. "That's actually good news. If the Smedleys didn't think something could be worked out, they wouldn't have bothered with a counteroffer. Get back to the Whimpsters right away. Tell them it's an encouraging sign, and work on reaching a compromise."

And there you have the two views of the negotiating process. The inexperienced salesperson tends to look upon any difference of opinion as a prelude to disaster—a sure sign that all efforts are about to go up in smoke and Junior's braces will have to be postponed for another year. The broker looks upon it as a necessary—and even stimulating—aspect of business life, and assumes that if folks weren't interested in striking a deal, they wouldn't be talking.

Of course, the broker is right. Negotiation in real estate is simply the process of managing a transaction with the objective of reaching an agreement among the participants. It should make your adrenaline flow, not give you stomach cramps.

But enough of the heavy stuff. Let's lighten up a little.

THE ULTIMATE, COSMICALLY DIFFICULT SITUATION

William Robert Dodd (or "Billy Bob," as he was known to his old friends) had died and gone to heaven. Billy Bob had been a successful real estate broker on the Mississippi Gulf Coast for more than forty years at Dodd's Bayside Realty. He passed on at a ripe old age, the way he always said he wanted to go. He was waiting to tee off on the ninth hole at the annual Realtor golf tournament at the country club. When Billy Bob got to heaven, he found a long processing line at the Pearly Gates. It moved quickly, but when he reached the front of it, the angel in charge told him to step to one side and wait. "Your papers are still in escrow," she said, but quickly added, "Oh, that's just a little heavenly joke. I am sure we will have everything straight in a moment." But Billy Bob was not amused, and he was definitely worried. Maybe they still held that 1993 tax return against him. Or maybe they didn't like his company slogan: "In Dodd You Can Trust." Or maybe . . . at that point St. Peter arrived, took Billy Bob by the arm and led him in. "Welcome to heaven, Angel Dodd," St. Peter said. "Sorry for the delay, but you see you are the first real estate agent we have ever had up here."

12

Client Follow-Up and Referrals

Your Insurance Policy Against Lonely Days, Sleepless Nights, and a Penniless Old Age

Traditionally, certain professions command a high degree of client loyalty. Real estate is not one of them.

Although it is entirely realistic for you to expect eventually to earn most of your money from repeat business and referrals, that idyllic situation doesn't happen by itself. You will have to work hard at it, and it will take time.

FOLLOW-UP

Here are some things you can do to help you achieve your objective. When discussing this topic, I use the word *client* to refer to <u>all</u> past contacts, whether customers or clients. As you recall, in legal terminology the client is the person in a real estate transaction whom you represent as an agent. A customer could be an unrepresented party or an individual represented by another agent.

Think Repeat

1. Do it right the first time. By far the most important factor in determining whether people come back to you for their future real estate business, or whether they recommend you to their friends, is how well you handle their original transaction. Do a good job, and it will then be mainly a matter of keeping in touch. Do a poor job, and it won't make much difference what else you do.

2. Make it the beginning of a beautiful relationship. A broker from Arizona got to the heart of the matter in this survey observation: "Too many agents view each closed transaction as the end of the relationship rather than as the start of it." When you automatically cross the street to chat with a former client you happen to see downtown (and he doesn't run when he sees you coming), you know you are doing things right.

3. Keep in touch. In the business world, and most particularly in sales, out of sight is absolutely, definitely, unequivocally out of mind. That doesn't pump up the old ego, but it is a basic fact of life you need to accept. You need to let folks know on a regular basis that you are alive and well and still in business.

People like to be remembered by the professionals with whom they have worked, and they like to feel that their welfare is a matter of personal interest to those professionals. I am certain you would enjoy it if your physician sent you a personal note telling you he appreciated the confidence you had shown in him, and that he looked forward to your future relationship (assuming your heart could stand the shock of getting such a message). Doctors do not need to do things like that to prosper. Real estate agents do.

4. Remember that the close is the opening. The formal part of client follow-up starts at the closing. Sending a thank-you note and a small gift is a good way to begin. If I was working with a buyer, I tried to get a good color picture of the house they had purchased, enlarge it, and frame it in a nice wood frame. Another possibility would be to find an artist who could do a sketch of the house and present that, assuming you can find an artist who would do it for an affordable price and turn out a good product. I never did come up with the perfect gift for sellers, but they were generally so thrilled about receiving their check at the closing that it didn't seem to matter much.

The Nitty Gritty

1. Maintain closed-deal files. By the time each transaction closes, you will have a substantial amount of information. Much of it could be on a computer program, but there will also be extensive paper files. For listings, you will have your original market analysis, the formal listing agreement, copies of advertisements, multiple listing documents, pictures, your chronological log of actions taken, records of open houses, special promotional flyers, results of pest and dry-rot inspections, copies of offers, the opening of escrow, a preliminary title report, a closing statement, and a variety of other miscellaneous records. For buyers, the file might be somewhat less extensive, but it will still contain vital documentation. It is important for you to keep each of these files in one folder identified by the client's name and filed in a separate location called "closed deals." (Don't confuse this with the official "deal file" that the office will maintain. Yours will contain copies of all the essential doc-

uments, plus a great deal more informal personal information about the customers or clients, such as the composition of the family.)

These records form an integral part of your client follow-up program. Often, a former client will simply call and tell you that they want you to list their home. Job transfers, health problems, changes in family relationships (discouragingly, divorces and separations alone generate a large amount of activity), a desire to move up or down in home size, and a host of other factors contribute to making ours a mobile society. When the call comes, if you can go to one source (your closed-deal file), it will save you an enormous amount of time. It is quite likely that in your real estate career you will sell the same property several times. Some houses will become old friends of yours.

2.   Keep them in suspense. Enter your clients' names in whatever kind of "suspense" file that works best for you. There are several computer software programs that are designed to handle client follow-up, and it's possible your broker will have one that handles the entire office. You should try to contact past clients at least three times annually, spaced throughout the year. The key is to make all contacts personal. Telephone calls are effective, but you should not use them exclusively.

I found that some of my most effective contacts occurred while I was driving around town previewing listings and showing property. Some meetings might occur on a random, unscheduled basis. Other times you might want to call ahead to see whether it would be convenient if you dropped by for a few moments to visit. If you happen to be working with a prospective purchaser who is seriously interested in a home in an area where a previous client of yours lives, you may wish to arrange for a brief meeting between them to discuss the neighborhood. Make sure you have a satisfied former client before you try this one.

3.   Remember, you can hire help. There are a number of national and regional companies that specialize in client follow-up programs. There are variations, and specific details change from year to year, but the principle is the same—someone else will handle your client follow-up for you, for a fee. For a time our real estate company used the services of two of these companies, and we found them to be honest and reasonably efficient. Based on my experience, however, my strong recommendation is that even if you subscribe to this type of service, you should still contact your former clients personally on a regular basis. You also need to do periodic checks to ensure the process is working as advertised. You have too much to lose not to give this job your close and constant personal attention.

REFERRALS: THE EASIEST MONEY YOU WILL EVER MAKE

The term *referrals* covers not only the kind of informal referrals your former clients make to their friends and associates but also the more formalized program that exists between real estate agencies. There are two basic types: outgoing referrals and incoming referrals.

Outgoing Referrals

Most people who sell their homes will buy another somewhere else. If that somewhere else is out of your service area, you have a potential referral; and if the referral results in a sale, you will earn a fee. Early in the process of taking a listing, find out where your clients will relocate. Ask them for permission to refer them to a real estate company in that city. Even if they have not decided to buy, ask for their approval. Almost every real estate company has a packet of information about the local area, including maps, which a newcomer will find useful.

If you are part of a real estate franchise operation or if you are in an independent office with membership in one of the national referral companies, you will have no problem in deciding where to make your referral, and on what basis it will be made. Most franchises have an elaborate system that provides toll-free telephone numbers for a national coordinating agency and agreed-upon administrative procedures and referral fees.

If you are in a completely independent and unaffiliated office, you must decide to whom you wish to make the referral and what type of fee you expect. When doing that, refer to agencies that are members of the National Association of Realtors, if possible, because they have agreed to be bound by a code of ethics in conducting their business.

There are some elaborate methods of determining referral fees, but we found it preferable to keep it simple. If we referred a prospect to another office, we expected 20 percent of the commission generated by the referral. Remember, you get nothing if the referral does not result in a closed transaction at the other end. We telephoned the referral and secured verbal agreement to the terms before we provided the name and telephone number of the people being referred. We also asked that the referral be handled by a full-time agent with experience in handling referrals. We further requested that a copy of the official closing statement be sent to us upon the culmination of any transaction. (If you do not see the statement, you have no verifiable way of determining whether you are receiving the agreed-upon fee.) Most real estate brokers are delighted to receive referrals and will gladly agree to your fee, since these are bonus transactions for them.

If you are personally acquainted with an agent in the office to which the referral is being sent, and are satisfied that she will do an aggressive and professional job, make the referral to that specific individual, after coordinating with her supervising broker. Insist that within twenty-four hours of receiving the referral the agent calls your clients on the telephone. Let her know when she can expect to catch them at home, and check to see that the contact has been made.

After each telephone conversation with the other agent, follow up in writing. Sometimes it may take months for a referral to pay off, so keep good records and keep asking for status reports for as long as the referral is active. In some cases, memories begin to fade when it is time to send you your check, so be ready to furnish written documentation of agreements.

Referrals can pay off for you. Let us assume that fifteen of your listings sell each year, and that you refer ten of the sellers to other real estate offices out of town. If five of those referrals result in closed transactions, your portion of the referral fees could go a long way toward paying MLS dues, postage, and any number of other items that have a way of increasing your overhead. There is a lot of money to be made for a minimal amount of effort and expense—and at the same time you will be performing a valuable service for your clients. Some offices even have a full-time relocation counselor paid for by the broker (from fees earned through referrals), who will handle all the administrative chores for you.

Incoming Referrals

You have only limited control over how many incoming referrals you receive. Your broker will decide who gets them, but they are ordinarily distributed on some type of rotation basis. Many offices (including most national franchises) are particular about who handles incoming referrals. It is not uncommon to use only agents who have closed a certain number of transactions and who have successfully completed specified in-house training courses. If that is the case where you work, proceed in all haste to qualify. Further, when you are at educational seminars out of town, particularly at GRI sessions, let agents from other offices in the state know that you appreciate referrals and that you will handle them efficiently.

Not all incoming referrals are of high quality so they need to be screened to make sure that they meet the following two minimum qualifications:

1. The people being referred know about and approve of the referral. "Blind" referrals (made without the knowledge or permission of the clients) are not worth your effort, and can actually result in resentment on the part of the persons who are unsuspectingly referred.

2. Be sure you are given some background as to plans, timing, and financial qualifications of the people involved.

Incoming referrals are quite often blue-chip, gilt-edged prospects. With just a little experience, you will be able to quickly identify the most promising ones and react accordingly.

Let's say that you have received a referral on a couple planning a house-hunting visit in the near future. How should you proceed?

1. Call the prospects. Call the prospects the same day you get the referral. If it is a weekday, you are more likely to catch them home after 7 P.M., their time. Your first order of business will be to identify yourself and relate your call to the agent who made the referral. Do not assume that you are the only agent with whom they will be in touch. Although that is often the case, you cannot depend upon it. Your goal will be to convince them that you can do the job for them better than anyone else. Further, do not assume that all of the information you have been given about them is correct. In a friendly way, try to verify what you were told.

The most important thing you will need to find out is whether their proposed trip is for house looking or house buying. If it is for the specific purpose of buying a home, you will need to arrange your schedule to stay with them for as long as necessary. To make their visit productive, you will need to know what they are looking for and what they can afford. Some people will tell you exactly the type of home they want and what they will pay, while others will be very noncommunicative. Do not press too hard if they seem reluctant. At this point, you are just a voice on the telephone, and some people find it awkward to discuss business matters with someone whom they have not met. If that's the case, you might get some insight by asking them about the house in which they are currently living, such as its size, style, location, and price range. If they have an e-mail address, you can send them specific information about certain properties, including pictures. Naturally, you will want them to check out your Web site. Your broker will unquestionably have a lot of information on the site about the community, as well as links to other helpful sites (if he doesn't, tactfully suggest he check out what your competition is doing).

If they are making specific plans for the trip at the time you call, ask if they need help with motel or hotel room reservations. Determine what days they will be in town, how much time they will have for you, and when you will be able to first meet with them.

2. Plan the visit. Schedule your time to be as productive as possible. Try to meet with your prospects briefly in your office before you start showing them houses. It will give you a chance to get to know them and you can provide an overview of the schedule you have planned. If you have a map of the city on your office wall, you can tell them a lot about your town in a short time, including the location of schools, hospitals, shopping centers, and major residential areas. I always tried to introduce prospects to my broker since he was a very positive, gregarious person who always made newcomers relax

and feel comfortable. I also made it a point to introduce them to a few of the more impressive agents on our staff to emphasize our professionalism and team spirit.

When you start showing homes, you must be very flexible, because it might become immediately apparent that you have misjudged what the prospects really wanted. It is crucial that you have an intimate knowledge of properties in various price ranges and locations to be able to shift gears quickly. Most people want time to themselves to explore the city and surrounding areas on their own. Make absolutely certain they understand that you can get them information on any property they see that has a real estate sign in front of it, because you do not want them calling other offices.

Buyers who are in town for only a short period rarely investigate homes for sale by the owner, but it happens on occasion. If it does, make it clear you could represent them as a buyer's agent, offer friendly general advice, wish them well, and keep in touch, for you want to make your association with them pleasant. If they do not hire you as their agent, do not give them detailed suggestions on how to put together a specific offer or how to negotiate because you could be getting into a sensitive legal area.

In one instance, a young couple with whom I was working on a referral ended up buying a house that was for sale by the owner. They were so distressed that I worked so hard with them and then got nothing, that they sent me Christmas gifts each year they were in town, and called me to list their home when they left. Not all stories like that have happy endings, so expect losses.

3. Follow up. If the visit results in a sale, you have accomplished your goal. If it does not, keep in close touch to be ready for the next visit or actual move. After having met and worked with the people, you should know exactly what they want and what they can afford. If something interesting comes on the market, immediately send them a picture along with descriptive information, either by e-mail or snail mail. Call them once a week or two to check on their status and to see if you can help in any way. If it will be several weeks or longer before they actually move, they might want to subscribe to your local paper. Send them the necessary forms. Some newspapers even have short complimentary subscriptions for prospective residents.

Keep the referring office fully informed. You may want to call the referring agent personally, because at that point, she probably has better rapport with the people than anyone else, and may be able to help from her end in working with them.

WHEN YOUR PAST CLIENTS GET AN ITCH

Let's say you move to a new city and shortly after you arrive you develop a horrible itch that won't go away. You check with your new neighbors and get their recommendation for a local physician who specializes in skin ailments. The doctor prescribes an ointment that quickly clears up your rash. On top of that, she seems like a decent, caring person. Chances are excellent that any time you develop a severe itch in the future you will go back to the doctor who treated you so well. You won't thumb through the Yellow Pages. You won't ask the service station attendant for his recommendations. You won't call Aunt Tillie, who is famous for her do-it-yourself home remedies. You won't even consult Cousin Fred, who sells ointments part-time when he isn't busy at the wrecking yard. Why should you? You know where to go to get professional service from someone you trust.

Any time anyone with whom you have worked develops even the slightest symptom of a real estate–related itch, you want to be the friendly professional whom that person calls. When that starts happening, you will know you are headed down the Yellow Brick Road.

13
Surviving

Strategies for Staying Solvent and Staying Sane

Certainly you will demand more from yourself and your career than mere survival. You will want to feel fulfilled in your work and earn an income that adequately reflects your abilities and rewards your efforts. But you will have to get the basics under control first, before you can concentrate on doing the things that will really make your career take off.

Most of the threats to your job survival in real estate are simply variations of problems traditionally encountered in any profession. None are insurmountable, but taken in combination they can be formidable and you need to understand them. If you have previously been a successful businessperson operating in a highly competitive environment, particularly in sales, you may not need all the information I present. But keep an open mind. The survival techniques you learned in a related field may need some fine tuning.

STAYING FISCALLY FIT

First, let's review the fundamental facts of life as a real estate agent. You are almost certainly going to be solely responsible for providing for your personal financial welfare. You will likely not be provided any company-paid medical, insurance, disability, or retirement benefits, although the brokerage may have plans in which you may enroll at your expense. These realities, plus the emotional pressures associated with any selling job, make it essential that you have a plan to keep your financial, physical, and mental health stable.

LIFE ON A ROLLER COASTER

Managing on a fluctuating commission income is quite a challenge, since the rest of the world seems to operate on such an orderly basis. You, on the other hand, may earn several thousand dollars one month, and then not have a payday for two or three months.

The solution? When you are just getting started you will need money to live on until the income starts. This is one of the greatest challenges to your longevity in the profession. To be safe you should have enough to last for several months. If you really wish to be safe, make that a year. If you do not you may quite understandably begin to let matters of survival cloud your judgment. As a recently licensed agent from Arizona expressed it in his survey: "You must be prepared to live without income for at least six months, or your integrity can be in jeopardy." Even if you make a sale the first day on the job (possible, but don't count on it), it generally takes 30 to 60 days or more for a transaction to close and for you to be paid. If you are married, it always helps to have a mate who is salaried. ("Get your husband a government job," was the sound advice from one survey participant.)

In rare instances, some affluent brokers may pay a new agent a monthly salary (called a "draw") while he's getting started; the amount is then deducted from later earnings. Many brokers who could easily afford this procedure don't do it because they do not feel it wise to place an individual in debt from the very start. I strongly advise against it, except in a dire emergency.

Like it or not (and I hate it), budgeting is an absolute must. About 75 percent of those who answered the survey said that *inability to budget to live on a commission income* was *very important* or *important* in contributing to failure (see Appendix A). Or, as a new agent from Missouri so aptly put it, "A fellow could starve to death!" The temptation is to assume that if you earn $7,000 in June you will earn at least half that much in July. That's not necessarily so. Most of us spend based upon what we earn and commit ourselves to debt based upon what we feel we *will* earn. Those who cannot discipline themselves to conserve their resources when paydays are frequent will find themselves scratching during the dry spells. Real estate agents have been known to visit the local bank around April 15 of each year to borrow money for their Uncle Sam, who is totally unsympathetic to anything other than receiving, by the deadline, a good check for the total amount due him. (Been there. Done that.)

GETTING PAID

Viewed from the outside, a job in residential real estate may appear to be glamorous, high paying, and not all that tough. That's how it looked to me. For example, most people know that, although commissions are negotiable, 6 percent is common. Let's see, sell just two $200,000 houses per month and you'll gross a tidy $24,000, or $288,000 per year! Wow! "Lifestyles of the Rich and Famous", here I come! You won't starve if you close two such sales a month, but it doesn't, in fact, put you in quite that high a tax bracket.

How does the commission system work? Let's illustrate by using the $200,000 sale. In most instances you will sell another agent's listing. If that agent is from a different company the commission will be split between offices, generally on a 50-50 basis. (It would work about the same if an agent from another office sold a listing of yours.) This means that the gross amount coming into your office will be $6,000.

Then there is the broker, who is providing everyone support and doing his best to make it all result in a profit so he can keep the doors open. Schedules differ, but a 50-50 split with him is common. That means that, of the $6,000, you personally gross $3,000. But remember, this is gross, not net.

From that, allocate roughly 15 percent as your cost of doing business. Automobile expenses, telephone calls, license fees, multiple listing fees, dues for professional affiliations, client relations expenses, clothing, business cards, postage, and office supplies all add up. Now consider federal, state and local income tax, and Social Security. You should also plan to allocate a portion of your income to retirement plans. Most of these things will not be deducted from your check—you will have to budget for them.

After the dust has settled and the euphoria of receiving the check subsides (I took a picture of my first commission check), you can expect to net somewhere between $1,200 to $1,600 in spendable income, depending upon your individual situation. So you may have to sell more than a couple of houses and a listing or two each month to live in the style to which you would like to become accustomed. It has probably also occurred to you that the numbers would come out a lot better if you both listed *and* sold a piece of property. That's true, and that's how many of the most successful agents got that way and stay that way.

There is a fast growing concept in the real estate profession, referred to informally as the "One Hundred Percent" office, in which real estate licensees retain all of their commissions, pay a set fee to a broker, and handle all their other expenses. I will discuss this further in Chapter 14. While affiliating with such an office has always been a viable option for an experienced agent, in the past it has not practical for most new licensees. However, there are new options being offered at those companies that would merit your investigation. There are also new business models emerging where licensees work on a menu or fee for service basis. We'll discuss those in Chapter 17. Suffice it to say that for the foreseeable future, the current commission system is likely to dominate.

BEING PREPARED FOR THE UNEXPECTED

There are always some things it is best to prepare for, even if they seem unlikely to happen. Among other things, these can include unanticipated illness, death, and tightness of cash flow.

When the Body Breaks

The cost of medical care is astronomical, and it will only get worse. It is essential that you have insurance to avoid the economic ruin possible because of illness to you or a member of your family. If you have good insurance coverage of any type from a previous employer, or from a spouse's employer, hang on to it. Even if you decide to switch there is typically a waiting period to cover "preexisting conditions." There are a number of companies that sell policies, many of whom advertise widely in professional real estate publications. There are similarities in coverage but there can be marked differences, particularly in responsiveness to claims. Your best bet is to investigate thoroughly by contacting several companies and comparing. If possible, talk to someone who is insured through the company. Find out how satisfied he is and how fairly and quickly claims are handled. You may also want to consider disability insurance to cover you if you are away from the job for an extended period. Your broker will have further guidance for you.

When There Is an Untimely Demise

If you never have anyone dependent upon you for financial support you will have no need for life insurance. A life insurance policy is certainly not the best way to save money, although some do have cash value features, which simply means that eventually you could surrender the policy for cash or borrow against it. If you compare the premiums that you would pay over a number of years for a policy that does build cash value with what you could realize by simply putting the same amount in a savings account at the going interest rate, you will quickly get the picture.

It is not easy to get sound advice about life insurance, for any agent you talk to will have a vested interest. The larger the policy you buy, and the more money you pay, the better it is for the agent. Educate yourself as to the various forms of life insurance and decide what is best for you. You get the most for your money by purchasing decreasing term insurance (insurance that decreases in later years of the policy as your need for coverage declines). If an agent urges you to buy any other type, make sure it is to your advantage, not his. These policies are widely available from companies affiliated with real estate professional associations. Investigate them first and use them as standards of comparison.

When Ready Cash Is at Issue

You will also need to have cash for emergencies. The best approach is to open a federally insured savings account and to establish as your goal an amount equal to about two months' income (that's been my goal now for about 30 years). The temptation will be to dip into this fund for non-emergency expenses, but the first time you have a real crisis you will appreciate being able to loan money to yourself, so to speak. If you own your own home and have a sizeable amount of equity in it, an equity line of credit would be worth exploring. The mortgage interest will most probably be deductible for you, but double check with your accountant. It's obviously a resource that could be abused, but it could also serve as a comforting safety net.

PLANNING FOR RETIREMENT

If you are in your mid-twenties, it is hard to get excited about an event that might occur thirty-five or forty years in the future. But the mathematical reality is clear—the sooner you start saving for your retirement, the more financially secure you will be and the more flexibility you will have in determining your future lifestyle. Even if you are getting into real estate late in life you need to plan for the day when you will retire completely. Here's how one veteran broker told me he advises his agents, young and old: "It's never too early to start and it's never too late, and no matter how much you save, you'll wish you had more."

The two major components to retirement planning are Social Security and do-it-yourself savings.

Social Security

You have no choice—you have to participate. If you are an independent contractor it will take a very sizable chunk out of your income, and if you are an employee both you and your broker will contribute. It would be extremely unwise, however, to depend upon Social Security as your sole source of retirement income. There are few issues of a more sensitive political nature than Social Security, and for that reason changes will be made slowly, but the evidence points to some drastic long-term revisions. Plan to have assets of your own.

You can get all the information you need about Social Security free from the Social Security Administration. Every city of any size has an office with an ample supply of literature that completely describes the program, and there are representatives who regularly visit smaller communities that do not have offices. They also have a very informative Web site at www.ssa.gov. Each year you are supposed to receive a statement in the mail approximately three months before your birthday. The statement is to include general information about Social Security, as well as information about your specific situation, including a historical record of your earnings and your projected Social Security benefits at various projected retirement ages. If yours doesn't arrive, or it arrives and you have questions, get on it immediately.

Make certain you know exactly how your retirement entitlement is computed. The amount of your retirement check will be based upon your average earnings over a specified number of years that is determined by your date of birth. Know how long you will have to work to get maximum benefits. Social Security also has disability and survivor benefits features, as well as hospital and medical coverage for those over age 65. You should integrate these into your long-term estate planning. It could turn out to be a great fringe benefit. For example, a friend of mine is roughly ten years away from beginning to collect his Social Security. He has a variety of other investments and a federal job with retirement benefits. He tells me he plans to use his monthly Social Security benefit to fund an annual European trip for he and his wife. On the other hand, I have an acquaintance who has been collecting benefits for about ten years. He tells me he invests it in the government's inflation-indexed Series I savings bonds to fund any possible long-term health care needs. His pitch for the I Bonds is that they are always exempt from state income tax (his state has a high income tax) and that you pay no federal tax until you cash them in.

Do-It-Yourself Retirement Plans

To encourage individuals to provide for their own financial independence the government has devised some very attractive programs. Details change but the basic concept is likely to remain. You will be given substantial tax incentives to save for your own future. Currently the two primary programs are Individual Retirement Accounts (IRAs), for both employees and independent contractors, and Keogh plans, for independent contractors only. There are a couple of different types of Keoghs, but the most popular for real estate professionals seems to be what is called a Profit Sharing Plan. The bottom line is that you can contribute a certain percentage of your net profit each year. These plans have to be set up prior to December 31, so do your research and take action. I've invested my Keogh (the maximum allowable each year) in a very conservative mutual fund. "Very conservative" is my strong recommendation no matter where you put your money. The rules on who may open tax-deductible IRAs are fairly selective, and change periodically, so keep up with them.

Let me make a special pitch for Roth IRAs. Subject to some very liberal income limitations, you can invest several thousand dollars each year in your Roth IRA—amounts will vary over time. The contributions are not deductible, but they accrue interest tax free and are not subject to tax when you start to withdraw funds, subject to certain limitations. I strongly recommend that if eligible you fully fund your Roth IRA each year and consider it a long-term investment. Again, make it conservative.

Stay turned in the event the ever-changing tax laws revamp the entire retirement plan landscape.

INVESTING YOUR MONEY

After you insure yourself, provide for emergencies, and establish a retirement plan, the next logical pillar in building your financial estate may be an investment in real estate.

A Home of Your Own

If you are in the business of selling homes it's a good idea (make that absolutely essential) to buy one of your own sooner or later—the sooner the better. You will be in a distinct minority among your peers if you do not. Among Realtors nearly 90 percent are home owners.

If you've never owned a home, here is some basic guidance: You will have two major obstacles to overcome—the down payment and the monthly expenses. If you are fortunate enough to have a relative who will help you, fine, but most folks have to come up with the cash themselves. Use as a very rough planning factor 10 percent for a down payment and another 5 percent for closing costs, including loan fees. For a $200,000 house (adjust up or down for your area) you would need $30,000 cash at close. You may be able to reduce that if you are earning a commission on the transaction. You will have to finance the balance of $180,000. Assuming you got a mortgage at 7 percent fixed rate for 30 years, your monthly principal and interest payment would be $1191.51, plus property tax and property insurance.

You can see that home ownership is not cheap, and that the hardest home to buy will be your first. On the positive side there are substantial income tax advantages in owning a home, because interest and property taxes are deductible items, and there is always the possibility of a profit when you sell. As a career Air Force officer we moved every three or four years. Each time we bought a modest home in a nice neighborhood, took care of it, and sold it for a very nice profit when we moved. Best monetary investments we ever made. You don't have to be in the military to follow the same plan, although not all families are anxious to uproot quite so often.

By the time you start looking at homes for yourself you will be well versed in the house-hunting process, for you will have worked with others in satisfying their housing needs. But because this will probably be the most important investment you will ever make, it won't hurt to emphasize a few very significant matters.

1. Get a firm handle on market value of the home. You will become very good at this very quickly. Decide what outcome you want to achieve and es-

tablish your priorities. Make an offer that reflects your ideal outcome. Typically, that will be somewhat less than asking price. This does *not* apply if you, or your mate, have decided that, if you don't get that little charmer on Harmony Lane, the world as you know it will crumble around your feet and life will not be worth living. While you are playing real estate tycoon the house might be sold to someone else! Just decide what it will take to buy it, and if you can afford it, make your first offer one that you know will be accepted. Even (gasp, groan) if that means a full-price offer? Yes. What is a couple of thousand dollars compared to twenty years of watery eyes or a mate with tight jaws every time you drive by that little dream house on Harmony Lane?

2. Be conservative. Look at every house not only as a buyer, but as a seller, for that is what you will eventually be. If a property has a flaw, but it is one that does not particularly bother you, remember that it might very well bother others when it is time to sell. The most important factor for you to consider in choosing your home is—that's right—location! Everyone seems to know this, but it is startling how often it is ignored, even by real estate agents when they are buying a home for themselves. Insist upon property that is in a nice residential neighborhood, away from busy streets. If there is not a high pride of ownership in the neighborhood, as evidenced by well-cared-for homes, look elsewhere. If possible, do not buy the most expensive house in the neighborhood.

3. Get an impartial inspection. Make your offer contingent upon a satisfactory pest, dry-rot, and structural inspection conducted by a licensed firm. In most areas, there are companies that specialize in generalized home inspections. It's worth paying for a professionally conducted inspection. By all means check out the home yourself as well. If the property is on a well, have it tested for potability and pressure. Take the water sample yourself and have it analyzed. If there is a septic system, have it inspected by the county sanitarian or someone he recommends.

4. Work to secure favorable financing. If interest rates are favorable, my first choice for financing would be a thirty year, fixed-rate loan. Over the years this has proven to be the most beneficial for home owners. Each payment remains the same, while hopefully the value of the home goes up. If mortgage interest rates skyrocket, assuming an existing loan may be a possibility. Assume a loan only with the concurrence of the mortgage holder. There are plenty of loans on the books that can be assumed, including older loans through FHA and VA. Just by keeping up with homes on the multiple listing service you will become aware of many. Do not take anyone's word that a loan may be assumed without checking yourself with the lender. Since there are frequently high equities involved in assumable loans (the difference between what the owner owes on the property and its market value) it is common for the seller to take back a second mortgage for a portion of that equity.

Balloon payments, in which the entire balance due to the seller is due to be paid in a few years, are also common. Be wary of these, particularly the ones that come due in just a year or so.

If you cannot qualify for standard mortgage financing because the monthly payments are too high, it may be wise to wait and save more money for a larger down payment, as opposed to trying to find a "creative" solution to your problem. Agree to an adjustable rate mortgage only if you could live with the highest possible rate.

Once you own the house take care of it. A well-tended home in a nice neighborhood is always in demand. Protect your investment by not deferring maintenance on items such as painting and repairs. If your interests and talents tend toward working outside, so much the better, for the "curb appeal" of a home with an attractive yard can translate into thousands of dollars and a quick sale when the time comes.

5. Remember that you are a licensed real estate agent. The fact that you have specialized knowledge will make it incumbent upon you to be unusually open and forthright in all your dealings. Laws vary from state to state so you will have to check on local ground rules, but expect to have your personal dealings closely scrutinized. Keep your broker informed about everything you do, including buying your own home.

Investment Properties

At some point successful real estate agents seem inevitably drawn toward investing in income-producing property, usually residential property. A significant percentage of all Realtor salespersons, for instance, own investment real estate. Single family homes are the first choice (we're talking rentals here), followed by vacant land, and multi-family units. There's a good reason for the interest in investment real estate. As an agent's income increases, so does the need for tax shelter, and few investments meet the need better than real estate (vacant land being an exception).

It is advisable, however, to enter your initial venture cautiously. First, do not be tempted to invest before you have a secure financial footing concerning your basic needs. Then decide on the kind of investment with which you would be most comfortable. Is it a small rental cottage that you can drive by each day and admire? Or is it a duplex in a good rental area? In either case, are you prepared to deal with tenants and their inevitable problems? Could you withstand a downturn in your local rental market and prolonged vacancies? Finally, make absolutely certain that you are aware of all tax laws as they relate to rental property. When we made our last move in the Air Force to our current location we used money from the profit on the sale of our former home to invest in a modest condominium, which we rented to my wife's mother. That was many years ago and we still own that property and another small rental. Both have been outstanding hedges against inflation. The rent my landlady wife collects on the condo is now roughly three times what it was originally, and the property is debt free. Very nice cash flow.

A nationally recognized author has sold thousands of copies of a book in which he outlines a system whereby he has turned a modest investment into millions in real estate. The plan is to buy old houses at bargains, fix them up, and sell them at huge profits. There is no question that money can be made by such an approach, but you can also lose your shirt. First, you have to have real expertise to judge whether a house is basically sound. Second, you must be able to estimate accurately how much work it will involve to make the repairs. If you are not handy and have to hire repairmen to do the work, it is most unlikely that the venture will be profitable (for you). And you must not only repair the house, you must also package a financing program that is attractive. Even experienced builders have difficulty putting an old house in order and selling it for a profit, so tread gently.

Other Investments

There will be no shortage of other investment opportunities, from stocks and bonds to government securities to rare gems and metals. The more successful you become the more tempted you will be to invest in such ventures. Everyone must learn their own lessons, but the old pros (the survivors of good times and bad) offer these suggestions: stick to something you know (in your case, probably real estate), diversify, and be cautious.

MAINTAINING YOUR PSYCHOLOGICAL BALANCE

In some professions you can leave your business concerns at the office at the end of the day, but that is just not the case in real estate. You will be under incredible self-imposed pressure to work late and put in extra time on weekends and holidays. There will always be some task that you could perform that might result in making more money. To compound matters, the more successful you become (the more sales in progress, the more listings) the greater will be the number of phone calls to you at home during your "off" hours.

Burnout

Burnout is a term that has come into vogue in recent years, but the phenomenon was common in real estate long before there was a name for it. If you do not establish some personal behavior patterns and guidelines and stick to them, you will be a prime candidate for a "career readjustment" after three or four years, perhaps just at the point when you are becoming well established and highly paid. Here are a few suggestions to help you avoid that happening to you:

■ *Don't be a slave driver.* It is just as important to schedule time off as it is to schedule business appointments, and it is just as important to honor your commitment to yourself as to honor commitments to others. You may hesitate to follow this advice because of the nagging feeling that you may miss a phone call or that a detail on a pending transaction may not get taken care of. Because either of these events could mean literally thousands of dollars to you, the temptation is to consider yourself indispensable.

To allay your fears, one of your top priorities should be to establish a special working relationship with another agent in your office. Pick one who shares your personal business views and whom you trust implicitly. When you are out of town or on vacation that agent will handle your affairs and you will return the favor. It is the same kind of situation that exists when a physician is "on call" for an associate.

■ *Establish a communications system.* As you will recall from our discussion in Chapter 6, it's absolutely essential to have an effective communications system. With all the whiz-bang technology we now have there's no excuse not to be fully wired. There will be times when you don't wish to be reached personally, but there's never a time when you won't want a message to be delivered for your future attention and action.

■ *Feel good and look good.* It is beyond the scope of this book or my expertise to offer detailed advice on diet and exercise, except to say that if you do not feel good physically and do not have a positive self-image, it will be hard for you to make the confident, successful impression that is so crucial.

It will be easy to fall into bad habits, for there will be so many occasions to celebrate and no shortage of frustrating experiences you would like to forget. If you do either by absentmindedly popping open a bag of candy (if life were fair, peanut M&Ms would be calorie-free), you'll find your spare tire gradually starting to inflate. It may be a constant battle, but the goal is to avoid becoming overly involved emotionally in your transactions and to vent your frustrations by exercising vigorously several times a week.

Here's what works for me: If I had a treadmill in my den it would gather dust. However, each academic term I sign up for 7 A.M. , five day a week, exercise classes at nearby Oregon State University. They provide enjoyable social interaction as well as being good for me. On my own I would never do it. And I know this will have absolutely no bearing on your decision on whether to follow my example or not, but over the years I've realized several thousand dollars in referral fees from contacts I've made in these classes, not to mention a lifetime supply of free cantaloupes in gratitude for the guidance I provided a woman and her husband in securing a farm property for their melon-raising operation.

A Commercial from the Surgeon General

Smoking is not only a hazard to your health, it could be harmful to your career. As nonsmokers assert their rights more and more and as business owners begin to conclude that smoking in the workplace can be bad for business, the smoker's freedom is being inhibited. Some brokers do not permit agents to smoke in the office at all, and some have "thank you for not smoking" signs even for customers. Smokers frequently seem unaware of the clinging nature of the smell of cigarette smoke. The aroma lingers on in the smoker's clothes long after the cigarette is gone. If you do smoke be prepared for criticism and expect some unpleasant glances from nonsmoking customers when they get a whiff of you. You could do your body and your career a great favor by giving it up. (You're right, there's nothing worse than a reformed sinner.)

IT'S A FAMILY AFFAIR

You come home after a twelve-hour day in your real estate job. You spent the last six hours showing homes to people who finally confided that they were just browsing, and that, if they did see something they wanted, they would wait until Nephew Clarence got his real estate license and buy through him. Your husband puts down his beer long enough to look up from the TV and complain that supper is late. Your daughter has had the phone tied up for forty-five minutes, even though she has been told repeatedly to "keep it short" so business calls can get through. Junior asks, "Sell anything today, mom?" Somehow it's not quite as much fun as you were led to believe it would be. The moral is clear. If you are part of a family, everyone has to understand how hard you work as a real estate agent and be prepared to make your job easier. The first four-figure commission check or two you bring home should go a long way in getting everyone's attention.

14

Where to From Here?

Long-Term Options For Your Career

To be a good general, you do not need to start as a private and work your way up through the ranks. But if you do, you will develop a perspective and understanding of your job you cannot achieve by any other means. Likewise, you do not need to sell a lot of houses to succeed in the more specialized real estate jobs. However, the experience you will gain as a salesperson in face-to-face contact with the home-buying public will be of immense value to you and cannot be duplicated in any other way. Whether or not you ever want to do anything in your real estate career other than work in residential sales, it is good to at least know what the possibilities are down the road. There's no shortage.

REMAINING IN GENERAL REAL ESTATE

Many agents spend their entire careers happily listing and selling residential property. They would not be content doing anything else, and they would not really consider it "being in real estate." There are some advantages to limiting yourself primarily to residential sales. First, if you are good at it, you will be well paid and you will know what it takes (in terms of time and effort) to meet your financial expectations. Further, the longer you specialize, the better you will become, the more repeat business and referrals you will have, and the more control you will exercise over your business and personal life.

There are some negative factors. Although your income might be substantial, you must continually put together a large number of transactions, and despite the fact that you have more control over your activities, your workload will always be large and demanding. Every buyer and seller is different, and each residential transaction will be unique, but there is enough repetition to begin to bother some agents after a few years. And certain people simply need a new challenge to stay motivated.

If you decide to remain in residential sales, let me suggest a goal that will add zest to your professional life and provide the continuing stimulant you will need, not to mention incredible income potential and the privilege hanging out with some of the profession's true super achievers. Let's assume you've been in the business for about three years. You've become a Realtor and have achieved your GRI designation (if you missed our discussion of the GRI designation in Chapter 4, now would be a good time to go back and review it). We'll assume that you earn a decent living, but you are looking for new horizons and new challenges.

The National Association of Realtors has a program tailored for you. It is offered by NAR's Residential Sales Council. It is the professional designation Certified Residential Specialist (CRS) and represents the highest designation awarded to sales associates in the residential field. Fewer than 4 percent of all Realtors have this designation. They also earn substantially more than their counterparts. As a matter of fact, according to recent statistics, they earn an average of $160,500 annually, roughly four times as much as the typical Realtor who specializes in residential real estate.

There are demanding production and educational requirements to earn the CRS designation, which undoubtedly accounts for the reason that such a minority of Realtors hold the designation. While there are different options, just to give you a preview, here is one path to gain the CRS. Production requirements (transactions you put together in the real world) would require 25 transaction sides (with no time limit) or $8 million with a minimum of ten transactions within any two year period. Educational prerequisites would require the completion of three core courses. Those are listed as: Business Planning and Marketing, Listings, Sales, Wealth Building, Technology, and Referrals. These courses are taught nationwide throughout the year by highly successful working professionals who have been down the same road you have. There are also some elective requirements you could satisfy in a variety of ways.

I have attended a number of Realtor conventions and educational seminars throughout my career. I can only imagine the quality of professional contacts you would make at a CRS educational session. To be honest, you're likely to learn as much from your fellow participants as you are from the presenters. Don't wait to investigate this program. Know what the requirements are early in your career. If you are at all attracted to residential real estate sales, I can't imagine you not being turned on by this opportunity. Had I remained active in this area, it would have been my next goal. For further information, your best source is the Web site at www.crs.com. For other contact information, write to Council of Residential Specialists, 430 North Michigan Avenue, Chicago, IL 60611.

GREENER GRASS

If you conclude that you enjoy what you are doing, but would prefer doing it in another office under another broker, make certain that you are actually improving your situation by moving. If you are making money where you are located, you are making money for your broker. You should be able to negotiate any reasonable changes you think might be necessary. Larger commission splits, more desirable office accommodations, increased broker support for high-producing projects, and more good-quality referrals are all possibilities.

Clearly, one of the most important factors in your success and contentment in real estate will be the personal and professional rapport you achieve with your broker. If you develop a good relationship, do not give it up without some serious thought. Those who leave a company because they have become dissatisfied with the environment (as opposed to those who leave on good terms to take advantage of a more attractive professional opportunity), seem to make several such moves and have trouble achieving a satisfactory relationship anywhere.

HAVING IT ALL

One special situation might tempt you to change offices even if you are happy where you are. We referred briefly in Chapter 13 to what is known generically as the "100 percent" concept, in which agents get 100 percent of all the commissions they earn. The broker provides the supervision required by law, acts as a general office manager, and supplies the necessary facilities support. In return, the agents pay a monthly fee for their office space, contribute to a salary for the broker, and are responsible for all their own direct support, such as office supplies and postage, as well as personal advertising.

RE/MAX International Inc. (P.O. Box 3907, Englewood, CO 80155, www.remax.com) is the leader in this concept. It is one of the most successful, vigorous franchises in North America and has 62 independently owned offices in sixty-two countries worldwide (by the time you read this, both numbers will likely be higher). The typical RE/MAX sales associate has more experience than other agents, and the average income for a RE/MAX agent over the years has exceeded the industry average by thousands of dollars. If you would like to read a complete history of RE/MAX check out the book *Everybody Wins—The Story and Lessons Behind RE/MAX* by Phil Harkins and

Keith Hollihan. In reviewing the book for *The Real Estate Professional* I received a press release from the publisher, Wiley. They made an interesting and very apt observation when they indicated that RE/MAX founder Dave Liniger was "cut from the same cloth as Sam Walton and Ray Kroc". That's Walmart and McDonalds in the unlikely event you didn't recognize the names.

If it's such a great deal, why wait? Why not affiliate with a 100 percent office right away? Several years ago while working on a previous edition of this book, I asked its cofounder Dave Liniger if it was practical for a newly licensed agent to consider going to work for RE/MAX. The short answer at that point was "probably not." There were a number of reasons, the most practical of which is that under the dominant RE/MAX compensation arrangement, associates pay a very healthy stipend per month for their share of office expenses. You would have needed to be very confident to commit to an annual overhead outlay of thousands of dollars before you even met a prospective client. Unless you were highly successful in a directly related sales position with a great deal of self-assurance and a healthy bank account, it would have likely been wise to file this one away for possible future reference.

However, several members of my most recent real estate licensing class interviewed with the local RE/MAX brokerage. What I learned was that RE/MAX now has a program tailored for new agents, including a mentor program and a revised compensation structure. One of my most promising former students went with RE/MAX immediately after getting her license and has done extremely well. The last time I had coffee with her she was about to head off to Las Vegas for a RE/MAX meeting to accept some type of rookie award. It would definitely be worth checking out.

REAL ESTATE SALES MANAGEMENT

If a management career appeals to you, you have two basic options: you can work for someone else or you can start out on your own.

Working as a Designated Broker or Sales Manager

A growing trend in the profession is for large real estate companies to hire one, or even two or more, brokers to run their offices. The term *designated broker* is widely used, although the exact title will vary. The concept is simple: you would be managing a real estate brokerage (alone, or with other brokers), while working for the owners of the company. Compensation would typically be in the form of a salary with other incentives for performance.

In large, active offices it is not unusual to encounter a sales manager whose job it is to supervise, train, and motivate the sales staff. The manager is generally paid a monthly or annual salary, as well as bonuses and incentives that are tied to the performance of the agents under him. In certain cases, he may do some selling, but the primary job is managerial.

If you are an outstanding salesperson, your broker (or another broker) might offer you such a position. It can be a tremendous opportunity, but do not automatically jump at it. On the plus side, you could expect to lead a more "normal" lifestyle (although, as a salaried employee, you would be expected to be available whenever your salespeople needed you, and that could be almost anytime). Your income will also be more stable, because you will not be entirely dependent on putting deals together to get paid.

The mistake most brokers make is to assume that top sales agents automatically make top managers. That is not necessarily the case. You see the same thing in sports, where the superstar athlete often fails as a coach. It takes special skills and personality traits to become a good supervisor.

Top producers in real estate sales often achieve their success by being fiercely independent and employing highly individualistic business techniques. If you cherish your freelance status, a job as a sales manager is probably not for you. If, on the other hand, you think you might eventually like to be a broker, and the thought of supervising your current associates does not give you a sinking feeling in the pit of your stomach, becoming a sales manager could be a good move.

Owning Your Own Brokerage

If you are suited for management and want to stay in the mainstream of general real estate and don't want to work for someone else, you may want to own your own company. How do you know whether you have the leadership potential to risk it all and do it all on your own? It's not hard to tell. Consider your pre-real estate experience. Were you involved in leadership activities in school, in your previous job, or in civic groups? During your early years in real estate, were you active in professional organizations? Did you enjoy attending courses in professional education and react with enthusiasm to those classes that explained areas new to you? During the staff meetings at your office, did you contribute enthusiastically to group problem-solving sessions and did the other members of the group seem to particularly value your suggestions? Did you often wish that you were in a position to make the final decisions on how the office was run? Be very clear on the fact that not all good real estate agents have the potential to become good brokers. You have to have a burning desire to be in charge, and the talent to do well when you are. If you are not certain, choose another course. A logical way for you to learn more about the real estate profession and your own place in it is to get your broker's license. If you're in a single license state, where your first license is some sort of broker designation, it simply means a step up to a higher form of broker. In Oregon, for example, it's called Principal Broker or Sole Practitioner Broker (on your own, no one under you). Doing so will likely involve additional course work covering such topics as office management, supervision, advanced financial and legal matters, and appraisal. As was the case when you got your salesperson's license, you must pass a test prescribed by the state licensing agency. Even if you decide that you do not wish to open your own office, having a broker's license is a logical career progression. You can still work in the same place under your current broker. Some organizations have several associate brokers. Having your broker's license opens the possibility of being able to take over and run a branch office of the company you work for; in this instance, you would operate in a separate physical facility, but you would still report to your broker.

If you decide you want to run your own company, you have two basic options. First, you can buy out an existing business. As you might expect, this approach will require some cash, sometimes quite a lot if there is real property involved in addition to the business itself. If you are buying into a franchise, the tab could be even higher.

More than any other factor, consider the reputation within the community of the company you are contemplating buying. If you buy a service station that has been poorly managed, you may be able to turn it around with new personnel and an aggressive, service-oriented approach. In real estate, however, public perceptions die slowly. If a company has a poor reputation, the bad rep is likely to persist despite the best efforts of new owners.

Another option is to start your own company from scratch. That does not necessarily mean you need to lease or buy your own office, purchase equipment and supplies, and secure agents. Some brokers start out as a one-person company, operating out of their own homes or in a very modest office. They expand as they gain confidence and capital.

Whether you opt for an existing company or start your own, you will eventually be in the position of recruiting sales agents. If you do a good job in this activity, it will be hard for you to fail. If you do a poor job, it will be nearly impossible for you to survive. If you don't think you are a good recruiter, be prepared to hire someone who is to work for you, because recruiting will be the key to your prosperity. For your long-range educational objectives, tuck away the fact that NAR's Real Estate Brokerage Manager's Council offers courses leading to the Certified Residential Broker (CRB) designation. It's the next logical step up from the CRS designation. You can get information by logging on to www.crb.com or calling 1-800-621-8738.

SPECIALIZED REAL ESTATE SALES

You may want to remain with the same company but concentrate your efforts in a particular activity. Here are three possibilities:

1. Exchanging. You will recall from our discussion of investment property exchanges in Chapter 9 that there are exciting income possibilities in this activity. Larger transactions may include several different high-priced properties with a total value in the millions. There are exceptionally prosperous agents who work exclusively on property exchanges. If you close three or four exchanges per year (or perhaps only one or two), you can earn an impressive income and be fully occupied.

If you believe you would like to do exchanges full-time, your first step is to learn the basics. Refer to the Web sites devoted to exchanging that we mentioned in Chapter 9 for additional information. Professional organizations also often sponsor educational sessions. If you are lucky, there may be a successful agent locally who specializes in real estate exchanges who teaches courses at your community college or university. If so, grab the opportunity. Make sure that any course you take is taught by someone currently active in exchanging and that the depth of instruction is adequate to get you beyond the initial overview stage.

There may be an exchange club organized through your local MLS. Members are typically agents who deal primarily or exclusively in exchanges and who meet on a periodic basis to trade information about specific properties. Meetings are an excellent source of networking contacts, and there are generally a handful of real pros in the group.

2. Commercial and Investment Activities. If you are fascinated by the prospect of dealing in commercial and investment transactions and you have genuine talent and true ambition, there is no limit to your potential earnings. This is not the arena for the timid or faint of heart, so be ready for life in the fast lane to take you straight to the high-rent district. A good starting point would be to contact the NAR affiliate to find the Realtors National Marketing Institute. You can also log on to www.ccim.com or write to them at 430 North Michigan Ave, Chicago, IL 60611. The professional designation of Certified Commercial Investment Member (CCIM) is conferred upon those who meet stringent educational and experience standards. Another good research tool is to visit the website of the Society of Industrial and Office Realtors, which offers the SIOR professional designation.

While I was active in residential sales, there was a young man in our city by the name of Jackson Cooper who was starting to branch out from residential into commercial activities. He eventually left his company and formed his own brokerage, specializing in commercial real estate. His company became the dominant commercial brokerage in our area. Everywhere you went you saw his sign. And I mean on big, big properties. He was a prime mover and investor in the building of a brand new Holiday Inn Express on the lovely Willamette River, and also the building of a large hotel complex adjacent to the local university campus. A few years ago he relocated his business to

Boise, Idaho. If you have not visited Boise lately, trust me it is a growing, robust economy. To quote from an e-mail he sent me shortly after relocating: "Boise is a fantastic real estate market!" To check it out for yourself, including some very impressive commercial listings visit his website at www.jackson-cooper.com. (When I visited the site there was a modest little office complex in Idaho Falls featured for an asking price of $3,915,000). Incidentally Jackson holds both the CCIM and SIOR professional designations we mentioned previously. And if you really want to be impressed, visit the website of the parent company of Cooper's local brokerage, Sperry Van Ness Commercial Real Estate Advisors: www.svn.com. Click on the "career opportunities" link. If Jackson can do it, why not you?

3. Farm and Land Sales. I listed and sold two large farms while I was a general real estate agent. The experience convinced me that there was a great deal more to know than I had originally expected. If you did not grow up on a farm, you will be operating in a strange world with a bewildering language. Soil types, water and mineral rights, crop values, federal and state income tax and incentive programs, land leases, equipment valuation, and animal appraisal are only a few of the subjects with which you may need to become conversant. Farmers do not bluff easily and are exceptionally wary of anyone other than another farmer, so do not say more than you know. Although you can use many of the skills you develop while working in residential sales, the differences are so great that you would be foolish to try to compete with those agents who specialize in this without first preparing yourself.

The properties you will be trying to list or sell will not be located just around the corner, and they will ordinarily have a high price tag with comparatively few qualified buyers. You can easily spend a year marketing a listing, but if you earn a commission of $15,000 to $20,000, it is obviously worth it, particularly if you have more than one transaction going at one time.

While doing research for another writing project I contacted a former college roommate of mine who owns several large almond orchard operations in California. Over the years he has bought and sold a variety of almond orchards. He indicated that his agent (and good personal friend) was one of the most prominent in that niche in Central California and typically grossed over twenty million in total sales yearly. He also said it was not uncommon for him to handle both sides of a transaction. Do the math on that and I'm certain you'll be as impressed as was I. By the way, we mentioned equipment valuation earlier as a topic of specific interest in this niche. My old Modesto Junior College almond growing buddy indicated he had recently sold his almond huller for around a million dollars.

If this career option peaks your interest, a good way to get information is by visiting the Realtors Land Institute (RLI) website at www.rliland.com to get a description of the professional courses they offer. Their professional designation is Accredited Land Consultant (ALC).

DIFFERENT FOLKS, DIFFERENT STROKES

For some of you, the overriding goal from your first day in the business will be to own your own real estate brokerage company. That's a noble and eminently achievable objective. The real backbone of the real estate industry in the United States has been the small "general store" office, looked over on a daily basis by a hardworking broker/owner. There are also tremendous brokerage opportunities available within the franchise systems, where many of the offices are independently owned and operated. Others will find their niche in an activity they knew about only vaguely before becoming a licensed salesperson. Still others will continue in general sales and wonder why anyone would ever want to do anything else. It's hard to think of a profession in which you would have so many options—all of them good.

You say you want more? There's plenty. Read on.

15

The Roads Less Traveled

Other Real Estate Career Possibilities

You will get a lot of mail as a real estate agent. Let me tell you about a packet I once received from an organization sponsoring an international conference on real estate. They were offering a one-week course in Geneva, Switzerland, for "the real estate professional who wants to become involved with the international real estate market." The faculty included people from the World Bank, Disney International, and Merrill Lynch Relocation Management International. The curriculum was intriguing, offering courses such as "International Manufactured Housing," "International Currency Hedging for the Real Estate Professional," and "A Case Study in Ecuadorian Real Estate Considerations." There was a hosted champagne mixer and a reception dinner sponsored by the West Midlands Industrial Development Association. (You can bet that wasn't weenies and beans.) I still have the color brochure, complete with pictures of Swiss castles and quaint European villages. Unfortunately, I couldn't convince my broker to fund my trip.

VARIETY OF OPTIONS

You will have opportunities outside of general real estate brokerage that are equally exciting. During your early years, you will have a chance to decide whether they have potential for you or not. If you have established a favorable reputation as a residential agent, or if you have a background from a previous profession that is particularly appropriate for a specific activity, it is not at all unlikely that someone will be contacting you concerning a career change. Or you may simply get a brochure in the mail. However it comes, you will have the opportunity—or more than one opportunity—to explore a wide range of options. Some of these possibilities are the subject of this chapter.

Real Estate Finance

One person with whom you will become very familiar is the mortgage loan officer. All lending institutions that make real estate loans, as well as certain government lending agencies, employ loan officers. Their job is to take loan applications, evaluate them, forward them to an underwriter for a final decision, and supervise the associated administrative work. When real estate is booming, there are tremendous opportunities in this field, but when times get tough and loan applications decrease, these specialists feel the pinch.

The job of mortgage broker is an interesting variation. A mortgage broker does not work for a specific lender. They take loan applications and place them with the lender that best meets the specific requirements and qualifications of the borrower. Not all lenders work with mortgage brokers, but enough do that they have a wide variety of possibilities to offer consumers. It generally costs the borrower no more to work with a mortgage broker than it does to go directly to a lender. If you opt for the mortgage broker job, you will survive on a commission income rather than a set salary paid by a lending institution. The Professional organization of mortgage brokers is the National Association of Mortgage Brokers, and their web site is www.namb.org.

If you are excited by the challenges and opportunities of real estate finance and believe you would enjoy the lifestyle, develop other financial skills as well as your real estate expertise so your versatility will provide insurance against the upheavals caused by the inevitable downturns in the economy. A college degree, preferably in finance or business, is a necessity if you are thinking in terms of the higher echelons of management in a lending institution.

The Mortgage Bankers Association of America (MBAA) at 1919 Pennsylvania Ave. NW, Washington, D.C. 20006 is a nationwide organization devoted to the field of real estate financing. They have an extremely informative website at www.mbaa.org, including career information links. More than three thousand mortgage companies, savings and loan associations, commercial banks, life insurance companies and others involved in mortgage lending belong to MBAA.

One of the subjects I teach as part of the real estate licensing program in Oregon is Real Estate Finance. Although my number one goal is to prepare my students to pass the State licensing exam, I also attempt to provide them with real world career information. In the area of real estate finance, the best source I've found is that of Jack Guttentag, who bills himself as the "Mortgage Professor". Visit his web site at www.mtgprofessor.com. It's incredibly informative and offers objective, easy to understand information.

Escrow and Title Insurance

In some areas of the country, real estate closings are handled by attorneys, who also perform title searches. In other places, the lending institutions themselves have an escrow department and hire an attorney to do the title search. Elsewhere, escrow and title companies perform both functions. The title search is done as a preliminary to issuing title insurance.

Both closings and title work should be performed by persons of intelligence who pay exceptional attention to detail. The escrow agent—the person who actually handles the closing—must be very adept in arithmetic functions and must have the ability to deal effectively with people who are in stressful situations. Real estate agents have the highest admiration for escrow (closing) officers, with whom they work closely. You see, if the escrow officers don't do their job properly, the agent never gets paid.

These are salaried jobs with more or less standard working hours. The best place to get additional practical information is your local title or escrow company. Community colleges often offer appropriate courses, as do some private schools. I typically have at least one or two students in my real estate salesperson licensing classes who are interested not in becoming a real estate salesperson but in learning more about the real estate profession in general to help them get a job in the escrow and title field.

The best book I have seen on the topic is *The Complete Guide to Your Real Estate Closing* by experienced escrow officer Sandy Gadow (see "Real Estate Reference" in Appendix C). Here is how she described the job to me: "Being an escrow officer is a combination of an accountant, a public relations personality, a legal assistant, and a salesperson." She suggested that an excellent way to get into the field and earn money at the same time would be to first attempt to secure a job as an escrow assistant or secretary in an escrow company, learn the ropes, and move up. Visit her Web site at www.escrowhelp.com for additional guidance.

Another excellent resource for escrow information is the California Escrow Association's website at www.ceaescrow.org. Click the Consumer link and then "Frequently Asked Questions" for a good basic escrow tutorial.

If you would like to know more about the title insurance field, a good contact is the American Land Title Association (ALTA), 1828 L Street, NW, Washington, D.C. 20036, website www.alta.org. The association is active in producing educational material designed to make the intricacies of the field comprehensible to real estate professionals.

Appraising

Fair or not (for the most part, not) appraisers got a lot of blame for the disastrous number of bad real estate loans that precipitated the savings and loan crash of the 1980s. The result, as might be expected, was federal intervention. By law, states must now regulate appraisal licensing, so if you are interested in this field, find out what the requirements are in your state.

If you enjoy doing the market analysis for a listing more than the other phases of listing and selling, you may be suited for appraisal. The real estate appraiser estimates, by as objective and scientific means as possible, the market value of real property.

In this field, you would have several options. Many appraisers are independent and either operate out of their homes or maintain an office. Some are salaried employees of government agencies, such as the county tax assessor's office, while others may be on the staff of financial institutions.

I should point out that there have been some predictions of dire downsizing of the appraising profession (more precisely, as it relates to the residential lending activity) based largely upon the impact of the computer. Lenders can now access real-time information of comparable sales in seconds. Since their main concern is to verify that the property on which they are considering making a loan has sufficient value, and since that is largely determined by what comparable properties are selling for, in many instances it is not necessary to hire an appraiser to do the research. They simply run the numbers and perhaps send someone out for a drive-by to ensure the property is still in place and standing. You should keep close tabs on how this plays out if appraising is your choice of career fields.

Appraisal courses are widely available, and there are several organizations from which you can get additional information about the profession. Here are a few:

- National Association of Independent Fee Appraisers, 401 N. Michigan Ave., Chicago IL 60611. Web site: www.naifa.com.
- Appraisal Institute, 550 W. Van Buren St., Chicago IL 60607. Web site: www.appraisalinstitute.org. This Web site has helpful links to individual state regulatory agencies.
- National Association of Real Estate Appraisers, 1224 North Nokomis NE, Alexandria, MN 56308. Web site: www.iami.org.
- Appraisal Foundation, 1029 Vermont Ave NW, Washington, D.C. 20005. Web site: www.appraisalfoundation.org.
- National Association of Master Appraisers, 303 Cypress St., San Antonio, TX 78212. Web site: www.masterappraisers.com.

Real Estate Counseling

If you list and sell real estate, you are, in essence, a counselor. How good you are determines how well you will be paid, for until you produce results, there is typically no compensation. Actual real estate counselors, however, offer their counseling services for a fee, and if they are expert enough, people will gladly pay it. Particularly when considering investment properties, many prefer to get advice from paid counselors.

Practically speaking, it is difficult to see how you could establish credibility as a real estate counselor without first having achieved great success as an agent. The Counselors of Real Estate (430 N. Michigan Ave, Chicago, IL 60611, Web site: www.cre.org) is affiliated with the National Association of Realtors, and is a leading professional organization. It awards the professional designation of counselor of real estate (CRE) upon meeting predetermined standards.

In Chapter 17 we discuss emerging new business models in real estate in which real estate professionals perform specific functions for set fees, including activities best described as counseling and consulting. At this point, the best introduction to the topic would be to refer you to www.narec.com, which is the Web site of the National Association of Real Estate Consultants. It's an organization founded by Julie Garton-Good, author of *Real Estate a la Carte*, (see "Real Estate Marketing" in Appendix C) in which she outlines her view of the brave new world of real estate. It awards the professional designation of Consumer-Certified Real Estate Consultant (C-CREC).

Corporate Real Estate

Many large corporations have developed an in-house real estate capability, since acquiring real estate, managing it, and disposing of it are functions of enormous magnitude for them. Job opportunities have increased as the trend toward corporate self-sufficiency has emerged.

The hiring process of any large business is tightly controlled, and as an applicant, you must prepare and submit resumes, conduct interviews, and draw on your previous contacts. A college degree with a record of achievement and a demonstrated potential for future growth are minimal qualifications. Proficiency in a foreign language or two would be a real asset (my top two recommendations would be Spanish and Chinese).

If the corporate world beckons, it would not be necessary to start by getting a real estate license, since as a corporate employee you would be exempt from normal licensing procedures. However, coupling your basic talents with several years of high-level performance in real estate sales might help the corporate doors swing open.

There are several excellent master's degree programs in real estate at colleges and universities throughout the United States, if you already have your bachelor's degree. The expertise you would acquire in such a program, coupled with the personal contacts you make, would be invaluable.

If you would like information about a possible career in the world of corporate real estate, an excellent source is an organization called CoreNet Global. The contact information is 260 Peachtree Street NW, Suite 1500, Atlanta, GA 30303, Web site: www.corenetglobal.org. In the organization's newsletter, I once read an article titled "How One Prepares for the Career" written by a young woman who was a real estate asset manager with Burger King Corporation. She had received a master's degree in business administration (MBA) in real estate and construction management (RECM) from the University of Denver. She was hired by Burger King upon graduation to help manage real estate holdings valued at more than $1 billion. As she relates it, her job was to "maximize return from the real estate portfolio through proactive asset management of approximately 200 properties." While no salary figures were mentioned, I'm guessing that such a job pays slightly more than that typically earned by the first-year residential agent.

International Real Estate

So, the conference in Geneva got your attention. Good. The International Real Estate Federation (FIABCI) is your best source of information. The headquarters are in Paris, but log on to the Web site at www.fiabci.com for an incredible amount of information, including how to join and get additional printed information. The federation has had world congresses in exotic places such as Copenhagen, Melbourne, Vienna, Athens, and London. Can interplanetary real estate—and "Beam me up Scotty, I've got the listing agreement signed"—be too far in the future?

Planning

If you are interested in the kinds of activity that city, urban, and regional planners engage in, there are ample opportunities for you. But unless you have a bachelor's or master's degree in planning or a related discipline, the chances are slim that you would be able to secure meaningful employment. Government agencies and educational institutions (for faculty positions) are the primary sources of jobs, but some larger corporations have a staff of planners also. The emphasis on environmental and social factors as they relate to planning has spurred development in this field. Almost every state has a university that offers a degree-granting program in some form of planning. For career information contact: The American Planning Association (APA), 1776 Massachusetts Avenue NW, Suite 400, Washington, D.C. 20036. Web site: www.planning.org. It offers the AICP professional designation to candidates who fulfill association requirements.

Property Management

There are enormous opportunities in property management. Owners of properties ranging from rented single-family residences to huge commercial complexes such as shopping malls are anxious to find reputable and efficient managers. The successful consummation of large real estate transactions sometimes turns on the quality of the company that is to manage the property. General real estate agencies often have a property management operation, so there is a chance that you will have gotten a taste of what is involved.

Management may involve specific bonding and licensing considerations so you need to investigate matters with your state licensing agency. Some enterprising real estate agents have formed their own residential property management companies and done very well. The profit margin on each individual account is typically quite small; therefore, to be successful, you must manage a large volume of properties or land a few big individual accounts, such as apartment complexes.

The Institute of Real Estate Management (IREM), 430 N. Michigan Ave, Chicago, IL 60611, website www.irem.org, a NAR affiliate, is the largest of several professional organizations concerned with the needs and interests of property managers. If you believe that managing a shopping mall has a certain glamour and appeal for you, the organization to contact for information is the International Council of Shopping Centers, 1221 Avenue of the Americas, 41st Floor, New York, NY 10020-1009, website: www.icsc.org.

Land Development

The general term *land development* covers a wide spectrum. The first thing most people think of is the development of land for residential building purposes. The most common form would involve developing land into residential building lots and selling them to builders or private parties. If doing this interests you, it would be wise to start on a very small scale on an experimental basis before you cut yourself off from other income. Just locating and developing land for a small residential subdivision could occupy most of your time and energy for months, and would no doubt test your business acumen in locating financing. Each state, county, and city has extensive requirements that must be satisfied before land can be converted to a residential subdivision. While these restrictions have served consumers well, they have made development an area where only the well-informed and astute players can prosper.

The Urban Land Institute, 1025 Thomas Jefferson St. NW, Washington, D.C. 20007, website: www.uli.org is a good source of information. They state that their mission is "to provide responsible leadership in the use of land to enhance the total environment."

Home Building

If your idea of the typical home builder is one who turns out two hundred to three hundred homes a year, you share a common misconception. Although there are some giants, the average homebuilder turns out much fewer homes than that. I'm aware of several local builders who construct four or five homes per year and do very well. Be advised, however, that this is a high-risk business, but one with tremendous opportunity.

Home builders, by and large, are entrepreneurs with a high tolerance for uncertainty and risk. If that describes you, investigate the opportunities. It is not exceedingly difficult to get started, assuming you have a buyer, have established yourself in the real estate profession, and have some cash plus good credit. It is generally easy to find a lot and the actual home building is primarily a managerial function. You must have the technical competence to judge the quality of the work being done and the supervisory skill to coordinate it, and it would be foolish to become involved unless you have some construction know-how, but your major tasks will be planning, organizing, controlling, and directing.

The National Association of Home Builders (NAHB), 1201 15th Street NW, Washington, D.C. 20005, website: www.nahb.com, with more than two hundred thousand members, is one of the most active of any of the professional associations in the country. Its membership is organized into state and local chapters that engage not only in professional development but also political action. The association produces a catalog of products and courses that is available by contacting them.

Home Inspections

Because home buyers are typically eager to have a prospective purchase inspected before they approve the final deal, home inspection is a rapidly expanding profession. Sellers are often motivated to have their homes inspected and repairs made before they place them on the market. Concern about exotic potential problems such as radon, lead, asbestos, buried gas tanks, mold, dry rot, and bugs that eat wood have fueled the interest. I have a friend who was a former builder who now specializes in inspection and does extremely well at it. His wife, an efficient and personable woman, sold real estate when I did, but now manages their prosperous family business. States are increasingly involved with licensing and bonding requirements, so check out any legalities. You can do that by visiting the website of the American Society of Home Inspectors, at www.ashi.org. There's a link there which summarizes each state's requirements. There's also a very interesting "virtual home inspection" you can take.

Real Estate Education

I'm sure you've heard it: "Those who can, do. Those who can't, teach." While I suppose that may have some element of validity in certain situations, my observation of real estate professionals who teach is that they are an incredibly talented group who know the nuts and bolts of the business.

There are several possibilities if you decide you would like to teach real estate. The first, and one of the most popular, is to teach at a community college where career-oriented courses are emphasized. Those who instruct usually have master's degrees in business or a related field. Sometimes, however, real estate agents with acceptable academic credentials are hired to teach specific courses. So if you want to supplement your income while enhancing your own professional competence (and make some good contacts), explore this possibility. A broker from Texas summarized the advantages in his survey reply: "I teach part-time at the community college, which forces me to stay abreast of the current state of the art in real estate. It also provides a forum for recruiting bright new agents. Then, too, the prestige of being a 'prof' enhances my professional image and attracts more business to me as a result."

There are also a number of jobs in the various independent real estate schools. Since the content of the courses is strictly monitored by the state licensing authorities, and the academic and professional credentials of the instructors are carefully evaluated, you need excellent qualifications to qualify. This is a growth industry, for each time a state experiences some widespread consumer discontent with real estate licensees, a standard reaction is to increase the educational requirements for licensing or to add to the continuing education requirement. Another rapidly developing set of opportunities involves online real estate licensing programs. For example, when a student enrolls in a course, an instructor is assigned, who will be available via e-mail to offer guidance. The instructor is typically compensated on a per student basis. I'm aware of one who currently handles over 300 at one time. That could get interesting.

Having taught live, classroom real estate licensing in the evening adult education department at our local community college for several years, I can assure you that if you choose that option, nothing you can do will keep your batteries charged more, or your ego in check better, than teaching prospective real estate licensees.

Another possibility is to present individual training seminars. Those who do are generally the real estate "fast burners," whose reputations for achieving staggering incomes ensures that when they speak, people pay to listen. Those who succeed in a big way, and command the big money, are generally dynamic public speakers who thrive on audience interaction. At another level, all of the franchises and many of the large independents have full-time trainers. These people typically instruct in the how-to techniques of real estate (listing and selling) and are ordinarily former agents (still with licenses) who were successful and who have a lively sense of communication. They may be on straight salary or on salary with incentive and bonus features.

Another possibility is to become a real estate coach. Again, these are typically agents who have excelled (really excelled) in the profession and who take on individuals as their paid mentor or coach. For your research, here are the names of three highly successful coaches and their websites. Each is a member of my personal network and I'm familiar with their work. Incidentally, each is also a published author whom we'll discuss in our "Write to the Top" section later in the chapter. The first is Dirk Zeller at www.realestate-champions.com. The next is Jim Remley at www.properformer.com. Finally, there is Bernice Ross at www.realestatecoach.com. I particularly like Bernice's company slogan: "Three percent of the agents do 97% of the business. The rest do not have coaches."

The Real Estate Educators Association (REEA), 19 Mantua Road, Mt. Royal, NJ 08061 (website: www.reea.org), is active in promoting communication and professionalism among real estate educators. If offers the opportunity to qualify for the professional designation of distinguished real estate instructor (DREI).

Write to the Top

If you have the desire to write, there are some interesting possibilities using your real estate expertise. Not to disillusion or discourage you, but there is typically not much money to be made in writing about real estate-related matters. There are, however, some notable exceptions. One is to write a textbook. A prominent example is Edith Lank, veteran New York real estate professional and syndicated newspaper columnist ("House Calls" for the *Los Angeles Times* Syndicate). For many years, she has written the New York state version of Dearborn's *Modern Real Estate Practice* (see "Real Estate Principles and Practice" in Appendix C). It's a widely used basic text. Bottom line: write a popular textbook and you will make a lot of money. Another money-making writing possibility is to author a best-selling trade book (one written for the general public). An excellent example of that would be veteran San Francisco real estate broker Ray Brown, who has co-authored several of the *Dummies* real estate books (see "Real Estate Marketing" in Appendix C for this book and the ones I mention in the next paragraph).

It is also fairly common for those who have become very successful in the profession to get published as a complement to their business and as an extra income generator. The three real estate coaches I mentioned earlier are excellent examples. Dirk Zeller is the author of *Your 1st Year in Real Estate* and *Success as a Real Estate Agent for Dummies*. (By the way, I highly recommend both of these books, even though they compete directly with the book you're now reading. Yes, I am incredibly objective.) Jim Remley is the author of *Make Millions Selling Real Estate*. While I'm not thrilled with the title (Jim said the publisher insisted), the book itself is an incredible real estate career guide. After you've gone through the process of getting your license and affiliating with a broker, this would be a "must have" book for you. Finally, Bernice Ross is the author of *Waging War On Real Estate's Discounters.* When I reviewed this book for my book review column in *The Real Estate Professional* magazine I observed that it would be useful to disregard the title. Even if you were a real estate discounter this would be a great basic reference for the real estate professional.

If you have the urge to write, my recommendation is that you first do a lot of reading. See how the real pros do it. There are a variety of possibilities, for example, Peter Miller is the author of *The Common Sense Mortgage* (see "Real Estate Finance" in Appendix C) and a number of other books. Log on to his website at www.ourbroker.com and also check out his articles at www.realtytimes.com. While you're on www.realtytimes.com, review the incredible array of exhaustively researched articles written by Blanche Evans, who has a number of real estate book titles to her credit, including *The Hottest E-Careers in Real Estate*; *Housing Bubbles, Booms and Busts*; and two National Association of Realtor publications, *Guide to Buying a Home* and *Guide to Selling a Home* (see "Real Estate Marketing" in Appendix C). The most widely syndicated of all real estate columnists is Bob Bruss, an attorney, educator, real estate broker, and investor. Other than your local newspaper, www.inman.com is the best place to review his work. Finally, log on to www. frogpondgroup.com for as diverse an array of real estate–related articles as you're likely to find anywhere. When I teach my real estate licensing class my primary objective is to prepare my students to pass the licensing exam. However, when I visit one of the websites I mention above and find a Blanche Evans, Peter Miller, or Bob Bruss article that deals with real life issues that illustrate an academic subject I have my students read it to see how the material we are studying plays out in real life situations.

If your writing aspirations are in the academic arena, you need to visit www.realsure.com. Here you will find a variety of articles written by Stefan Swanepoel. Many you can download free from the website. Swanepoel has over 13 publications to his credit (more by the time you read this), most relating to the future of the real estate industry. Perhaps his most recognizable title is *Real Estate Confronts the Future,* widely regarded as one of the most insightful books written on that subject—and there are many. In addition to a variety of other real estate related activities, Swanepoel is the chairman of RealtyU, the nation's largest network of Real Estate Educators and the executive director of the Real Estate Apprentice program (www.realestateapprentice.com), which we discuss further in Chapter 16.

Hank Williams, Sr., the legendary country singer, was quoted as saying: "You've got to have smelt a lot of horse manure to be able to sing like a hillbilly." It's the same with writing. Trust me, if you sell residential real estate you will smell a . . . well, you know. And there's absolutely no evidence to support the notion that if you can't do or teach, you write about the whole thing.

Radio Real Estate

There are many real estate professionals around the country who host radio shows. Some are active brokers while others are in allied fields. I interviewed several for an article I did for *The Real Estate Professional* and I've encountered others while browsing the internet. If you're within radio range, listen in to one of these to see how you might structure a radio show of your own.

■ *"Real Estate Corner,"* KCOH 1430 AM, Houston, Texas, 6 to 7 p.m. Tuesdays. The host is Shadrick Bogany, owner-broker of ERA Bogany in Houston. If you would like to hear how Shad does it, log on to his Web site at www. ERABogany.com when the show is on and you can listen to it.

■ *"Ray Brown on Real Estate,"* KNBR 680 AM, San Francisco, 9 to 10 a.m. Saturdays. Although Ray has his California broker's license, he no longer has his real estate company. He does this show and writes the *Dummies* books as his major real estate-related activities now.

■ *"Keepin' It Real,"* KECO 1000 AM, Carlsbad, CA. 7 to 8 a. m, Tuesdays. Host George Mantor bills himself as the "Real Estate Professor" and directs his show toward the small real estate investor. Mantor is the CEO of Associates Financial Group in Carlsbad (www.myafg.com), and also contributes articles to Broker Agent News (www.brokeragentnews.com).

■ *"Real Estate Coast to Coast."* www.realestatecoasttocoast.com. 12 p.m., Wednesdays, Eastern Standard Time. The site is billed as "Internet Radio's Weekly Residential Real Estate Magazine". The host is Evanston, IL real estate agent and author Mark Nash (www.marknashrealtor.com). The list of past guests is very impressive.

■ *"Real Estate Insiders."* www.realestateinsiders.com. The website's banner caught my eye: "America's #1 Real Estate Radio Show." The program is hosted by four real estate professionals, most of whom specialize in mortgage and finance issues. It airs Sunday's from 9 a.m. to noon eastern. You can type in your area code and find where the program is aired. If it's not available you can log on to the website and listen or read the text.

■ *"Real Estate Focus."* www.jerryfowler.com. This is an excellent example of an active real estate broker (Jerry Fowler & The Results Team Realtors) who uses his radio program to enhance his professional real estate activities. You will see when you visit the web site there are several company listings prominently displayed. The program, which has been on the air for 14 years, airs

11:00 a.m. to noon on WVOC a.m, Columbia, S.C. Check out Jerry's very impressive bio when you visit his website.

Government Job

There are many jobs at the state and federal level in which a knowledge of real estate would presumably help. In each state, for instance, there is a real estate commission (or an equivalent) that oversees all the real estate activity within the state, including licensing, education, inspection, and enforcement of rules and regulations. As an example, a former student of mine is now on the staff of the Oregon Real Estate Agency after her transition from a very successful real estate career. I would personally like to made it mandatory that any employee of a state real estate regulatory agency have practical experience as a real estate licensee, but don't hold your breath. The combined workforce across the nation in this niche is substantial, but entry is through competitive exams and state civil service channels.

Other Possibilities

I know a broker who now spends almost all his time producing weekly Homes on Parade magazines. He started by turning out one for the local company where he maintained his license. He did such a good job that he now produces them for dozens of other brokerages throughout the United States. Brokers send him photos and listing information, and he creates a finished product, prints it up, and sends copies back. If you have similar interests, there may be untapped opportunities worth exploring in your area.

MORE?

You say you want even more? The possibilities are almost limitless, but I don't want to take away all the fun of discovery for you. Entrepreneurs (that's you) are supposed to have great imaginations.

16

Special Messages for Special People

From Fast Trackers to Retirees

The real estate profession is truly a mansion with many rooms. No matter what your background, there is definitely a place for you—if you want one. My purpose in writing this book was to offer you the information you need to make an informed choice about a career in real estate. Much of what I have covered to this point should pertain to people from a variety of backgrounds. But there are challenges and opportunities that are unique to specific groups, so in this chapter I offer "special messages for special people."

WOMEN IN REAL ESTATE

More than half of all licensed real estate agents in the country are women and an increasing number are progressing to the broker ranks. Successful role models abound, and it would be difficult to find an occupation where you would encounter fewer barriers because of your gender—it is an equal opportunity profession in the truest sense of the word.

Unfortunately, the opportunity for failure is just as great as the opportunity for success. Here are some questions it would be good to ask yourself:

■ *What is your motivation?* Here is a survey comment from an honest, if not tactful, male broker: "Give me a woman who is divorced, supporting two kids, with house payments to make. Now *she* can sell real estate!"

Women come into the profession for widely different reasons. Many simply want to supplement the family budget. Others are looking for a meaningful challenge in life, with the money being a nice, but incidental, feature. Many others need to earn a living, pure and simple. If they don't succeed, they don't survive—and they'll have to find another job. If you fall into this category, be very honest in assessing your talents and determination, and in recognizing the demands of the job. It is not nearly as easy as some success-ful women agents make it appear. Be certain, also, that you have the resources to see you through the predictably lean first six months (or more).

■ *What is your work experience?* When I was a new agent, my "big sister" was a woman who, many years before, had been a waitress. She was—and still is—an outstanding real estate agent. We developed a close professional relationship and eventually covered for each other during absences. There are probably many ex-waitresses who are earning very comfortable livings sell-ing real estate. On the other hand, it has to be counted as a definite plus if you have had previous successful work experience in a more closely related job.

While on the subject of former waitresses who did reasonably well in real estate, let me cite the experiences of Barbara Corcoran. Barbara was the founder and chairperson of The Corcoran Group in New York City. She ended up with 700 salespeople in 11 offices with over $2 billion in annual rev-enues. She eventually sold the operation and is now occupied with speaking, writing and consulting (and appearing frequently as a guest on TV money shows). In her book *Use What You've Got* (see "Real Estate Resources," Appen-dix C) Barbara relates that she got straight D's in high school and college, and failed at twenty-two other jobs before borrowing a thousand dollars from a boyfriend, quitting her waitress job, and starting a tiny real estate office in New York City. The part of the book I liked the most was her description of her negotiating sessions with Donald Trump.

■ *How tough are you?* When I was a corporal in the U.S. Air Force, the first sergeant of our outfit was a woman master sergeant (six stripes—the highest enlisted grade at that time). For those who are not familiar with the term, an old-time first sergeant was expected to be the toughest and meanest sergeant in the outfit, and could generally lick anyone in it. Our first sergeant certainly could have, although she never had to prove it. Her karate experience was a sufficient deterrent. She had come up through the ranks in World War II, and the image of her Sherman-tank figure bulging in a too-small khaki uniform, with stripes running up and down her sleeves, is one that lives vividly in my memory. Now she was tough—physically and emotionally. I can't imagine a situation she couldn't handle, but she had the benefit of years of leadership training and experience.

How tough do you need to be in real estate? You certainly don't need to be a battle-hardened combat veteran with a karate chop that can shatter bricks, but you must be able to remain calm when things get tense. Let me give you a hypothetical situation (based on fact, embellished only slightly for dramatic impact), to stimulate your thinking.

Take This Offer and . . .

Let's suppose that one of your first listings is a nice little three-bedroom home on five acres on a hillside in a peaceful country setting. The owner is a young, recently divorced woman with two children who works full-time. You got the listing as a result of her calling your office one day when you were on floor duty. She explained that the place was too much for her to handle alone and that as soon as she sold it she would be looking for a small home to buy in town near her work. You do a thorough market analysis, ask several of the more experienced agents for their input, arrive at what you believe is a realistic price, meet with the young woman, and take the listing.

She assures you that her divorce is final and that the property is in her name alone. Your research confirms that to be the case. She mentions her ex-husband only once ("He was OK when he wasn't drunk"), but you learn from other sources that he spent time in jail for an incident in a barroom fight, and that he still visits on occasion.

You receive an offer on the property almost immediately. Although it is several thousand dollars below the asking price, it comes through a respected agent from highly qualified, motivated buyers. Indications are that they would be willing to negotiate and that a mutually satisfactory solution is entirely possible.

You make an appointment to present the offer, along with the other agent. The three of you are sitting around the kitchen table and have just about agreed upon the structure of a counteroffer at a substantially higher price but with somewhat better terms for the buyers. The other agent says she is confident that the proposal will be accepted.

Suddenly, from the back bedroom, stumbling and cursing, emerges one of the most thoroughly reprehensible-looking men you have ever seen. He is well over six feet tall and must weigh 250 pounds, or more. He is wearing a dirty tee shirt that smells of whiskey and beer, and looks as if he hasn't washed or shaved in days. The seller sweetly announces, "Ladies, this is my ex-husband, Linus."

Linus lurches toward the table where you are sitting, grabs the offer to purchase agreement out of your hands, and reads no further than the offering price. "So you're the little *bleep* who's trying to steal my wife's house," he screams in your face. "This place is worth twice this *bleeping* much. If you don't get your skinny *bleep* out of here, I'm going to stuff this where it won't never get no sunlight!"

To the woman you hastily mumble, "We'll talk later," grab your stunned associate by the hand, and get to the car as fast as possible. As you drive from the house, you see Mr. Wonderful in the rear-view mirror shouting at you and making obscene gestures. His snarling and barking German shepherd escorts your car the quarter of a mile to the main road, doing his best to get at you through the car window.

Not every day in real estate will be that exciting (let's hope none will be), but you meet all types and you must expect some rough-and-tumble situations. Not taking things personally, staying cool, and knowing when to retreat are valuable traits.

How Informed Are You On Personal Safety Issues?

While the topic of personal safety obviously applies to everyone in the real estate profession, it is particularly critical for women to understand the seriousness of the subject. Your best course of action is very early in your career to become well versed in the nature of the possible threats and the most effective preventive measures. I recently attended an educational session at a local real estate company. The guests were two officers from the local police department. They gave an outstanding, if somewhat sobering, presentation on personal safety for real estate agents—particularly women. My strong recommendation is that you suggest to your broker that a similar session be scheduled for your company.

Another excellent reason to become a Realtor is that NAR has an active and ongoing program focusing on Realtor safety. For example, each year they have a Realtor Safety Week and they have produced a very informative video titled "Don't Be A Victim: Personal Safety for Realtors". Here are a couple of websites you can visit for a preview of Realtor safety resources. First, log on to the website of the Washington Association of Realtors, www.warealtor.com and click the "Realtor Safety Council" link. There's a short list of safety tips as well as a 22 page safety guide you can down load. Another informative site is NAR's www.realtor.org . When I logged on I simply typed "safety" in the search box and up came an incredible amount of information on the subject.

Here's a suggestion. When you are interviewing for your initial job with a real estate company, ask the broker what type of policies they have regarding personal safety for the agents. On a personal note, if my wife were still actively listing and selling, and was going to hold an open house, I would absolutely not permit her to be there alone. It's always wise in these matters to envision worst case scenarios.

What Do You Know About the "Business Birds and Bees?"

There is a certain element of glitz and glamour in the real estate business, and even an experienced person's head could get turned. Agents understandably try to present the best possible appearance and attempt to stay psyched up when dealing with the public and associates. You will find yourself in situations, such as sales rallies and conventions, that promote socializing and revelry. You are also likely to meet a few super salespeople who specialize in selling themselves. If you have a good grasp of who you are and clearly defined standards of conduct, you will find it all mildly amusing and view it with friendly detachment.

If you are especially good-looking, you might find some of your male customers paying more attention to you than to the transaction at hand. (I've heard it works that way with male real estate agents and female customers too, but I have no firsthand knowledge). Taking a friendly, no-nonsense attitude will keep things on an even keel.

Keep in mind that, in most home-buying situations with married couples, the woman often makes the final decision, or at least exercises veto power. Even if you are getting good vibes from the husband, remember that you have to sell them both, and a jealous wife is a mighty poor prospect to buy from you.

The Women's Council of Realtors (WCR) was formed to provide specialized guidance to women in their real estate careers. Their mission statement is: "We are a community of real estate professionals creating business opportunities, developing skills for the future, and advancing our individual potential for success." Their primary professional designation is the LTG (leadership training graduate), which is awarded after completion of courses that emphasize communications, management, and leadership. Men are eligible to join. Information on WCR programs and products can be obtained by contacting the organization at 430 North Michigan Ave., Chicago, IL 60611-4093 (Web site: www.wcr.org).

As a final note, let me emphasize that women are excelling in all phases of real estate, many of them nontraditional. As an example, a former female student of mine is a full-time employee at a local educational institution. She took the entire licensing sequence just to learn more about real estate. She would be able to operate gracefully and successfully in the most refined circles. A year or so after she completed the courses, I was working with an associate in finding a starter home for a newly assigned associate professor at Oregon State University. The house he and his family settled on was one that my former student had purchased, renovated on weekends and after regular work hours (much of it herself—we're talking sanding, painting, the whole works), and put on the market. She informed me that her motivation was to establish a fund for her daughter who was heading to college in a couple of years. She has successfully repeated similar projects several times.

HUSBAND-WIFE REAL ESTATE (OR, HOW MUCH TOGETHERNESS CAN YOU TAKE?)

Real estate presents an ideal opportunity to work together with your spouse, if that is what you both want. There are several possible arrangements and a few important cautions.

In what may be the most common situation, both husband and wife work as licensed agents in the same office, but function independently. There are all sorts of variations possible. At one very successful local company, the principal broker is a woman whose husband works there full-time as an associate broker. If both partners are successful, there is the potential for a very healthy family income. Another advantage is that each spouse can take pride in individual accomplishments.

The arrangement my wife and I had illustrates another possibility. We were both licensed agents in the same company and functioned as a team. I worked at it full-time while my wife was part-time. She developed some specialized prospecting programs and administered them, whereas I did most of the actual listing and selling. She was also the company's relocation coordinator and on occasion listed property. As a matter of fact, she listed the most expensive piece of property (a large farm) that I ever sold, resulting in a very impressive family payday (yes, she does remind me of that on occasion). It was an arrangement with which we were both comfortable and which utilized our individual strengths.

There are some predictable problem areas. First, we are talking about a whole lot of togetherness, and, unless the relationship is exceptionally strong to begin with, a bad case of overexposure can develop. Second, each individual ego must be delicately preserved. It is entirely possible that the woman might emerge as the more successful agent, so if you are a man with any male chauvinistic hang-ups, you are in big trouble. In the same light, duties at home need to be shared, which could come as a shock to some men. If you can handle these matters maturely, I can assure you that you will come to regard this phase of your married life as among your most cherished. Two of my former students are a husband-and-wife team. She is by far the more successful. He has absolutely no problem with that. "We have a joint banking account," he said with a satisfied smile the last time I talked to him.

RETIREES AND REAL ESTATE

Many people look forward to retirement with eager anticipation and make a satisfactory adjustment to it. A significant number, on the other hand, become bored. They may never admit it, but they actually miss working! Still others find that the Golden Years require slightly more gold than they have stored up, and they need to do something to earn extra cash.

There are a variety of excellent options for retirees in real estate. There is sales, of course, and many seniors have become successful agents and continue to carry a full workload well into their seventies and beyond. For example, two of the most delightful students I've ever had in my Oregon real estate licensing class were Dolores and Ed Hodge. Ed reluctantly admitted to being over 80 and his younger wife wouldn't divulge age related details, but she does qualify for the senior discount at our local bagel shop. They had previously pursued real estate careers in both Florida and California. I've never had more focused, serious students. Incidentally, they both aced the exam and are now affiliated with a local brokerage.

Two other possibilities exist that you might consider. One is property management. Pick up almost any newspaper in the country and you can generally find an advertisement that goes something like this: "Help wanted. Couple to manage apartment complex in exchange for rent and salary. Must be mature, dependable, and have experience with minor household maintenance and gardening." If you pursue this option, I strongly advise that you prepare by taking some of the property management courses offered by professional organizations. Many are available at the local level. If you wish to get into property management full time, check out your state's licensing requirements. Finally, if you are really good at household maintenance chores, such as fixing dripping faucets, repairing commodes, painting, unsticking doors, and replacing broken windows, you could earn a healthy income as "Fred, The Fix-it Man" or "Fern, The Fix-it Lady."

There is a negative stereotype or two about retirees that you will need to overcome. If you are considering real estate sales, your prospective broker may be worried that what you really want is a nice comfortable place to "hang your hat." The fact that a retiree probably already has a steady (albeit modest) income makes the motivation for entering real estate even more suspect.

It is best to meet the problem head on. Muster all the enthusiasm of a young college graduate interviewing at IBM. Prepare a resume, buy new clothes, give it the works. Assure the broker that you have always carried more than your share of the workload and that you fully intend to do the same in real estate. Make a special point of telling her that you are definitely in it for the money, and not just to have a place to come when your golf game is rained out or your bridge game canceled.

A final suggestion: If you sold real estate several decades ago and have reactivated your license to give it another try, be very frugal with your advice and criticism. Saying, "That's not how we did it in the San Fernando Valley in 1986," is not likely to win friends or influence brokers.

REAL ESTATE FOR MILITARY RETIREES

If you are a military retiree with the right temperament, and you are willing to get out among the troops and hustle, a second career in real estate can turn out to be one of the most exciting and well-paying jobs you ever had. There are some features of the profession that ex-military people are typically quite enthusiastic about, along with a few that generally don't thrill them nearly as much.

First, the positive. In the military, your effectiveness was based largely on subjective evaluation. That can be frustrating, because we all naturally think we do a better job than we are given credit for. In real estate, it is wonderfully simple. You are paid when you produce results. You are paid *every time* you produce results! For someone who is accustomed to receiving the same pay each month, regardless of how well or poorly you do, that is an exhilarating experience. There is even a danger that you can lose control and become a workaholic.

Then there is the excitement of being your own boss. You can come to work when you want, quit when you want, and dress how you like. Men, you can throw custom and caution to the wind and wear your hair long if that pleases you, and (may the Pentagon forgive you) even grow a beard and wear beads! As it turns out, the years of straight-arrow training will probably have left its mark, and you will no doubt continue to act like a good soldier should, but it is fun to have the option.

There are some potential frustrations. If you have spent twenty years or more getting to meetings on time, recognizing the chain of command, and generally following every accepted precept of good management and human relations ever conceived, the freewheeling, fiercely competitive nature of real estate can leave you perplexed. After the initial shock wears off, and after you get your nose pushed in the dirt once or twice, you will learn the ground rules and will be able to more than hold your own. Little things will always bother you, though. You will still grit your teeth when half the staff saunters in ten minutes late to a sales meeting, or someone clips his nails while the broker is talking. You will adjust.

You will also likely conclude that the level of professionalism among your new associates is not as high as that in the military. "My word is my bond" has no direct counterpart in the business world. But do not be too impatient. After a while, you will come to know who you can trust and who you would not leave alone in the supply room without an armed guard. Progress is being made on this front, particularly through the National Association of Realtors. You know how a professional outfit should act, so pitch in and help them out with their efforts.

A cordial admonition is also in order. You will be happier if you accept the fact that you are starting over as a buck private in the rearmost rank. I have talked to dozens of ex-military people who are currently in real estate about their careers, and I have corresponded with many others. Their suggestion for success: Forget your rank. Or, as one ex-NCO put it: "RHIP-RIP (Rank Has Its Privileges—Rest in Peace)." Even if you had been the officer in charge of procurement at Humongous Air Force Base and had handled multimillion-dollar projects so often that it all became a trifle dull, it will earn you no special privileges in real estate. You still need to deposit that $1,000 earnest money check the same as everyone else.

You will also need to overcome some negative stereotyping. Some of your coworkers are likely to see you as a saber-rattling automaton who will try to organize them into 0600 calisthenics every morning. You will eventually get most of the respect you deserve, but there is no rank insignia on your sleeves or shoulder to pave the way, and do not ever expect the same kind of courtesies and perks you enjoyed in the military, no matter how successful you become.

If you're active duty military and stationed in a location where you plan to retire, there are some other interesting possibilities. Log on to www.coldwellbanker.com and type in "Rake" in the "Agent Search" link. Two entries that will appear are Elsa and Jim Rake, both agents with Coldwell Banker Elite in Stafford, Virginia. Elsa got her real estate career going while Jim was still on active duty and he joined her as part of the "Rake Team" when he retired. As is apparent from reviewing her achievements and credentials, Jim enlisted in a very impressive outfit.

To make you feel welcome, here is a little story that is told about a former military man who went into real estate. A broker invited an ex-Army career type to join his real estate agency. The Army man seemed to be doing well enough, but it bothered the broker that the fellow did not show up for work until after 10 A.M. Finally, the broker could not stand it any more, and said, "Clyde, what did they say in the Army when you came in at midmorning every day?" "Oh, not much," Clyde replied. "They just stood up and said, 'Good morning, Colonel.'"

REAL ESTATE FOR MILITARY SPOUSES

If you are a military spouse there's a strong likelihood that you've moved a few times in your lifetime. Nothing could prepare you better for a career in real estate. Let me cite one example to illustrate. Sue Guenther is the wife of Lynn Guenther, Colonel, USAF, retired. Sue is an agent with Don Nunamaker Real Estate (www.donnunamaker.com) in the beautiful community of Hood River, Oregon. I've known both Sue and Lynn personally for several years since Lynn and I were on the Air Force ROTC staff together at Oregon State University.

Visit Sue's company's website and check her agent's page. You'll find that she and Lynn moved 19 times during their 26 years together in the Air Force. In my 28 year Air Force career my wife and I moved six times and I marvel at how much I learned about buying a home, selling a home, and working with real estate agents. As a matter of fact, it was largely a result of those experiences (plus the incredible profit we make on each transaction) that motivated me to enter real estate as a second career. Compare that to what Sue must have learned in her 19 relocations! You'll also note that Sue has the advanced Realtor designation of Certified Residential Specialist, clear evidence that she has excelled in her chosen profession. Incidentally, you'll also note that Lynn, after eight years as City Manager for Hood River, got his license and works at the same company. I'm guessing his experience as a POW in the Hanoi Hilton during the Vietnam War prepared him reasonably well for any stress he might encounter in his real estate career.

If you are a military spouse considering your career options, let me recommend an outstanding resource for you. It's the book *Help! I'm a Military Spouse—I Want a Life Too!* It's written by Kathie Hightower and Holly Scherer, both of whom are military spouses. Check out their activities at www.militaryspousehelp.com.

ALL MILITARY TROOPS AND SPOUSES HEADS UP!

Don't miss my "Go For The Gold" discussion in Chapter 18. There I describe the incredible past and current achievements of a woman by the name of Bernice Green, an award winner in the Real Estate Apprentice program. Bernice is a retired Army troop who is now active in real estate.

YOUR FIRST JOB?

If you are young and real estate is your first full-time job, you will find yourself in a distinct minority. If you are typical of other newcomers to the workplace, you will bring with you a refreshing enthusiasm and an apparently inexhaustible supply of energy. Couple those admirable traits with the type of systematic and creative approach suggested in this book, and it will be only a matter of time until the paydays become frequent and predictable. What at first was bewildering and incomprehensible will start to fall into place, and soon you will be one of the old timers graciously offering advice and counsel to befuddled newcomers twice your age.

As you are getting started on the job, you will represent an extremely valuable asset to your broker in a way that you may not have anticipated. You will be reacting for the first time ever to the traditional ways things are done in the business world in general and the real estate business in particular. You will be unencumbered by a familiarity with the standard, the accepted, and the traditional. Because of this freshness, you will be an excellent sounding board. You will not have been conditioned by the old accepted arguments, and you were not around when "we tried that once before and it didn't work." If a policy or procedure seems questionable to you, do not be passive—express your reservations. If it doesn't seem to make sense or to be fair, it probably poses problems for others also and it needs to be examined. You may even have to tell your Emperor Broker on occasion that he has no clothes on. He might not always listen, but he deserves your honest opinion.

THE "FAST TRACKERS"

There are some people in real estate who seem to have been born to the profession. Everything they touch turns to gold. When I was very young, I had a short and undistinguished career selling *The Saturday Evening Post* magazine. The standard procedure for most of us was to meet in front of J.C. Penney and wander amiably but aimlessly down Main Street, hoping someone would approach us and offer to buy one. Not my friend Rees. He had a system. He visited all the barbershops, doctors' offices, automobile dealers, restaurants-any place that might need a magazine each week. He also knocked on every door in the residential neighborhoods within biking distance of his home. Lord, that kid sold magazines. My ultimate put down was when I visited my barber and tried to sell him a magazine, only to be informed that he got his from Rees (who, by the way, was not his customer). Rees was definitely several cuts above the rest of us as a salesperson. (I do admit, however, that his incredible nine-year-old cuteness probably played somewhat of a role in his success.)

Here's a real world real estate example: A member of my network is Oregon Realtor Jim Remley. Jim is the co-owner of one of the largest networks of independent real estate companies in southern Oregon. Check his operation out at www.allstaterealestate.com. Jim started that impressive operation at age 23, four years after "I walked through the doors of that first office as a rookie agent". In addition to his duties in running All State Real Estate, Jim is a speaker, trainer and author. You can check out his real estate coaching operation at www.properformer.com. Finally, as I mentioned in Chapter 15, Jim has written what I consider to be one of the most practical, down-to-earth real estate career guides on the market, titled: *Make Millions Selling Real Estate: Earning Secrets of the Top Agents* (AMACOM Books). After you get your feet solidly on the ground it will provide an outstanding training guide for the remainder of your career. Remember, all of these accomplishments by a young fellow who walked through the doors of that first real estate office at the tender age of 19.

Be assured that if you are a fast tracker, there are ample opportunities for you in real estate, and that the potential for material reward and emotional fulfillment are as great as any other in the business world.

For the past several years, *Realtor Magazine,* the official publication of the National Association of Realtors, has done a "30 Under 30" feature article. It puts the spotlight on thirty Realtors under age 30 who are doing well—really well. I mean incredibly well. In the event you might not have access to the printed version of the articles, log on to www.realtormag.com, where you can access the articles through the magazine's archives. They have the lists going back to the year 2000. You can learn a lot by reading the impressive resumes that are included with each selection, along with the person's website. Of course, many of these young super achievers are likely over age 30 at this point and approaching geezerdom, but if you're looking for inspiring role models, they will still be worth your attention.

OPPORTUNITIES FOR TEACHERS

Because they have most of their summers free, and because the traits that make for good teachers also tend to make for good real estate agents, many educators are attracted to real estate. Some work at it on weekends and holidays during the school year, and even after school. Many go into it on a full-time basis when they leave teaching.

One of my survey respondents, a high school social sciences teacher, described this arrangement: She was affiliated with a brokerage firm that was active in new home sales. She spent most of her time when school was not in session in sales offices located in the model homes of various new-home subdivisions. She did not need to spend time prospecting, since her prospects came to her. She also taught several sections of personal finance at school, so she felt that the on-the-job experience she got in real estate gave her added credibility in the classroom.

Here is her brief comment about handling two demanding professions at the same time: "A lot of my friends are into skiing, stained glass, quilting, and other hobbies. Real estate gives me an emotional charge and it makes me a better teacher."

I got additional feedback from a former student of mine who was a former secondary school teacher. She has done very well in real estate. Her view of the sales process in real estate is basically one of educational counseling. For example, in working with a home seller she gathers the information, presents it in a well organized, unbiased manner and lets the client make the decision. "For me, it's one teaching project after another" she indicated on a survey form I asked several of my former students to complete.

As a rookie real estate agent, I briefly shared office space with an ex-high school football coach who had left teaching to join our real estate company. It was an incredible experience, and it gave me an inferiority complex from which I had great difficulty recovering. His telephone rang constantly. People called our secretary to make appointments just to talk to him on the phone. It seemed to me that everyone in our little community was beating down the doors to work with "the coach," while I was spending most of my time studying and getting ready to spring into action—should the need ever arise. So if you have celebrity status, even if it is of the small-town athletic variety, it can be a big boost to your fledgling real estate career. Remember, though, that the initial contact with the prospect is only the first step in your lesson plan.

MID-CAREER JOB CHANGERS

A prominent real estate educator from New York State made this comment when I asked her if she thought there was a need for the kind of real estate career guide I was writing: "Yes. Everyone and their brother thinks they can sell real estate."

It's true. There is a widespread fascination with the profession and there are probably thousands of people in the middle of other careers who would just love to chuck it all, get their real estate licenses, and start doing something they think they would really enjoy. Many people do just that. Almost 90 percent of all real estate agents were previously in another occupation. While it's true that a small percentage of these people are retirees (notably from the military), and some were not actively engaged in their previous occupation when they came into real estate, there is a still a large number of people who simply got the real estate bug badly enough to change careers in midstream. You will have plenty of company if you make the same decision.

HIGH SCHOOL STUDENTS

An owner of a real estate proprietary school told me that he frequently receives queries from high school students asking about a career in real estate. My primary guidance to anyone still a high school student would be this: First, if you are able to work part-time, do your best to land a job with a local real estate company. Many top producers hire a variety of assistants to perform various functions. Of course, that could be anything from pounding "For Sale" signs in the front yard to helping with administrative chores, but you'll get an insight into the profession that attending a career night won't even approach. I would also counsel you to become as computer savvy as possible and take business-oriented courses. Learning a foreign language would also be helpful.

A former student of mine, who had graduated from high school several years prior to enrolling in my class, looked as though he was about sixteen years of age. He complained to me that it was tough for people to take him seriously, since he looked so young. About all I could do was encourage him to hang in there. He got a job in a mortgage lender's office, and after a short time emerged as a successful mortgage loan officer. The last time I ran in to him he still looked young, but he had matured considerably. "Tell them they'll outgrow it" was his advice to me on counseling other young people who are worried about their apparent adolescence.

NON-LICENSED INVESTORS

Over the past few years, an increasing number of students have enrolled in my real estate classes to learn more about how the profession operates with the objective of becoming more astute investors. They are interested in gaining the knowledge, but do not want to be burdened by the restrictions placed on real estate licensees who buy for their own account. That involves mandatory disclosure and being held to a higher standard than nonlicensees. One former student who followed this path has been particularly successful. He's in a type of service business that puts him in contact with many owners of real property who are planning repair work. Some are doing that in anticipation of selling. He's informed, articulate and honest—and he's purchased many good real estate investment properties by being there "the fustest with the mostest."

REFERRAL AGENTS

Let's say you get your real estate license, but for some reason you do not wish to become active in actually listing and selling. A fairly new business model has emerged that incorporates what has always been possible but sometimes difficult to arrange in traditional brokerages—simply refer your leads to an office for a referral fee. Referral Associates of New Jersey, an affiliate company of The Prudential New Jersey Properties (twenty-seven offices in eleven New Jersey counties) has emerged as a leader in this activity. They conduct an aggressive recruiting campaign to sign on new licensees or those who are active but desire a change of pace. They have been very successful in their efforts and have a large and impressive array of referral agents. The advantage to the licensee is that they do not need to belong to any professional organizations and do not need to pay multiple listing and associated fees. If there are state continuing education requirements for license renewal, they must satisfy them; but basically, they merely refer leads. When they result in a closed transaction, they collect a fee. I predict that you will be seeing more of these operations come into existence in the future.

A LICENSE TO INVEST

There are also a handful of individuals who get their real estate license and affiliate with a broker with only one objective in mind—to find great real estate investment opportunities. No listing, no selling, no floor duty, no nothing but investing. Of course, there are some formidable hurdles. First, you need to find a broker who would let you hang your license in his office. That could be tough, but possible. (You would likely have to pay multiple listing and professional organization fees.) Next, you would need to disclose your license status in any transaction and your actions would be held to a high professional standard. The advantages being that you would be on the ground floor of many good opportunities and you would have your share of the commission to work with. Get guidance from seasoned pros before you even consider this one.

DIVERSE BACKGROUNDS—COMMON QUESTION

While it's clear that there are special opportunities and unique challenges for members of different groups, there is one question that faces us all: Where is the real estate profession headed? We'll look at that next.

17
Change Happens

The Real Estate Profession's Brave New World

Yogi Berra is given credit for this wise bit of advice: "There will be times in your life when you will come to a fork in the road. Take it." That's pretty much what you will face if you become a member of the real estate profession. There is solid evidence that we're approaching some dramatic forks in the road. You will need to make choices and take action. Of course, had Yogi elaborated, I'm certain he would have counseled trying to get as much information as possible as to where those roads might lead you. My goal in this chapter is to help you to identify some of the major challenges facing the profession so that you will be able to make choices that result in the most satisfying and rewarding career for you.

WHAT WILL NOT CHANGE

Through world wars, civil unrest, economic depressions, and every other type of turmoil know to humankind, one thing has remained constant in the United States: Its citizens want to own their own homes and our economic system encourages that. Every formal survey that has ever been done indicates that among those who rent rather than own, over 90% aspire to home ownership.

From the time I was born until I was twelve, my parents rented. We moved every two or three years. They finally scraped up enough money for a down payment after my father landed a federal government job at a nearby Air Force base. It was 1940 and they paid $5,000 for a nice little three-bedroom, one-bath home on a lot large enough for a chicken coop and my dad's annual WWII Victory Garden. My parents had achieved the American Dream, and were they proud. Times have changed and prices of homes have escalated somewhat, but that dream remains constant. People want to own their own homes, the U.S. government is wise enough to encourage that, and the country's free enterprise system responds vigorously to the demand. It would be impossible to overestimate the positive influence upon the societal structure that a high rate of home ownership has.

Despite what may from the outside look like a fairly easy task, the home-buying process can be complicated and even minor mistakes can result in major long-term consequences. There will always be a role for professionals who know how to work with consumers in satisfying their housing needs. And now for the tough stuff.

WHAT ABSOLUTELY WILL CHANGE

While you are studying for your real estate license, you will undoubtedly cover the subject of "supply and demand" as it relates to real estate. The basic concept, of course, is that when a product is in short supply and the demand increases, prices will escalate. If you stay in real estate for any period of time, you will undoubtedly see both "buyers' markets" and "sellers' markets" for that's how supply and demand plays out in real estate. What you need to know is that marketing challenges are dramatically different in each situation. In a buyer's market, for example, qualified buyers are scarce and in order to be competitive, sellers must price their properties reasonably and be very flexible in the negotiation phase of the transaction. It's during these periods that creative financing becomes a dominant strategy, for it's tough to qualify for a loan when interest rates are high. The point is that in order to be able to counsel buyers and sellers to achieve their goals, you must understand the challenges and appropriate marketing responses during both situations. Don't be lulled into a false sense of security if, when you enter the business, mortgage interest rates are affordable and the entire real estate market very stable. It's not a matter of whether the economic climate will change, but when it will change and how much. Be prepared. Be flexible.

There's another challenge when market instability occurs. There are more situations in which it is sometimes tempting to put your interests ahead of your client's. The best example of that is when interest rates skyrocket and creative financing becomes a dominant feature. Quite frequently buyers, in their quest for home ownership, agree to mortgage financing that could work to their long range detriment. When adjustable rate mortgages first appeared on the scene, for example, they were not as stable and consumer friendly as they now are. Many buyers did not anticipate worst case scenarios and loan defaults became all too common.

WHAT ABSOLUTELY WILL (OR MAYBE COULD) CHANGE

Rest assured that serious attention is being paid to what might change about the real estate profession. For example, the National Association of Realtors recently conducted an extensive formal study in which the association's strategic issues subcommittee conducted formalized and structured sessions with focus groups of active Realtor brokers from around the country. Their goal was to identify key trends in the industry. This is how they described those which they believed are certain to impact every aspect of the profession:

1. Consumers will have new expectations. The report indicated that there has emerged a "new consumer who is technically competent, has access to deep pools of information, and who demands to be included in the decision process." All the research that has been done on this subject, as well as common sense observations, support the notion that an increasing number of consumers are using technology to aid them in achieving their real estate goals. For example, one NAR study showed that in 1995, only 2 percent of buyers used the Internet to search for a home, while a more recent estimate put it at over 80 percent and that number goes up each year.

2. Whether those statistics are precise or not, they clearly identify a growing trend that will ultimately result in almost total immersion in the Internet by home buyers—and sellers. There is so much incredible information on the Internet—and real estate companies are so engrossed in responding to consumer expectations to capture clients—there's little doubt that, in a few years, surfing the Internet will be as old hat as opening the classified section in the newspaper to check out the real estate advertisements. Eventually it will be rare to encounter consumers who have not immersed themselves in the Internet in their home buying—or home selling—quest.

3. The innovations in technology that empower consumers will impact upon the services demanded of brokers. The informed consumer will have not only information about the home buying and selling process but also the ability to compare services offered by brokerages. To compete, brokers will likely have to add more value to the transaction, such as offering extra services for the money.

I might add that it's equally vital that real estate professionals make absolutely certain that consumers realize the extent of the services they are being offered under the current model. When taking a listing for example, it is very instructive to provide the home owner with a detailed check list of all the services that you will be providing. Trust me, the list will be long and impressive.

4. As competition between brokerages becomes more intense, commission levels will fall. This relates basically to the profitability of real estate of-

fices. The net profit per real estate transaction has moved downward in recent years. Part of the reason is that top agents are taking higher commission splits. Since you will be entering the profession at ground level, this will not be of immediate concern to you, but it certainly will be when you become a top agent. However, it's obvious that brokers must turn a profit, so agents need to have an arena in which they can operate.

There's also going to be an incentive for brokers to add services for which they can charge a fee. The "one-stop transaction"—which would include mortgage lending, title and escrow services, insurance, and home-warranty programs—is a growing trend. Whether this is actually in the best interests of the consumer is still a matter of debate. There is a school of thought that completely independent service providers are more likely to offer objective, dedicated service.

5. Experimentation with new business models will continue, with new definitions of what is "traditional real estate" emerging. The task groups mentioned:

    a. The concierge model, where brokers provide services beyond basic brokerge services to enhance profitability.

    b. The Internet model, in which e-companies serve the cost-conscious FSBO market.

    c. The P- to - P model, in which peer-to-peer brokers cooperate in sharing information as an alternative to the MLS cooperative model.

    d. The NASDAQ model, in which brokerage companies buy homes from sellers and resell them to buyers.

Perhaps the most dramatic real world example of repercussions from the "experimentation with new business models" trend is the legal clash between the real estate profession, as represented mainly by the National Association of Realtors, and the federal government, as represented by the U. S. Department of Justice. Several states have recently passed what is known generically as "minimum service" laws relating to real estate brokerage. Basically, it requires real estate licensees to provide a minimum level of service to clients when they enter into a contractual relationship. This obviously impacts upon those brokerages who offer the "menu of services" option we discuss later in the chapter. In response, the Department of Justice filed an anti-trust law suit against NAR. This could take years to make its way through the legal system, but the end result will undoubtedly have a major impact upon how real estate brokerages conduct their business. An attorney friend of mine, who is much more versed in these matters than I, offered me this prediction of outcome: "NAR has violated the oldest legal axiom: 'choose your adversaries wisely.' " You do not want the Department of Justice as an adversary. I predict NAR will lose this one, big time." We'll see.

BRAVE NEW WORLD REAL ESTATE

Speculation is great, but how is all this playing out in the real world of real estate, right now? Your best evidence is to take a close look at real estate operations that are adapting and prospering. There are hundreds of them all around the country. One is John L. Scott Real Estate, a Pacific Northwest organization with 128 offices and more than 4,000 sales associates. Fortunately for us, company president J. Lennox Scott has documented his company's approach in his book *Next Generation Real Estate* (see "Real Estate Marketing" in Appendix C).

It is clear from reading his book that Scott is a hands-on manager and is responding to trends identified by the Realtor focus group. He is the third generation to run the family business, which was founded in 1931 by his grandfather, John L. Scott. Lennox took over the company upon the passing of his father, W. Lennox Scott. Twice he has been recognized by *Realtor Magazine* as being one of the nation's top twenty-five most influential people in real estate. In 2001, he was honored as one of the top five most-admired individuals in real estate in the nation by the publication *REAL Trends*.

Scott's viewpoint is made clear early in the book when he states: "This is the most exciting time in the history of real estate because everything is changing as it remains the same. What's changing is the process; what remains the same is the trusted relationship that exists between the agent and the client." Chapter headings give a good feel for how the author's message is developed: "Real Time Real Estate," "Personalized Service Enhanced with Technology," "Broker Management," and "Life Plan." The title of the first chapter, "Real Time Real Estate," needs further explanation. Here is what Scott said about real time real estate:

> "Real time is the only time. It's now, it's instant, and it's all about offering the ultimate level of customer service. In real time, what formerly took three or four days now takes only seconds, thanks to the Internet. The Internet is the greatest communication tool in the history of real estate."

You can get further insight into the company's philosophy by visiting its Web site at www.johnlscott.com. The site has an incredible mount of information and is easy to navigate. Company sources claim it gets more than a million hits a month. You can see that the company is aiming at the technologically savvy consumer.

Another basic theme is developed in the chapter titled "Customer Relationship Management." The objective here is "to establish a long-term relationship with clients throughout the home owner experience." It's designed to "deepen and maintain customer loyalty." A unique feature is that the brokerage takes the lead in operating the system, but the agent is the focus of attention and must participate. Clearly, since home owners have a habit of moving every few years, the advantage of having kept in touch and establishing loyalty is apparent. There's been a lot of lip service paid to client follow-up, but all too often, it becomes a perfunctory, poorly administered, or completely ignored function. With competition between brokerages escalating and the profit margin shrinking, there should be little debate as to the wisdom of designing and implementing a program to which both the brokerage and the agents are genuinely committed.

The term "survival of the fittest" has been around for a long time, and it obviously has a clear application to our free enterprise society. Those who survive and prosper among real estate companies will be those who clearly identify the challenges ahead and respond appropriately. It will obviously be to your advantage to affiliate with a brokerage that seems to be doing exactly that.

MEET ANOTHER GURU

Stefan Swanepoel has emerged as one of the dominant prognosticators for the real estate profession. With over 13 publications to his name, he has established himself as an objective and accurate evaluator of where the real estate profession may be heading. His resume is much too long to include here, so I suggest you log on to www.swanepoel. com to check out his credentials. My primary contact with him has been in my role as a judge in the Real Estate Apprentice program (www.realestateapprentice.com) and working with The RealtyU Group (www.realtyu.com). As you will see, he is the primary administrator for both. As I was immersed in preparing this edition of my book, Stefan released a report titled: "Top 15 Real Estate Trends". With his permission, I have included a summary of those in Appendix E. As you read these projected trends, let me suggest this: Place yourself in the position of an aspiring real estate professional (which, of course, you are). If these trends actually develop, how would you adapt your marketing strategies to take advantage of each?

MODEL T TO MODEL Z

We discussed the concept of agency in Chapter 5, so you know where we've been and where we are now. The question is, of course, "Where are we going?"

Most industry observers believe that the business model in which real estate companies run operations that work with both buyers and sellers will continue to dominate. Company policies will need to be put in place to ensure that proper agency roles are understood and practiced, but the full service real estate brokerage business model appears likely to continue to prevail in the future.

That does not mean that the exclusive buyer's agent (EBA) movement will disappear. There are companies now that work with buyers only and take no listings, and professional organizations that promote the business model. If that approach appeals to you, there's likely to be an office with which you could affiliate. Remember, though—no listings. That would take a lot of the fun out of it for me, but it's obviously your choice.

FRIES WITH THAT?

Another business model that's getting a lot of attention is the fee-for-service model. As we noted earlier, it's demanded so much attention that there's a major league, national level, legal battle underway. The model is not new. It's been around for years, with national franchise operations specializing in it. Although there are many variations, I'm certain you know how one aspect of it works. A home seller can hire a real estate professional to perform a specific task—for a set fee. I once had a student in my class who was going to sell his home himself. However, he hired a local company to do some specific functions for him, such as getting the property on multiple listing, doing a market analysis to help determine an asking price, and helping with negotiations when an offer was made. He actually had a menu, with a price next to each function.

The current manifesto for the fee-for-service model, or "unbundled services," is the book that we referred to in Chapter 15, *Real Estate a la Carte* by Julie Garton-Good, a veteran real estate broker and educator. She has enunciated the rationale for the concept very convincingly, and as we pointed out, she has formed a professional organization, called the National Association of Real Estate Consultants, that awards the designation of consumer-certified real estate consultant (C-CREC). The Web site is at www.narec.com. If you would like a preview of Julie's message, log on to Amazon.com and check out the "search inside" feature for her book.

Where is fee-for-service headed? It obviously fills a need, and as consumers become better informed and more demanding, it might very well increase its market share. The outcome of the legal battle between the Department of Justice and NAR we discussed above will clearly have an impact upon this business model, but it is highly likely that some form of it will emerge as a viable option. You might want to visit the following websites to become better informed on the subject: www.helpusell.com and www.assist2sell.com. These two sites have an amazing array of options for both home sellers and home buyers—and real estate professionals.

FIND A NICHE AND FILL IT

There have always been great opportunities for real estate professionals in identifying and working in specific niches. You have agents who specialize in everything from marketing bed-and-breakfasts to selling large rural properties. There are two niche markets that deserve special attention.

Senior Power

I mentioned working with retirees briefly in Chapter 8, but the topic deserves elaboration. Americans are living longer, and living more vigorously. Retirement has taken on an entirely different meaning for a large segment of the senior population. Statistics also show that roughly 80 percent own their own homes. So we've got a booming population with somewhat similar attitudes, goals, and values who overwhelmingly value home ownership.

It's a hot niche, and one that's being responded to. There's even a certification for agents who gain advanced knowledge called the seniors real estate specialist (SRES). Visit www.seniorsrealestate.com/sarec to find out more. And the following advice is from someone who reluctantly admits to being close (really close) to qualifying for "seasoned" citizen status: You don't need to be a senior to relate effectively to them. Just work with senior citizens as you would wish someone to work with your parents.

Diversity Reigns

According to mortgage industry giants Fannie Mae and Freddie Mac, through the year 2010, it is expected that ethnic minorities will account for three of every five first-time home buyers. Currently, less than half of all minorities own their own homes, but there was a 24 percent increase in black home ownership and a 39 percent increase in Hispanic ownership between 1994 and 2000.

The fact that the real estate profession has a small minority membership presents a special challenge. For example, the latest NAR statistics indicate that among Realtors, 85% are white, 4% are African American, 4% are Hispanic, and 4% are Asian. Those figures are likely representative of the entire profession. Brokers are going to need to be actively seeking practitioners who understand cultural differences and who may have special language skills.

Let me suggest a few good sources of further study on this subject. One is the book by Michael D. Lee CRS, GRI, called *Opening Doors: Selling to Multicultural Real Estate Clients* (see "Real Estate Marketing" in Appendix C). Lee, an Asian American, has spent more than a decade learning his craft as a broker in California, and you can see that he has excelled because he is both a GRI and a CRS. He is also a master instructor with the California Association of Realtors. The book contains invaluable information on working with people from different cultures, especially as it relates to every aspect of the real estate transaction. If you visit his website at www.ethnoconnet.com you'll find this quote: "Multicultural marketing is not enough to sell to Hispanics, African-Americans and Asians in the U.S. To sell to minorities in America your sales staff must be trained to provide culturally competent sales presentations and customer service or they won't buy from you."

Hispanics are projected to be the largest minority group in the United States in the near future. You can learn more about the opportunities and challenges related to that trend by visiting the website of the National Association of Hispanic Real Estate Professionals at www.nahrep.org. I ran across a very informative article while visiting their site entitled, "Targeting Hispanics of Mexican Heritage to Expand Your Business." With their permission, the article is reprinted in Appendix E of this book. There is also a link to agents who are members. To see how well represented the association is outside the major metropolitan areas, I entered my old home town of Turlock, California (small town in central California) and up popped the names of nine agents, including website addresses.

When I checked out my old home town I encountered a website I simply had to visit. It was that of Genaro Pulido, whose website address is www.TheHandsomeManOnAMission. com. Face it, how could you possibly resist checking that out? What you will find when you log on to Genaro's web site is not only a very impressive display of real estate marketing, but a real estate success story that is truly inspiring. The next time I head down for my high school reunion I hope to meet with Genaro.

Next, log on to www.nareb.com, the Web site of the National Association of Real Estate Brokers. This is an organization generally composed of African-American real estate brokers. A member of the organization is known as a Realtist. Founded in 1947, it is the oldest and largest minority trade association. Realtists subscribe to a code of ethics for working toward better housing in communities they serve. You will recall we mentioned real estate broker Shadrick Bogany in Chapter 15, when we were discussing real estate professionals who had radio shows. A visit to Shad's website at www.erabogany.com reveals that he was Realtist of the Year for 2001, as well as the number one ERA agent in Houston. You can learn a lot by navigating his Web site. It's incredibly informative and well designed.

GAME TIME

So you've memorized the play book and you've honed your skills. Game time approaches, and you are chomping at the bit to go out there and "sell one for the Gipper." But hold on for just a minute. The grizzled old coach, who has been there himself and is obviously moved by the moment, has a few final inspirational words for you before kickoff.

18

A Final Encouraging Word

How to Succeed in Real Estate by Really Trying

Whoever observed, "I've been rich and I've been poor—I'll take rich," expressed the viewpoint of most of us. To those sentiments you may add the often quoted observation of Guru Ken (that would be me): "Money will not buy happiness. However, the list of the things that it will buy is long and impressive." Although we might never have been truly destitute or ever aspired to be Rockefeller rich, we are reasonably confident that there is no particular virtue in poverty.

Barring an unlikely run of dumb luck or the bequest of an affluent relative, becoming prosperous and staying that way takes a lot of hard work and an ability to manage success when it comes. In real estate, for example, there are those who are comfortable in administering a modest amount of achievement but start to lose control and confidence when things really start to hum and the demands intensify. A major objective of this book has been to put you in the position to decide for yourself exactly how successful (and rich) you would like to be, based on your priorities, the amount of effort you want to expend, and the lifestyle you want to lead. No matter which fork in the road you decide on, here are a few final thoughts to help you in your journey.

YOUR PRESCRIPTION FOR PROLONGED PROSPERITY

You will likely attend several megahype sales seminars and rallies during your real estate career. The search for the magic formula for success is endless. New marketing ideas will burst on the scene, remain in vogue for a while, and, mercifully, fade into well-deserved obscurity. Some of them will truly boggle your mind. The most incredible I ever heard involved a form of hypnotism. ("When you hear the word *blue,* you will have warm and loving thoughts about that beautiful little home I showed you on Tranquility Circle and have an uncontrollable urge to buy it.") Most are not that bizarre and will have at least a few useful elements.

In reviewing my old course notes from the Realtors Institute, I came across the following comments of a now-forgotten (by me) speaker. "To get rich and be happy in real estate," I recall him saying solemnly to a suddenly attentive audience, "it will take a whole lot of perspiration and once in a great while a little inspiration. There is only one rule you ever need to worry about following. You will recognize it by its golden color." In response to a few scattered groans, he finished with something like, "Well, what do you want—originality or good advice?" In my notes, I wrote, "Hokey, but true." There is no magic formula for success, but I do have some suggestions I hope you will consider. If, as you read what follows, you think to yourself, "Hokey, but true," I'll be happy.

1. Above all, keep in mind what creates the need for real estate agents. As long as you have anything to do with residential real estate, remember that it is first, last, and always a people business. With all the technical advances, organizational innovations, and intramural squabbles within the profession, it can be easy to lose sight of the primary reason real estate agents exist, which is to help people solve their housing problems. Those who stress service—honest, efficient, courteous, and above all, individualized—will have people lining up to see them. The same will apply in principle no matter where in real estate your career ultimately takes you.

2. It is absolutely incredible how widespread the interest in real estate is. Let me illustrate. A year or so ago, I attended a small social gathering at a local restaurant. It was my wife's swimming class from Oregon State University. There were twelve people sitting around the table. After dinner, the word somehow got out that I was in real estate. From that point on, real estate dominated the conversation. One woman, who was a widow, asked me how she should go about finding out how much her home was worth in the event she decided to sell it. Her husband had handled those things. Another woman had a current listing in Arkansas and needed guidance on how that transaction was progressing so she would be able to buy a home locally. A third wanted to know the difference between a mortgage broker and a regular lender, since she was in the process of determining how much home she could afford. There were probably other questions, but those are all I could handle that evening. When the word gets out that you're in real estate, get ready to rock.

Here's another quick example: Recently, I'm sitting in my dentist's chair for my first root canal since I was a teenager (a few decades ago). My head was numb and I was having difficulty concentrating. My locally renowned orthodontist knew I was in real estate. First, he fondly recounted the experiences of his uncle, who went from farming in eastern Oregon into real estate sales and who enjoyed a long, prosperous and tremendously enjoyable career. Next, he asked questions which related to our local real estate market and the advisability of investing in rental property. Fortunately, my head cleared up well enough to be able to respond to his interests.

3.   Take the long view. When the nation's economy is healthy and the housing industry robust, folks tend to think and act like the good times will last forever. When interest rates skyrocket and unemployment soars, the doomsayers are certain things will never get better. But, whether times are good or bad, the urge for home ownership is so deeply ingrained in the American character that there will always be a need for real estate professionals. One reason the dropout rate among agents is so high is that they allow themselves to ride an emotional roller coaster. Those who retain their enthusiasm, yet develop a sort of mature detachment born of a good grasp of historical perspective, will be the contented and prosperous survivors.

4.   Follow your heart. It is highly unlikely that your plan to enter real estate is a result of your parents' lifelong dream to have a licensed salesperson in the family, and that they scrimped, saved, and made sacrifices for years just to pay for your training. It is much more probable that you are attracted to it because it sounds a little exciting and because you believe you will be good at it. In fact, you are much more likely to succeed if you *are* happy at what you are doing. If that means selling modest homes in Topeka for the rest of your career, wonderful. On the other hand, if marketing condominiums on the French Riviera has a certain appeal to you, go for it. And someone has to be the first real estate agent in space, right?

5.   Listen to the little voice. There are little voices, and then there are *little* voices. I am talking about the one that whispers, "Sultan's Delight in the third at Pimlico." I am talking about your conscience. No matter how much we try to bury it with rationalization or self-deception, it is always there, ready to tell us clearly what is right and what is wrong. So when you are showing the home to those nice people from out of state, and the little voice says quietly but firmly, "Better mention the lake in the basement," it is a good idea to pay attention.

6.   Also pay close attention when that little voice is advising you to "always put your client's interests first." There are times when it may be tempting to do otherwise. One of my favorite entertainers was the singer Ray Charles. When the movie Ray was released I naturally attended. Here's what impressed me relative to our current discussion. As you know, Ray was blind. In the movie, there was a scene in which a nightclub owner was paying Ray for a performance. Of course, Ray could not see, so the owner counted the money out so Ray could hear, but he shortchanged Ray dramatically. It's

somewhat the same in real estate. Much of the time your clients will have no clue as to what is transpiring. That's particularly true when they are reviewing the final closing paperwork. They will be depending upon your honesty and integrity. Make certain other professionals in the transaction follow your example.

7. Forget the commission. Forget the what!? You read correctly. Forget the commission. I can understand your confusion. But here is the reason I'm advising this drastic course of action:

Your success will be determined by how well you solve problems. Solve a lot of problems and you will make a lot of money. If you try to steer people toward solutions that result in the biggest payoff for you, as opposed to the best possible solution for them, you will become confused, ineffective, and transparent. People will lose confidence in you—and you will lose respect for yourself.

Now, if a $500,000 farm you know about seems perfect for that rich Canadian who is looking for a ritzy horse set-up, you'll automatically spend a minute or two calculating what your potential earnings might be. That's only natural. But, when you are making your decisions, the only question you should ask yourself is: "How well does this fit my customer's or client's needs?"

Am I saying that, in deciding what properties to show a prospective purchaser, it should make absolutely no difference to you whether the commission is 5 percent, 6 percent, or 10 percent? Am I further saying that you should not even be influenced by thrilling enticements such as, "Sell this turkey and win a trip to Pango Pango on the luxury barge *Condemned*?" You have definitely got it. Solve the problems and the commissions will take care of themselves. It works that way. Trust me. (If you happen to be working on a fee-for-service basis, I would rephrase my guidance as "Forget the fee! Do what's best for number one—your client.")

8. Develop your network and keep it up-to-date. Networking is really old wine in a new bottle. It simply means keeping in close contact throughout your career with those people on whom you know you can count to help you get a job done, and who can count on you to help them. Professional organizations provide potentially fertile ground. Start early and stay with it. Networking is absolutely critical; it pays incredible dividends.

9. Let your little light shine. I am not saying that if you think good thoughts, smile a lot, put in ten hours a day, and have good contacts, you are certain to be hugely successful in real estate. Those are admirable traits, but it takes more in a highly competitive business. The phrase, "Early to bed, early to rise, work like hell—advertise," captures the spirit of the point I am making. I always sincerely felt that people were fortunate to have me handling

their real estate affairs. I knew what kind of a job I would do. I never felt even the slightest inclination to hide my light.

10. Don't sell yourself short. I thoroughly enjoy teaching real estate licensing courses at the local community college. It is disheartening, however, when I encounter a student with tremendous potential who is convinced that he is capable of only modest achievement. I have seen some of the great ones operate, in real estate and other professions. A rare few are gifted. Most are simply people of average abilities who are determined to succeed and who are, to resort to a cliché, "willing to dream the big dream."

11. Go For The Gold! You're Hired! For the past two years I've served as a judge in an elementary school speaking contest. Young contestants from the fourth through the eighth grade representing about a dozen elementary schools converge on the bucolic little town of Sweet Home, Oregon to compete. I have been a judge in the fourth and fifth grade group, and it is absolutely inspiring to see these youngsters stand before a large audience, as well as judges, and deliver their presentations. Imagine how intimidating that must be for them, but they accept the challenge. I'm guessing it will be an excellent indication that throughout their lives they will be accepting daunting challenges. How does this relate to your real estate career?

12. Here's a challenge I would like for you to consider even while you are participating in your license training. Compete in the Real Estate Apprentice program. You can learn all about it, including how to get started, by visiting www.realestateapprentice.com.

As a preview, here is how you'll find the program described:

"The goal is to assist newly licensed real estate agents starting a new career in real estate to enter the industry by overcoming their fears and obstacles, and to facilitate the creation of top producing real estate sales associates by providing quality real estate education, guidance, products and services to expedite a successful fast track to profitability. The grant is designed to spotlight the importance of real estate apprenticeships for the enhancement and betterment of the U.S. residential real estate brokerage industry, and to raise the standards and levels of professionalism for real estate agents in general."

In addition to the professional distinction it would be for you to be selected as an award winner, the monetary incentives are substantial. They are described on the website, as well as the specific eligibility requirements, which are time sensitive so you need to become informed early. In 2006 I was honored to have been selected as a national judge in the competition. We as national judges evaluate the 30 semifinalists. Each candidate must submit an extensive report in which specific questions must be answered (For example: "Explain why you will succeed in real estate while others around you may fail") and a biography submitted.

To say I was impressed by the biographies of the 30 semi-finalists would be a monumental understatement. When you visit the Real Estate Apprentice website, click the "awardees" link. Anita Lam, now an active Realtor, was the Grand Prize Winner in the first group I evaluated. As you will see from her biography, she rose from being a shop girl in her native Hong Kong to attaining a master's degree and working as a school administrator in the U.S. Other biographies of the other award winners, also available on the website, are impressive as well.

You will face many challenges in your real estate career. The most severe typically occur early (like surviving). Getting involved with the Real Estate Apprentice program will prove stimulating and motivating and should get you headed in the right direction. Make sure you check out the "important dates" at the website so you'll be able to compete when you're eligible.

13. Do it all with a little class. As a young U.S. Air Force officer, I was stationed in Alabama when legendary coach Bear Bryant returned to his beloved alma mater to coach. ("Mama called," said the Bear.) Along with the rest of the state, I watched each Sunday afternoon during football season when Bear narrated the 'Bama game from the day before. On those infrequent occasions when the Tide lost or didn't win by as much as was expected, the inevitable question posed by the moderator was "what happened?" The typical growling response went something like this: "That was the sorriest job of coaching I've ever seen. We just have to suck it up and hunker down." No whining. No complaining. No looking for someone else to blame. Just work harder. Bear was, as they say, a class act, and one worthy of emulating in any profession, real estate included.

14. Keep in touch with reality. If you work in general residential real estate, you will have absolutely no difficulty in staying humble. There is something about showing houses to the great American home-buying public that tends to discourage any inclination you might have to develop a godlike image of yourself. And when a customer's child wets his pants on the back seat of your nice new car, you will be reminded that you are not in total control of even your own little universe. If you end up selling chalets to the beautiful people in Aspen or shopping centers to oil-rich Middle Eastern sheiks, it is entirely possible that you may need to develop some other techniques of reminding yourself of your mortality. An honest mate, or a very good friend, is your best bet for performing that vital function.

15. Remember, it's still the "land of opportunity." There are so many rags-to-riches stories from real life real estate that it's hard to know who to cite as the best example. I'll mention just a few briefly.

One is Danielle Kennedy. She started selling real estate in 1972 at age 27 when she was six months pregnant with her fifth child and facing a personal crisis. Although she had little formal sales training, she was driven by the most compelling of all motivations—to provide for her family. After a rocky start, she listed and sold more than one hundred homes yearly, which put her in the top 1 percent of all real estate professionals in the nation. She is currently one of the most successful real estate trainers, authors, and speakers in the country. (If you ever have the opportunity to listen to her, grab it. I've also included information on her educational material under "Real Estate Marketing" in Appendix C.) In addition to her other remarkable achievements, she has handled with equal distinction and grace the demands of being a wife and the mother of eight children.

Another example is provided by Dave Liniger, the cofounder (with his wife) and now chairman of RE/MAX International Inc., which I mentioned in Chapter 14. Liniger was a college dropout who joined the Air Force and taught ROTC at Arizona State University in the mid-1960s. While in Arizona, he began buying single-family homes as investments, and is said to have owned twenty of them by age 24. He got a real estate license to save the commissions on his deals, and the rest, as they say, is history. The first company he worked for allowed agents to keep all their commissions in exchange for a monthly fee. It was the inspiration for the 100 percent concept that he perfected and franchised. Under his leadership, RE/MAX has emerged as one of the largest, most prosperous, and vibrant real estate operations in the United States, Mexico, Canada, and other exotic locations around the globe. There are currently more than fifty eight hundred independently owned RE/MAX offices in fifty eight countries worldwide with well over one hundred thousand sales associates. Each time I do a new edition these numbers go way up.

Here's a more recent example: In 2001, former Vietnamese refugee and current RE/MAX agent Chris Nguyen was honored by NAR with an award known as the NAR President's Medal. In 1975, when he was fifteen years old, Nguyen and his family escaped from Vietnam in a leaky, crowded boat. After an incredible odyssey that included four days on the South China Sea and six months living on a Malaysian beach, they obtained sponsorship from a U.S. church and moved to Littleton, Colorado. Nguyen started in menial jobs, earned a business degree, and obtained a managerial job in a grocery store. He entered real estate in 1985. He's done well. He was named to the RE/MAX Hall of Fame for practitioners who have earned $1 million in commissions over the course of their careers. He now primarily serves the Denver Vietnamese community out of the RE/MAX Southeast office. In his acceptance speech for the award, Nguyen thanked the audience for accepting him into this country, adding: "Twenty-five years ago I was a boat person. Today, I'm proud to be an American and a Realtor."

Here's a personal example: A few years ago I'm teaching session number one of my real estate licensing class at the local community college. In that initial meeting I ask class members to stand and tell us something about themselves. There were two young Vietnamese students in the class. They were brothers and both were students at Oregon State University, one majoring in accounting and the other in business. One had a New York Yankee baseball cap on and the other a Los Angeles Laker sweat shirt. They both spoke absolutely impeccable English. When they came to the U.S. one was in the fifth grade and the other in the fourth. When I asked them how much English they spoke at that time, they replied: "Basically, it was 'Hello', 'Goodbye', "my name is . . .', 'Please', 'Thank you', and 'Where is the rest room?'" Their parents opened a laundry in an Oregon community that is still very successful. Their older siblings (it's a big family) opened a Vietnamese restaurant in a shopping center next to the Oregon State University campus that is still one of the most popular in town. While they did not go into real estate (they took the class to learn about investing strategies), both the Yankee fan and the Laker fan are doing well in their chosen careers.

If you do not firmly believe that this is still the land of opportunity, where vision, persistence, and hard work will pay off for you, you simply have not been paying close attention.

16. Get your priorities straight. The story is told of two men who were attending the funeral of Andrew Carnegie, one of the wealthiest men in U.S. history. "How much did he leave behind?" asked one of the men. "He left it all," replied the other. How you order your life's priorities will be a personal matter. This much, however, is incontestable: Unless your physical and emotional health are good, nothing else matters much. And if Mr. Carnegie couldn't take it with him, what chance do you think you have?

WHEN YOU BECOME SUCCESSFUL BEYOND YOUR WILDEST DREAMS

As you are getting started, it will be hard for you to imagine that there will come a day when your biggest challenge will be to take care of all your business and still have time for a personal life of your own. That will happen if you have the right stuff and you use it properly. When it does, be ready to make some changes in how you conduct your affairs. Here are two suggestions:

It's About Time

First, you need to make a major adjustment in your attitude toward the value of your time. Just to give you a point of reference, assume that in your third year you net $100,000. (You did pay attention, didn't you?) Based upon a forty-hour week, with two weeks off for vacation, that means your net hourly wage would be roughly $50. You may make less than that, or you could make more, but the concept is the same. The time you spend on any needless task costs you money.

It is not enough just to develop a general sensitivity to the fact that "time is money." Remember what a terrific deal you offer people. If you are like most real estate professionals specializing in residential sales, you will work on a commission basis. You can look listing prospects straight in the eye, for example, and honestly pronounce: "Folks, if I don't produce results, you will owe me nothing. It makes no difference how much time I spend trying to help you solve your problem; if I don't deliver the goods to your satisfaction, I will thank you for allowing me to try, and we part friends, but no money changes hands." (Try asking your doctor, lawyer, CPA, or auto mechanic for that kind of guarantee.) I assume it is redundant to encourage you to be results oriented.

Help Wanted

Beyond the normal things you can do to manage your time more effectively, there is another step you might want to consider—hiring help. I do not make this suggestion lightly. One of the exhilarating aspects of being a Lone Ranger Independent Contractor Real Estate Agent is that you are your own boss with no one else to worry about. You're in complete and total control of a dedicated, one-person operation—you. When you employ someone, you introduce all sorts of ugly words into the equation—words like overhead, span of control, bureaucracy, and employee relations (I had better stop—I don't want to stir up more snakes than I can kill).

Here's an example of how hiring an assistant can pay off. I once had a referral to make on a young couple who were heading to Montgomery, Alabama. I recalled a fellow I was associated with there when I was in the Air Force who had gone into real estate upon retirement. I called his office to place the referral and was put in touch with his administrative assistant, who, after screening my call, patched me in on his cell phone to the Old Sarge himself. He handled the referral faultlessly, I received my fee, the couple found a home they were happy with, and Sarge earned a healthy commission. I learned from other sources that he had emerged as one of the most successful agents in the area. I'm sure he more than paid for his assistant's salary that month with my one referral.

The point is that you can vastly increase your earnings, and take a lot of pressure off yourself, by paying someone to help you. An increasing number of successful agents—and those who wish to become successful—are doing this. It takes a leap of faith, but the payoff can be substantial. (Remember, even the Lone Ranger eventually teamed up.)

To give you a preview of tasks that a personal assistant might perform for you, here's a "Tasks Performed by Personal Assistants" list from NAR's Member Profile report, listed in order of frequency. Be aware up front that all tasks must be supervised by the responsible real estate licensee and that licensed personal assistants may perform a variety of jobs not permitted for those who are not licensed. Here's the list: Process new listings and enter them in the MLS; photograph listings; send mailings to past clients or prospects; manage closing paperwork; schedule listing presentations, closings, and appointments; order inspections; prepare comps; place/track advertising of listings; write ads; send progress reports to sellers; prepare escrow files; check MLS for expireds; check newspapers for FSBO's; and prospect FSBO's.

You will recall that we referred to Allen Hainge in Chapter six as a leader in the world of technology as it relates to real estate. Here is his view regarding personal assistants, as reflected on his website www.cyberstarts.net. "My thinking is that your Personal Assistant should be sharing the major load where technology is concerned. Remember, your job is meeting people, letting them know what you do for a living, and asking if they need your service, not slaving away at a keyboard and mouse."

These are the specific tasks Hainge believes a Personal Assistant should be able to do for you if you're technologically challenged. Again this information is from his website.

1. Install, learn and use all software necessary for you to run your business.
2. Teach you what you need to know about the software.
3. Do all of your printed presentations, from design to printing.
4. Do all of your multimedia presentations, using programs like Photo-Share, PowerPoint, etc.
5. Make additions and updates to your website, using a program such as Microsoft Front Page 2000, etc.
6. Use your digital camera to take photos for your presentation.
7. Keep current on new technology that will increase your market share.

Ready For a Virtual Suggestion?

In working with Allen Hainge on a previous writing project, I learned that he employs a Virtual Assistant. Her name is Kim Hughes, and you can learn about her operation specifically and Virtual Assistants in general by visiting her website at www.kimhughes.com. This is how Hughes defines a Virtual Assistant: "Virtual Assistants are independent contractors who provide administrative support or specialized business services from a distance, through the internet, fax, telephone, or other methods of communication."

Since Kim operates out of Mineola, Texas ("The Birding Capital of East Texas") and Allen's seat of operations is in Reston, Virginia, it's apparent she's meeting the virtual challenge very well.

Finally, here's a reference to the Real Estate Virtual Assistant Network website—www.revanetwork.com. It describes its function in these terms: "REVA Network is a unique community providing an online forum where Real Estate Professionals and Virtual Assistants who specialize or wish to specialize in real estate assistance can collaboratively support each other in the pursuit of maintaining high levels of ethics and professionalism while also increasing the capabilities and business opportunities for all its members."

ON PRIDE AND PROFESSION

Is real estate a profession that commands a high degree of public confidence and respect? If you believe Mr. Gallup and Mr. Roper, there's a great deal of room for improvement. It does not rate highly on public opinion surveys. In my own survey, 25 percent of the respondents thought that the *feeling that the real estate profession lacks public respect* was *very important* or *important* in causing people to leave the profession. For that matter, is real estate actually a profession? It all depends on how you define profession. But that is not the point, nor is it really that critical where people place it on their hierarchy of respect. The important thing is your attitude toward what you do for a living. You have as much right to be proud of your job in real estate as those in law, teaching, accounting, or medicine.

In our quiet little town alone, I can take you to any number of real estate licensees who are consummate professionals by any definition you wish to use. They observe the highest ethical standards in their business and personal affairs, they treat their clients and their competition with respect, and they keep up-to-date on the latest developments in the field. I am certain the same is true in all parts of the country. This does not mean that the overall level of professionalism within the industry cannot be raised. It needs to be, and you will be disappointed and discouraged by the conduct of some of your associates. At times, you will be appalled. But the foundation for improvement exists within organizations such as the National Association of Realtors and through state licensing agencies. Much more critical a task is the need to attract quality people into its ranks in the first place. If you have come this far with me, I can assure you that you would fit in nicely.

ALL THIS AND MONEY, TOO

When I was starting out in real estate, another new agent in our office (who was having a little trouble earning that first commission) was fond of saying that real estate would be a lot of fun if you only got paid for it. It is a lot of fun, and you can get paid for it—and paid extremely well. In the event your ultimate ambition is to be among the "soarers" of the real estate profession, I'll close with my "Top Ten Things to Remember If You Want To Soar Like an Eagle."

Good luck in *your* successful real estate career!

Top Ten Things to Remember if You Want to Soar Like an Eagle

10. You must conquer your fear of heights.
9. No matter how gross the vultures and other subspecies may act, emulate the actions of the highest and noblest soarers, and always conduct your affairs in a manner befitting a national symbol.
8. Don't be afraid to go out on a limb—after you've invested a few dollars in soaring lessons.
7. Keep your beak to the grindstone, but remember that longevity is enhanced by periodic flights of fancy somewhere over the rainbow.
6. Feather your nest for your post-soaring years.
5. Let the early birds fight over the worms—you go for more regal fare.
4. Map out a flight plan before you take off and learn to soar in both good weather and bad, but avoid tornadoes, hurricanes, lightning storms, and large airborne objects with "Boeing" written on the side.
3. Keep an eagle eye out for opportunities over distant horizons, but remember that hunting will likely be best in your own familiar domain.
2. Avoid associating with turkeys.
1. If at first you fail to soar—fly, fly again.

Appendix A
Survey Results

Question: Based on your experience, please indicate how important you think each of the following is in causing people to leave the profession of real estate.

	Very Important or Important	Neutral	Very Unimportant or Unimportant
1. Lack of "self-starter" and "self-motivator" personality.	91%	5%	4%
2. Unrealistic income expectations.	85%	4%	11%
3. Unwillingness to work hard enough to produce results.	84%	10%	6%
4. Inability to budget to live on commission income.	75%	15%	10%
5. Lack of objective information about the career field before they entered it.	73%	18%	9%
6. Inability to plan and manage time.	72%	19%	9%
7. Inability to establish specific goals.	70%	18%	12%
8. Lack of long-term supervision and motivation by brokers.	63%	28%	9%
9. Inadequate preparation in practical real estate matters during prelicense activities.	60%	27%	13%
10. Pressures generated by problems typically associated with real estate transactions.	56%	31%	13%
11. Erratic and unpredictable work schedule.	53%	11%	36%
12. Disenchantment with high-pressure sales techniques they were expected to use.	43%	38%	19%
13. Feeling that the real estate profession lacks public respect.	25%	40%	35%
14. Overregulation of activities by state licensing agency.	2%	31%	67%

The purpose of the survey was to examine possible causes of attrition in real estate. Three hundred forty-nine active, licensed real estate salespeople and brokers participated. To show major trends, "Very important" and "important" responses were combined, as were "very unimportant" and "unimportant."

Appendix B
State Real Estate Commissions

Note: The source of contact information is the Association of Real Estate License Law Officials (ARELLO), 4170 Carmichael Court, Montgomery, AL 36106. Phone: (334) 260-2902. The ARELLO website www.ARELLO.org contains links to the websites of each of their member regulatory agencies listed below. In the first session of my real estate licensing classes I pass out to each student the state's official Real Estate Agency "Real Estate License and Examination Information" booklet. No matter how much prior research you've done, it's critical to get a copy of your state's official licensing and testing guide. It would also be important to visit your state regulatory agency's website. Many of them also contain the contact information of approved license training.

Alabama Real Estate Commission
1201 Carmichael Way
Montgomery, AL 36106
(334) 242-5544

Alaska Real Estate Commission
550 W. 7th Ave., Ste. 1500
Anchorage, AK 99501
(907) 269-8197

Arizona Department of Real Estate
2910 N. 44th St., Ste. 100
Phoenix, AZ 85018
(602) 468-0562

Arkansas Real Estate Commission
612 South Summit St.
Little Rock, AR 72201-4740
(501) 683-8010

California Department of Real Estate
Post Office Box 187000
Sacramento, CA 95818-7000
(916) 227-0782

Colorado Division of Real Estate
1900 Grant St., Ste. 600
Denver, CO 80203
(303) 894-2166

Connecticut Professional Licensing
    Division
165 Capitol Ave.
Hartford, CT 06106
(860) 713-6150

Delaware Real Estate Commission
861 Silver Lake Blvd.
Dover, DE 19904
(302) 744-4519

District of Columbia Board of Real
Estate
941 North Capitol St. NE
Washington, DC 20002
(202) 442-4528

Florida Division of Real Estate
400 West Robinson St., Ste. N801
Orlando, FL 32801
(407) 481-5662

Georgia Real Estate Commission
Ste. 1000—International Tower
229 Peachtree St. N.W.
Atlanta, GA 30303-1605
(404) 656-3916

Hawaii Real Estate Commission
335 Merchant St., Room 333
Honolulu, HI 96813
(808) 586-2643

Idaho Real Estate Commission
P.O. Box 83720
Boise, ID 83720-0077
(208) 334-3285

Illinois Office of Real Estate
500 East Monroe St., Ste 200
Springfield, IL 62701
(217) 785-9300

Indiana Professional Licensing
Agency
302 W. Washington St., E034
Indianapolis, IN 46204
(317) 234- 3009

Iowa Real Estate Commission
1918 S. E. Hulsizer Ave.
Ankeny, IA 50021
(515) 281-7393

Kansas Real Estate Commission
Three Townsite Plaza, Ste.200
120 SE 6th Ave
Topeka, KS 66603-3511
(785) 296-3411

Kentucky Real Estate Commission
10200 Linn Station Road, Suite 201
Louisville, KY 40223
(502) 429-7250

Louisiana Real Estate Commission
P.O. Box 14785
Baton Rouge, LA 70898-4785
(225) 765-0191

Maine Real Estate Commission
State House Station #35
Augusta, ME 04333
(207) 624-8603

Maryland Real Estate Commission
500 N. Calvert Street
Baltimore, MD 21202-3651
(410) 230-6200

Massachusetts Real Estate Board
239 Causeway St.
Boston, MA 02114
(617) 727-2373

Michigan Bureau of Commercial
Services
P.O. Box 30243
Lansing, MI 48909
(517) 241-9265

Minnesota Department of
Commerce
85 7th Place East
St. Paul, MN 55101
(651) 296-6319

Mississippi Real Estate Commission
Post Office Box 12685
Jackson, MS 39236-2685
(601) 932-9191

Missouri Real Estate Commission
P.O. Box 1339
Jefferson City, MO 65102
(573) 751-2628

Montana Board of Realty Regulation
P.O. Box 200513
Helena, MT 59620-0513
(406) 444-2961

Nebraska Real Estate Commission
Post Office Box 94667
Lincoln, NE 68509-4667
(402) 471-2004

Nevada Real Estate Division
2501 E. Sahara Ave.
Las Vegas, NV 89104
(702) 486-4033

New Hampshire Real Estate
    Commission
25 Capitol St., Room 434
Concord, NH 03301
(603) 271-2701

New Jersey Real Estate Commission
Post Office Box 328
Trenton, NJ 08625-0328
(609) 292-8280

New Mexico Real Estate
    Commission
5200 Oakland Ave. NE, Suite B
Albuquerque, NM 87113
(505) 222-9820

New York Division of Licensing
    Services
84 Holland Ave.
Albany, NY 12208-3490
(518) 473-2728

North Carolina Real Estate
    Commission
P.O. Box 17100
Raleigh, NC 27619-7100
(919) 875-3700

North Dakota Real Estate
    Commission
P.O. Box 727
Bismarck, ND 58502-0727
(701) 328-9749

Ohio Division of Real Estate
77 South High St., 20th Floor
Columbus, OH 43215-6133
(614) 466-4100

Oklahoma Real Estate Commission
2401 N.W. 23rd St., Ste. 18
Oklahoma City, OK 73107
(405) 521-3387

Oregon Real Estate Agency
1177 Center St., N.E.
Salem, OR 97310-2505
(503) 378-4170

Pennsylvania Real Estate
    Commission
P.O. Box 2649
Harrisburg, PA 17105-2649
(717) 783-3658

Rhode Island Real Estate Division
233 Richmond St.
Providence, RI 02903
(401) 222-2255

South Carolina Real Estate
Commission
Post Office Box 11847
Columbia, SC 29211-1847
(803) 896-4400

South Dakota Real Estate
Commission
221 W. Capitol, Ste. 101
Pierre, SD 57501
(605) 773-3600

Tennessee Real Estate Commission
500 James Robertson Parkway
Davy Crockett Tower, Ste. 180
Nashville, TN 37243-1151
(615) 741-2273

Texas Real Estate Commission
P.O. Box 12188
Austin, TX 78711-2188
(512) 465-3900

Utah Division of Real Estate
P.O. Box 146711
Salt Lake City, UT 84114-6711
(801) 530-6747

Vermont Real Estate Commission
81 River Street, Heritage 1 Bldg.
Montpelier, VT 05609
(802) 828-3228

Virginia Department of
Occupational Regulation
3600 West Broad St.
Richmond, VA 23230
(804) 367-8526

Washington Real Estate Division
P.O. Box 9015
Olympia, WA 98507-9015
(360) 664-6500

West Virginia Real Estate
Commission
300 Capitol St., Ste. 400
Charleston, WV 25301
(304) 558-3555

Wisconsin Real Estate Bureau
P.O. Box 8935
Madison, WI 53708
(608) 266-2112

Wyoming Real Estate Commission
2020 Carey Ave., Ste. 100
Cheyenne, WY 82002
(307) 777-7141

Appendix C
Real Estate Resources

Note: The three largest publishers of real estate career material are: Dearborn, 30 S. Wacker Drive, Chicago, IL 60606-1719, telephone: 800-621-9621, website: www.dearbornRE.com; South-Western, 5101 Madison Road, Cincinnati, OH 45227, telephone: (513) 271-8811, website: www.realestate.swcollege.com; and Wiley, 111 River Street, Hoboken, NJ 07030, telephone: (201) 748-6000, website www.wiley.com. You can also gather an incredible amount of information from the online book stores, such as www.amazon.com and www.barnesand-noble.com. The "Search Inside" feature at Amazon permits you to browse the actual contents of many books.

REAL ESTATE LAW

Hinkel, D.F. *Practical Real Estate Law,* 4th ed. Florence, KY: Delmar Thomson Learning, 2003.

Jennings, Marianne. *Real Estate Law,* 7th ed. Cincinnati: South-Western, 2004.

Reitzel, J. David, Robert B. Bennett, and Michael J. Garrison. *American Real Estate Law.* Cincinnati: South-Western, 2002.

Siedel, George J. *Real Estate Law,* 6th ed. Cincinnati: South-Western, 2005.

REAL ESTATE FINANCE

Dennis, Marshall W. *Residential Mortgage Lending,* 5th ed. Cincinnati: South-Western, 2003.

Garton-Good, Julie. *All About Mortgages,* 3rd ed. Chicago: Dearborn, 2004.

Gkuttentag, Jack. *The Mortgage Encyclopedia.* New York: McGraw-Hill, 2004.

Miller, Peter G. *The Common Sense Mortgage.* New York: McGraw-Hill, 1999.

Sirota, David. *Essentials of Real Estate Finance,* 10th ed. Chicago: Dearborn, 2000.

Wiedemer, John P. *Real Estate Finance,* 8th ed. Cincinnati: South-Western, 2001.

REAL ESTATE MATH

Armbrust, Betty, John W. Armbrust, and Hugh H. Bradley. *Practical Real Estate Math,* 2nd ed. Cincinnati: South-Western, 1995.

Gaines, George, David Coleman, and Linda Crawford. *Real Estate Math: What You Need To Know,* Chicago: Dearborn, 2005.

Tamper, Ralph. *Mastering Real Estate Mathematics,* 7th ed. Chicago: Dearborn, 2002.

REAL ESTATE PRINCIPLES AND PRACTICE

(Note: the following are basic real estate texts in widespread use for licensing courses. Review any for good overview of what to expect in license training.)

Cortesi, Gerald R. *Mastering Real Estate Principles,* 4th ed. Chicago: Dearborn, 2003.

Galaty, Fillmore W., Wellington J. Allaway, and Robert C. Kyle. *Modern Real Estate Practice,* 17th ed. Chicago: Dearborn, 2006.

Geschwender, Arlyne. *Real Estate Principles & Practices,* 7th ed. Cincinnati: South-Western, 2003.

Jacobus, Charles. *Real Estate Principles,* 10th ed. Cincinnati: South-Western, 2005.

REAL ESTATE REFERENCE

Abbott, Damien. *Shorter Encyclopedia of Real Estate Terms,* Washington, D.C.: Delta Alpha Publishing, 2004.

California Department of Real Estate. *Real Estate Law.* Department of Real Estate, P.O. Box 187006, Sacramento, CA 95818-7006. Updated frequently A variety of other helpful products also offered. Website orders: www.dre.ca.gov.

Cox, Barbara. *Learning the Language of Real Estate.* Cincinnati: South-Western, 2002.

Dahlheimer, Charles M. *20/20 Vision—A Focus on the Future of the Real Estate Industry*. St. Louis, MO: North American Consulting Group, 2000. A leading real estate guru peers into the crystal ball. www.nacgonline.com.

De Heer, Robert. *Realty Bluebook,* 33rd ed. Chicago: Dearborn, 2003. You will likely see this little book around real estate offices more than any other. Written by a pioneer in the field and kept up-to-date. It has a little of everything. You can get updates to the current edition by visiting www.realty-bluebook.com.

Frascona, Oliver E., and Katherine E. Reece. *The Digital Paper Trail In Real Estate Transactions*. Boulder, CO: Real Law Books, 2003. Orders/information: (303) 494-3000. Web site: www.frascona.com. Great website for real estate law information.

Gadow, Sandy. *Your Complete Guide to Your Real Estate Closing*. New York: McGraw-Hill, 2003. Web site: www.escrowhelp.com. Latest version of classic *All About Escrow.*

Harris, Jack C., and Jack P. Friedman. *Dictionary of Real Estate Terms,* 6th ed. Hauppauge, NY: Barron's, 2004.

Harris, Jack C., and Jack P. Friedman. *Real Estate Handbook,* 6th ed. Hauppauge, NY: Barron's, 2005.

Reilly, John W. *The Language of Real Estate,* 6th ed. Chicago: Dearborn, 2006. An indispensable reference.

Swanepoel, Stefan, and Tom Dooley. *Real Estate Confronts the Future*. Cincinnati: South-Western, 2004. Two industry stalwarts gaze into the future of the profession.

Tuccillo, John. *New Business Models For the New Economy—Remaking the Four Businesses of Real Estate*. Chicago: Dearborn, 2002. The former chief economist for NAR looks ahead to emerging business models in the real estate profession.

REAL ESTATE ETHICS

Long, Deborah H. *Ethics for the Real Estate Professional,* 2nd ed. Cincinnati: South-Western, 2001.

REAL ESTATE INDUSTRY STATISTICS AND HISTORY

Association of Real Estate License Law Officials (ARELLO). *Digest of Real Estate License Laws*. Montgomery, AL (annual publication). Website:

www.arello.org. This is an annual publication. In addition to statistical information, it contains a summary of prominent real estate legal cases for each year.

National Association of Realtors (NAR). *Membership Profile*. Washington, D.C.: National Association of Realtors. Annual publication. One of a series of reports issued periodically by NAR.

EXAMINATION PREPARATION GUIDES

Garton-Good, Julie. *Real Estate Licensing Super Course*, 2nd ed. New York, NY: ARCO, 1995.

Lindeman, J. Bruce, and Jack P. Friedman. *How to Prepare for the Real Estate Examination*, 7th ed. Happauge, N.Y: Barron's, 2005.

Reilly, John W., and Paige Bovee Vitousek. *Questions and Answers to Help You Pass the Real Estate Exam*, 7th ed. Chicago: Dearborn, 2005.

Yoegel, John A., *Real Estate Licensing Exams for Dummies*. Hoboken NJ: Wiley, 2005.

REAL ESTATE APPRAISAL

Appraisal Institute, *The Appraisal of Real Estate*, 12th ed. Chicago: Appraisal Institute, 2001. www.appraisalinstitute. com.

Betts, Richard M., and Silas J. Ely. *Basic Real Estate Appraisal*, 6th ed. Cincinnati: South-Western, 2005.

Ratterman, Mark. *The Student Handbook to the Appraisal of Real Estate*. Chicago: Appraisal Institute, 2004.

Venetolo, William L., and Martha R. Williams. *Fundamentals of Real Estate Appraisal*, 8th ed. Chicago: Dearborn, 2001.

REAL ESTATE PROPERTY MANAGEMENT

Griswold, Robert. *Property Management for Dummies*. Hoboken NJ: Wiley, 2001.

Reed, John T. *How to Manage Residential Property for Maximum Cash Flow and Resale Value*, 5th ed. Danville, CA: Reed Publishing, 1998. Reed also publishes a newsletter and other property management and income tax material. Website: www.johntreed.com.

Robinson, Leigh. *Landlording,* 9th ed. El Cerrito, CA: ExPress, 2004. www.landlording.com. Great practical reference. Continually updated.

Taylor, Jeffrey. *The Landlord's Kit.* Chicago: Dearborn. 2002.

REAL ESTATE MANAGEMENT

Cyr, John, and Sobeck, Joan. *Real Estate Brokerage: A Management Guide,* 6th ed. Chicago: Dearborn, 2004. If your broker does not have this book, give it to her as a birthday present.

REAL ESTATE MARKETING

Allen, George. *How to Find, Buy, Manage, and Sell a Manufactured Home Community.* Indianapolis, IN: PMN Publishing, 1998. Allen is the guru of manufactured homes. This is a great basic reference. Check out www.mfd-housing.com/gfa.

Brown, Ray, and Eric Tyson. *Homebuying for Dummies Third Edition.* Hoboken, NJ: Wiley, 2006. All of the *Dummies* books on real estate coauthored by Brown are exceptional.

Cook, Frank. *21 Things I Wish My Broker Had Told Me—Practical Advice for New Real Estate Professionals.* Chicago: Dearborn, 2002. Down-to-earth guidance on avoiding the typical rookie pitfalls.

Corcoran, Barbara. *Use What You've Got and Other Lessons I Learned From My Mom.* New York: Portfolio Books, 2003. This is a "rags to riches" must read. Visit Barbara's website at www.barbaracorcoran.com.

Cox, Danny. *Leadership: When The Heat's On.* New York: McGraw-Hill, 2002. This is not a book about real estate, but author Cox learned his leadership lessons largely as a result of his career as a real estate broker. www.danny-cox.com. Great motivational speaker

Cross, Carla. *Up and Running in 30 Days: A Proven Plan for Financial Success in Real Estate.* Chicago: Dearborn, 2001.

Cross, Carla. *The Real Estate Agent's Business Planning Guide.* Chicago: Dearborn, 1994. Both Cross books would be excellent choices for your training program.

Dorris, Tamara. *See How They Sell! Success in Real Estate Sales.* New York: Writer's Club Press, 2001. Contains extensive case study scenarios from successful Realtors. Exceptional research. A California Association of Realtors project; www.car.org. Author Dorris's website: www.asharpedge.com.

Evans, Blanche. *The Hottest E-Careers in Real Estate.* Chicago: Dearborn, 2000.

Evans, Blanche. *Homesurfing.net.* Chicago: Dearborn, 1999.

Evans, Blanche. *Housing Bubbles, Booms and Busts.* New York: McGraw-Hill, 2006.

Evans, Blanche. *National Association of Realtors Guide to Buying a Home.* Hoboken, NJ: Wiley, 2006.

Evans, Blanche. *National Association of Realtors Guide to Selling a Home.* Hoboken, NJ: Wiley, 2006.

Garton-Good, Julie. *Real Estate a la Carte.* Chicago: Dearborn, 2001.

Hainge, Allen F. *Dominate!: Capturing Your Market with Today's Technology.* Springfield, VA: Allen F. Hainge Seminars, 2001.

Irwin, Robert. *The For Sale By Owner Kit.* Chicago: Dearborn, 2004.

Keller, Gary. *The Millionaire Real Estate Agent.* Austin, TX: Rellek Publishing Partners, 2004. Keller is a cofounder of Keller Williams Realty and currently chairman of the board. An incredible amount of great career information. www.millionaireagent.com.

Kennedy, Danielle. *How to List and Sell Real Estate: Executing New Basics for Higher Profits.* Cincinnati: South-Western, 2003. Also refer to www.danielle kennedy.com.

Kennedy, Danielle. *Seven Figure Selling: Proven Secrets to Success From Top Professionals.* Cincinnati: South-Western, 2003.

Knox, David. *The Mentor Series.* Minneapolis, MN: David Knox Seminars. This is a series of twelve DVD's on the basic topics of listing and selling. I've used them in my real estate prelicense classes for years to illustrate "real world real estate." They are incredibly well done. Visit www.davidknox.com for a variety of other products, including a "Real Estate Live" series of training DVD's.

Lee, Michael D. *Opening Doors: Selling to Multicultural Real Estate Customers.* Winchester, VA: Oakhill Press, 1999. Lee specializes in multi cultural topics as a speaker and writer. Website: www.seminarsunlimited.com.

McCrea, Bridget. *The Real Estate Agent's Field Guide.* New York: AMACOM, 2004.

McCrea, Bridget. *The Real Estate Agent's Business Planner.* New York: AMACOM, 2005.

Moore-Moore, Laurie. *Rich Buyer, Rich Seller: The Real Estate Agents' Guide to Marketing Luxury Homes.* Dallas, TX: Institute for Luxury Home Marketing, 2003. www.luxuryhomemarketing.com. Great read if this is your niche.

Murphy, Terri. *E-listing and E-selling Secrets for the Technologically "Clueless."*

Chicago: Dearborn, 2001. A working real estate professional outlines how technology interfaces with listing and selling. www.terrimurphy.com.

Remley, Jim. *Make Millions Selling Real Estate*. New York: AMACOM, 2005.

Richard, Dan Gooder. *Real Estate Rainmaker*. Hoboken, NJ: Wiley, 2000. The intent is to design a system that makes it rain prospects. Highly recommended. www.gooder.com.

Richard, Dan Gooder. *Real Estate Rainmaker: Guide to Online Marketing*. Hoboken, NJ: Wiley, 2004.

Rosenauer, Johnnie, Michael D. Hennessey, and James M. Mullen. *Farm and Ranch Marketing*. Cincinnati: South-Western, 1998. If this marketing niche appeals to you, this is a solid reference.

Scher, Les, and Carol Scher. *Finding and Buying Your Place in the Country*, 5th ed. Chicago: Dearborn, 2000. Les Scher is an attorney with practical experience. Best consumer-oriented source I've found on this topic.

Schwarz, Barb. *Home Staging: The Winning Way to Sell Your Home For More Money*. Hoboken, NJ: Wiley, 2006.

Scott, J. Lennox. *Next Generation Real Estate*. Crete, NE: Dageforde Publishing, 2002.

Stefaniak, Norbert J. *Real Estate Marketing*. West Allis, WI: Walker-Pearse Ltd., 1998. Great career information. Written by an industry legend.

Sullivan, Marilyn. *The Complete Idiot's Guide to Success as a Real Estate Agent*. Indianapolis, IN: Alpha Books, 2003.

Swanepoel, Stefan. *Real Estate Confronts the E-Consumer*. San Diego, CA: RealSure Inc., 2000. Exhaustive research on the impact of technology on real estate.

Zeller, Dirk. *Your 1st Year in Real Estate*. New York: Random House, 2001. Practical roadmap for that critical first year. www.realestatechampions .com.

Zeller, Dirk. *Success As a Real Estate Agent For Dummies*. Hoboken, NJ: Wiley, 2006.

Ziegler, Holly. *Sell Your Home Faster With Feng Shui*. Arroyo Grande, CA: Dragon Chi Publications, 2001.

Ziegler, Holly. *Buy Your Home Smarter With Feng Shui*. Arroyo Grande, CA: Dragon Chi Publications, 2004. If you wish to learn more about Feng Shui, visit author Ziegler's website at www.hollyziegler.com. Even without the Feng Shui element, these are excellent home selling and home buying books.

REAL ESTATE TAXES

Hoven, Vernon. *The Real Estate Investor's Tax Guide*, 4th ed. Chicago: Dearborn, 2005.

Reed, John T. *Aggressive Tax Avoidance for Real Estate Investors*, 18th ed. Danville, CA: Reed Publishing. Annual editions since 1981. Orders/information: www.johntreed.com.

REAL ESTATE PERIODICALS

Realtor Magazine. National Association of Realtors, 430 North Michigan Avenue, Chicago, IL 60611. Official publication of NAR and included in membership. www.realtormag.com.

The Real Estate Professional. Wellesley Publications, 1492 Highland Avenue, Needham, MA 02192. Subscription information: 781-729-0935. www.TheRealEstatePro.com.

REAL ESTATE–RELATED WEB SITES

www.realtor.com—This is NAR's official website, designed for both consumers and real estate professionals. An incredible array of information, including links to state and local Realtor organizations. When you become a Realtor you can log on to www.realtor.org.

www.inman.com—Click on the "Today's Real Estate News" link for the current developments in the profession. Bob Bruss and Dian Hymer are featured columnists. For complete access to all articles you must become a member.

www.realtytimes.com—Another outstanding real estate news website. An impressive array of columnists, including Peter Miller, Blanche Evans, Kenneth Harney, Lew Sichelman, and attorney Benny Kass. Marketing support opportunities for real estate professionals.

www.reintel.com—This site is run by Frank Cook, widely published author. You can get a free trial subscription to his newsletter, *The Real Estate Intelligence Report*. The "calendar" link, documenting real estate related events, is the most exhaustive of its kind I've seen.

www.frogpond.com—This site features an elaborate file of real estate articles by top real estate professionals.

www.ired.com—*The International Real Estate Digest*. An impressive array of information and valuable links.

www.ourbroker.com—This is author Peter Miller's website. He is one of the profession's most accomplished and respected writers.

www.realestateABC.com—Information for consumers and real estate professionals. If you're interested in learning more about developing your own real estate website, refer to columnist Barbara Cox's link, http://www.real estateabc.com/webmarketer/select.htm

www.recyber.com—The Real Estate Cyber Society has a number of tools and educational ideas for online agents.

www.waltersanford.com—Sanford is one of the leading real estate educators in the country. He has a wide variety of products that are described on his website.

www.rismedia.com—An independent provider of news, information, and reference publications for the real estate and relocation industry.

www.realtyU.com—Promotes itself as "largest network of real estate educators in the nation."

www.internetcrusade.com. Responsible for delivering training for National Association of Realtors—sponsored E-PRO certification course. Objective: "To help real estate professionals thrive in the competitive world of online real estate." Also hosts "Real Talk," an online real estate discussion forum.

www.joeklock.com—This is the website of Joe Klock, veteran real estate professional and former dean of Coldwell Banker University. Klock is a prolific, entertaining, and provocative writer. An abundance of free material here, including periodic newsletters.

REAL ESTATE PRODUCTS

In most instances, the website designation will tell you what's being promoted. I've included several to give you a feel for the variety of resources.

www.talkinghouse.com

www.360house.com

www.colorcardsdirect.com

www.harmonhomes.com

www.stayintouchsystem.com

www.safeshow.com

www.topagentsecrets.com

Appendix D

Real Estate Pre Test

The story is told of a lion in the jungle who was constantly roaring "Who is the king of the jungle?!" He went on and on, repeating the same question. An elephant who was grazing nearby became agitated, walked over to the lion, grabbed him by the tail with his trunk, twirled him around and hurled him about twenty yards in the air. The lion hit the trunk of a large tree with his head, and slid down to the ground. As he sat dazed and confused, he said to the elephant: "Hey man, don't get mad just because you couldn't answer the question." That's my guidance to you for this Pre Test and all the academic material you encounter in your licensing program. You're essentially learning a new language. Relax, study hard, and enjoy. By the way, if you would like brief explanations for each of these questions, e-mail me at DoctorKenisin@aol.com.

REAL ESTATE PRACTICE

Listing agreements; sales agreements; offers to purchase and counter offers; federal fair housing; and Americans with Disabilities Act.

1. A listing agreement is essentially
   A. an employment contract.
   B. a purchase contract.
   C. an option to sell.
   D. all of these.

2. To create a valid listing for the purpose of selling real estate, a principal broker must have
   A. two witnesses to the contract.
   B. a written contract.
   C. a general power of attorney.
   D. a signed deed by the sellers.

3. When a broker terminates his association with his principal broker, all of the current listings written by the broker
   A. may be transferred with that broker to his new office.
   B. are retained by the principal broker.
   C. immediately terminate.
   D. must be renegotiated with the broker's new principal broker.

4. An oral agreement to sell a parcel of residential real estate for a commission is
   I. unenforceable.
   II. contrary to the Statute of Frauds.
   A. I only B. II only C. Both I & II D. Neither I nor II

5 A principal broker's listing contract in the form of a letter addressed by the owner to the broker provides that the principal broker will be paid a commission if within 30 days the real estate is sold for $130,000 "by you, by me, or anyone else." This
   A. creates an open listing.
   B. creates an exclusive agency listing.
   C. creates an exclusive right to sell listing.
   D. does not comply with the Statute of Frauds.

6. Once an offer to purchase real estate has been signed by both buyer and seller, the buyer acquires an interest in the property known as
   A. legal title.
   B. special title.
   C. equitable title.
   D. sole title.

7. When an earnest money agreement has been signed by the purchaser and given to the seller's broker with an earnest money check
   A. the transaction constitutes a valid contract by law.
   B. the purchaser can sue for specific performance if the seller refuses to sign the agreement.
   C. the transaction is considered an offer until the seller accepts the agreement and the acceptance is communicated to the buyer.
   D. the earnest money must be returned to the purchaser if he withdraws the offer after the seller signs the agreement.

8. Where do you find the "time is of the essence" clause?
   A. Closing documents.
   B. Earnest money agreement.
   C. Employment contract.

D. Listing contract.

9. A particular savings and loan association has blocked out certain regions of the community where it will not place loans because of ghetto conditions. Such a practice is called
   A. redlining.
   B. steering.
   C. warehousing.
   D. relocating.

10. Which of the following is an example of steering?
    I. Leading prospective purchasers to or away from certain areas.
    II. Refusing to make loans to persons in certain areas.
    A. I only B. II only C. Both I & II D. Neither I nor II

REAL ESTATE LAW

Forms of ownership; purchase and sale of real property; easements and encumbrances; nature of real property; and ways to legally describe real property.

1. All of the following are tests to determine whether personal property becomes a fixture **except** the
   A. initial cost of the item.
   B. intent of the person placing the item.
   C. manner of annexation.
   D. nature of use or adaptation.

2. In terms of basic physical characteristics, land may properly be described as
   A. immobile.
   B. indestructible.
   C. nonhomogeneous.
   D. all of these.

3. A riparian owner is one who owns lands bounding on
   A. municipal property.
   B. a national forest.
   C. the seashore.
   D. a waterway.

4. Public powers in private property include which of the following?

I. The right to tax.
II. Zoning codes
III. Deed restrictions in a subdivision.
IV. Eminent domain.
A. I & II only B. II & III only C. I, II, & IV only D. II, III, & IV only

5. When an owner of land refuses to sell his land to the government or
   any governmental agency under the right of eminent domain, the
   name of the proceeding to require the owner to sell his land is
   A. escheat.
   B. estoppel.
   C. condemnation.
   D. constructive eviction.

6. A standard title insurance policy would give coverage for which of
   the following?
   A. A governmentally imposed restriction on the use of the property.
   B. A claim on the title that the purchaser could have discovered upon
      a physical inspection of the property.
   C. A missing heir.
   D. All of the above.

7. To acquire title by adverse possession, the adverse claimant
   I. must maintain actual, open, hostile and continuous possession for
   the statutory period set by the state.
   II. may tack the time of his possession to that of a previous adverse
   possessor if the two were successors in interest.
   A. I only B. II only C. Both I & II D. Neither I nor II

8. Which of the following is correct regarding tenancy in common?
   A. Each party must have acquired interest at the same time.
   B. Each party may sell his interest without the consent of the other.
   C. Parties may have unequal rights of possession.
   D. Each party's interest must be equal.

9. A farm, described as the "NW 1/4 of the SE 1/4 of Section 10, Town-
   ship 4N, Range 4W of the Gila and Salt River Base and Meridian,"
   sold for $500 per acre. The sale price would be:
   A. $10,000
   B. $20,000
   C. $25,000
   D. $40,000

10. Under the rectangular survey system, the legal description of a particular land unit is based on
    A. one township line.
    B. one range.
    C. One meridian and one base line.
    D. metes and bounds.

REAL ESTATE FINANCE

Government lending policies; conventional financing; government lending laws; Truth-in-Lending; Equal Credit Opportunity Act; Real Estate Settlement procedures Act; competitive market analyses; mathematical calculations.

1. In a so called "tight money market," one would expect to find
   A. potential borrowers delaying projects, expecting interest rates to fall.
   B. lower interest rates than in an "easy money market."
   C. marginal borrowers forced out of the credit market.
   D. Both A & C.

2. If the Federal Reserve Bank feels that there is an inflationary trend developing in the U.S., it can do which of the following?
   I. Increase the discount rate.
   II. Adjust the amount of reserves required of member banks.
   A. I only B. II only C. Both I & II D. Neither I nor II

3. A borrower obtains a home improvement loan which is neither insured nor guaranteed by a government agency. The security for the loan is the borrower's house which he owns free of any encumbrance. This borrower has obtained which type of loan?
   A. Wraparound.
   B. Package money
   C. Subordinated.
   D. Conventional.

4. When a grantee takes title to real property "subject to" an existing mortgage, what is his maximum risk?
   A. Loss of his equity.
   B. Possibility of a deficiency judgement.
   C. No risk, since he did not agree to assume and pay the mortgage.
   D. the threat of specific performance.

5. A purchase money mortgage can sometimes be used as
   A. a warranty of title.
   B. a junior financing instrument.
   C. a valid deed.
   D. an equity of redemption.

6. A mortgage that includes both real and personal property is called
   I. a package mortgage. II. a blanket mortgage.
   A. I only B. II only C. both I & II D. neither I nor II

7. In researching records at the county clerk's office, a first mortgage and a second mortgage on the same piece of property can usually be distinguished by
   A. the date of the instrument.
   B. the words "first" or "second" preceding the phrase "this indenture".
   C. notations made by the recorder.
   D. date of recording.

8. A financing arrangement under which the buyer does not immediately become the legal owner of record is a
   A. trust deed.
   B. land sales contract.
   C. purchase money mortgage.
   D. quitclaim deed.

9. Regulation Z of the Truth in Lending Act
   A. establishes loan interest rates.
   B. limits loan amounts.
   C. requires loan cost revelations.
   D. restricts closing costs.

10. A mortgage company agrees to loan a sum of money equal to 90 percent of their appraised value, at an effective interest rate of 7 percent. This rate can only be achieved after a discount of 6 percent is paid on the actual face amount of the note. What sum of money does the borrower actually achieve if the appraisal of the property is $98,250?
    A. $83,120
    B. $88,425
    C. $91,372
    D. $92,355

REAL ESTATE CONTRACTS

Basic contract law; required provisions for listing agreements; earnest money agreements; options; and leases.

1. Essential elements of a contract include, among other things
   I. consideration in the form of money.
   II. competent parties.
   III. mutual agreement.
   A. I & II only B. I & III only C. II & III only D. I, II & III

2. An amount predetermined by the parties to an agreement as to the total amount of compensation a party should receive in the event that the other party breaches a specified part of the contract is known as
   A. just compensation.
   B. liquidated damages.
   C. consideration.
   D. deferred damages.

3. Taylor contracts to sell some land to Hamilton and thereafter refuses to sell. Since Hamilton wants the land he should bring suit against Taylor for
   A. rescission.
   B. specific performance.
   C. dollar damages.
   D. novation.

4. A broker in court to collect a commission on an exclusive right to sell listing must allege and prove which of the following?
   I. He had an agency relationship with the seller.
   II. He was licensed.
   III. He introduced the buyer and the seller.
   A. I only B. II only C. I & II only D. I & III only

5. An option in a contract by which the owner of property gives another person the right to purchase his property for a stated sum within a given period of time is
   A. a voluntary lien.
   B. an involuntary encumbrance.
   C. a voluntary encumbrance.
   D. none of the above.

REAL ESTATE PROPERTY MANAGEMENT

Economics of property management; leases; record keeping; and anti-discrimination statutes.

1. With reference to the function of a property manager, which of the following is the responsibility of a property manager?
   A. Obtain the best possible return on the owner's investment.
   B. Preserve the owner's investment.
   C. Provide financial records and accounts.
   D. All of the above.

2. Leasehold estates that continue for an indefinite period of time include
   I. estate for years.
   II. tenancy at will.
   A. I only B. II only C. Both I & II D. Neither I nor II

3. A tenant who pays rent plus some or all of the property taxes, insurance and maintenance is under which of the following lease agreements?
   A. Percentage lease.
   B. Sale and leaseback.
   C. Net lease.
   D. Proprietary lease.

4. In a sale-leaseback arrangement
   I. the seller retains title to the real estate.
   II. the purchaser receives possession of the property.
   A. I only B. II only C. Both I & II D. Neither I nor II

5. A lease can always be terminated by
   I. selling the building.
   II. death of the tenant.
   III. abandonment of the leased premises by the tenant.
   IV. expiration of the term of the lease.
   A. II & IV only B. II & IIII only C. I, II, III & IV D. IV only

REAL ESTATE AGENCY

Common law of agency including fiduciary requirements.

1. The position of trust assumed by the principal broker as an agent for the client is described most accurately as a
   A. trustee relationship.
   B. trustor relationship.
   C. confidential relationship.
   D. fiduciary relationship.

2. Commingling occurs when the
   I. client's funds are mixed with the agent's personal account.
   II. agent's funds are mixed with the clients' trust account funds.
   A. I only B. II only C. Both I & II D. Neither I nor II

3. Which of the following would be considered "dual agency"?
   I. Two principal brokers who are cooperating with each other to sell the same piece of property.
   II. A principal broker who acts for both the buyer and seller.
   A. I only B. II only C. Both I & II D. Neither I nor II

4. Which of the following is a duty of the agent?
   A. Completely truthful dealings with the client.
   B. Accept only those tasks which he can skillfully perform.
   C. Assume full liability for any wrongful act committed or permitted by himself or his employees.
   D. All of the above.

5. It is improper for a principal broker representing the owner to
   A. tell a buyer that a house has a leak in the roof.
   B. reveal that a house has a drainage problem during the winter.
   C. confide to a buyer that a homeowner will take less than the list price.
   D. None of the above are improper.

REAL ESTATE BROKERAGE—REAL ESTATE CLOSINGS; ADVERTISING; OFFICE MANUALS; FINANCIAL REPORTS.

1. A proper escrow, once established, should be
   A. managed by a licensed broker.
   B. void at the seller's option.
   C. voidable at option of either buyer or seller.
   D. not subject to the control of any one interested party alone.

2. A buyer assumes an existing loan when purchasing a single family residence. The loan assumption on the closing statement would be shown as
   A. debit to the buyer.
   B. debit to the seller.
   C. credit to the seller.
   D. credit to the buyer and credit to the seller.

3. Which of the following belongs in the debit column of a seller's closing statement?
   A. Prepaid property tax proration.
   B. Prepaid rent.
   C. Earnest money.
   D. Loan origination fee.

4. A principal broker would have the right to dictate which of the following to an independent contractor?
   A. Number of hours the person would have to work.
   B. Work schedule the person would have to follow.
   C. Minimum acceptable dress code for the office.
   D. Compensation the person would receive.

5. GHI Realty has adopted a 100 percent commission plan. The monthly desk rent required of associate brokers is $900, payable on the last day of the month. In August Associate Broker Mary Johnson closed an $89,500 sale with a 6 percent commission and a $125,000 sale with a 5.5 percent commission. Johnson's additional expenses for the month were $1,265. How much of her total monthly income did Johnson keep?
   A. $10,080
   B. $10,980
   C. $11,345
   D. $12,245

Answers:

REAL ESTATE PRACTICES

1. - A, 2. - B, 3. - B, 4. - C, 5. - C, 6. - C, 7. - C, 8. - B, 9. - A, 10. - A.

REAL ESTATE LAW

1. - A, 2. - B, 3. - D, 4. - C, 5. - C, 6. - C, 7. - C, 8. - B, 9. - B, 10. - C.

REAL ESTATE FINANCE

1. - D, 2. - C, 3. - D, 4. - A, 5. - B, 6. - A, 7. - D, 8. - B, 9. - C, 10. - A.

REAL ESTATE CONTRACTS

1. - C, 2. - B, 3. - B, 4. - C, 5. - C

REAL ESTATE PROPERTY MANAGEMENT

1. - D, 2. - B, 3. - C, 4. - D, 5. - D

REAL ESTATE AGENCY

1. - D, 2. - C, 3. - B, 4. - D, 5. - C

REAL ESTATE BROKERAGE

1. - D, 2. - B, 3. - B, 4. - D, 5. - A

These questions are from the *State of Oregon Questions and Answers In Real Estate*, Ninth Edition, copyright 2003. Used with permission. You can order a copy of the book by logging on to the Oregon Real Estate Agency website at www.rea.state.or.us, and clicking the Publications and Forms Link.

Appendix E

Stefan Swanepoel Real Estate Trends Report

The following is from *Swanepoel Trends Report, Top 15 Real Estate Trends* by Stefan Swanepoel, copyright 2006 by RealSure, Inc with permission. Remember, your assignment is to analyze each of these projected trends and to anticipate how you might integrate your marketing strategies.

15. Trend: Development of the Internet

Executive Overview: Technology has significantly influenced the way the real estate marketplace operates. The pace of technological change has been startling. However, the Internet is a very dynamic beast, and although we as an industry have advanced with e-mail and e-commerce, we have more coming down the pike, including ASP, Wi-Fi, and blogging.

14. Trend: Changing Consumer Characteristics

Executive Overview: There is not one single customer type. Increasingly we are learning that different generations and different grops behave differently and have differing needs based upon a wide variety of factors. Specialization, coupled with niche marketing, will provide agents an excellent opportunity to gain a competitive advantage in the future.

13. Trend: Advancement and Sophistication of Real Estate Agents

Executive Overview: Gone are the days when agents were the gatekeepers of a wide range of real estate information. They are now, by default, broad experts in the home buying and selling process. The pace and extent of change in the real estate business has been escalating faster and faster. The challenges facing the agent of today are more complicated and complex than ever before. To succeed in the new world of real estate, agents will have to learn some new skills, be very technology proficient, offer a broader base of services, and learn to adapt quickly.

12. Trend: Evolution of Multi-Listing Services

Executive Overview: Although MLS's continue to play an essential role in the US real estate market, migration to the Internet has opened a myriad of complexities. The industry has worked through data ownership, but still struggles to ensure the security of data. The next hurdles include data exchange, territorial issues, and uniformity.

11. Trend: The Realignment of Marketing Strategies

Executive Overview: The Internet has become the most powerful tool in real estate, both as a research device and as a marketing medium. The Web has totally changed the consumer's focus in selecting a media containing the desired data. The challenge for brokers and agents is to find a dynamic blend of print and Internet advertising in order to create one balanced channel that meets the specific needs of their segmented and fragmented real estate consumers. The potential for those who succeed may be a significant increase in market share.

10. Trend: The Franchising Revival

Executive Overview: Franchising is one of the most popular ways to expand your company. The Internet has also fueled the growing need for a recognizable online brand, providing a competitive advantage and increased market recognition. Globalization is an added bonus for franchising. So whether a real estate agent wishes to expand their brand, or quickly acquire another brand, franchising is currently one of the best opportunities to achieve that end.

9. Trend: To Those Who Have, More Will Be Given

Executive Overview: Size, previously considered by many as more cost-prohibitive than effective, has demonstrated to the world just what sheer volume is capable of overcoming. Economies of scale have changed the financial landscape and dominated industries. For the first time in history the residential real estate brokerage industry has a mega company with the power to really effect change.

8. Trend: Integrating And Managing The Real Estate Transaction

Executive Overview: While the 2000 dot.com crash rained destruction on the one-stop-shop parade, the integration of transaction components, the effective management of the transaction, and the drive toward a more seamless real estate transaction is still very much alive. However, transaction management is different today, as title companies lead the way by laying a solid foundation for an automated real estate transaction.

7. Trend: A Population On The Move
Executive Overview: Although our population has always moved and impacted our industry, Baby Boomers have caused or changed more trends than any other group. As a result of the cost of living and the availability of affordable housing, a significant group of Boomers are likely to move during the next few years. The potential geographic relocation places us at the initial stages of a huge population shift, one that could have a national impact, redefining cities across the US, and creating opportunities galore for the smart broker and agent.

6. Trend: Impact of Immigrants And Minorities
Executive Overview: Many immigrants come with little or no knowledge of the inner workings of the American real estate transaction, nor do they understand the vast number of terms used during the process. In many cases, this is compounded by a lack of proficiency in the English language. Yet, they desire to and increasingly do buy homes. This poses multiple opportunities for real estate brokers and agents.

5. Trend: The Growing Knowledge And Skills Vacuum
Executive Overview: During the last five years the real estate industry has absorbed an influx of newly licensed agents at a rate and number that has shattered all records. Simultaneously, brokers and agents have been bombarded with new business models, the Internet, bundled services and specialization. The need for true knowledge and fundamental sales skills has never been more prevalent and essential than today.

4. Trend: The Entry of "Outsiders"
Executive Overview: The industry's current fear of entry by outsiders is not new. Every time it's rumored that some large player is going to enter the industry "the end" is predicted, and scenarios of how the paradigm will change seems to appear out of thin air. As the industry continues its consolidation over the next five years, very large outsiders may be afforded an opportunity to enter and change the rules of the real estate transaction.

3. Trend: The Proliferation Of Business Models
Executive Overview: Competition in the residential real estate brokerage industry is immense and intense. Brokers and agents are increasingly assailed by a large selection of business models, products, and commission structures and Internet options. In reflection, one can see that previous business models and trends significantly influenced the industry. For example, the growth of

multiple listing systems in the 60's, the franchising of the 70's, the 100% concept in the 80's, and technology in the 90's. There can be little doubt that something different will again cause a major shift in the industry.

2. Trend: Rebirth Of A New Middleman—Lead Generation

Executive Overview: Numerous attempts to reduce the role of the agent in the home selling and home buying transaction will continue. The recent strong growth of the lead generation initiatives are raising concern among some, since they feel the existing commission pie is being pre-sliced. Increasing dependency on these leads may also allow for price increases that will further exacerbate the situation.

1. Trend: Electronic Devices Take Center Stage

Executive Overview: We've been dazzled with palm pilots, blackberries, bluetooth, m-life, t-mobile and more. Now the time has come to simplify and integrate all these individual devices into fewer, multi-function, more multi-task-enabled devices. REDtablets, iPods, and GPS devices are just some of the items currently making the news and providing a promise of saving time and increasing productivity, For those who love gadgetry, heaven has a name on earth: CompUSA.

Appendix F

Targeting Hispanics of Mexican Heritage to Expand Your Business

[The following article is reprinted with permission from the Web site of the National Association of Hispanic Real Estate Professionals at www.nahrep .org. Membership information is available at their website or you may write: NAHREP, 1650 Hotel Circle North, Suite 215A, San Diego, California 92108.]

With the Hispanic population growing faster than any other ethnic group in this nation, Hispanic consumers are becoming increasingly important to the real estate industry. Lower interest rates, better housing programs, and the realization that home ownership is the cornerstone of a family's wealth are all factors that contribute to greater participation of Hispanics. According to projections by the U.S. Census Bureau, the Hispanic population will nearly triple from 35 million in 2000 to 98.2 million in 2050. Under this scenario, the percentage of Hispanics in the total population will rise from 12 percent to 24 percent over this period. By 2005, Hispanics will become the nation's largest minority group.

Mexico is the United States' largest source of legal immigrants, constituting one-fourth (27 percent) of foreign-born residency. Nearly two-thirds (65 percent) of the nation's Hispanics in 1999 were of Mexican origin.

To expand your business to Hispanics of Mexican heritage, a real estate agent must first establish trust with a client. Case studies show that the Mexican customer, in particular, might have reason to be suspicious of American businesses.

Skepticism toward North Americans is supported by the following evidence: Although 39 percent of Hispanics are foreign-born and most have lived in the United States long enough to qualify for citizenship, fewer than 18 percent are naturalized citizens. We have compiled some information to aid you when dealing with Hispanics of Mexican heritage:

- Hispanics of Mexican heritage tend to form strong bonds with the family, and they support their community. Approximately 90 percent of Mexicans are religious, which bonds the community even tighter and serves as a foundation for many cultural attitudes and beliefs.
- Families play a dominant role in Hispanic society and are a major influence on individual behavior. What is in the best interest of the family will dominate any decision, including home selection, school proximity, safety of the neighborhood, and projected monetary appreciation of one house over another.
- Mexican business culture has a warm, friendly atmosphere with a slower and more thoughtful pace, which may result in a greater amount of time needed for decision making. Be patient and understanding.
- Mexican-Americans place a high value on personal relations. They will do business only with people they know or through an acquaintance. Cultivating personal relationships is crucial to a real estate agent's success.
- The telephone is considered an informal means of communication. It should be used only to set up appointments and to ask general inquiries. Transactions are never closed over the phone.
- The dignity of the individual is highly respected, so there will be no gain in telling a Hispanic client that you are busy. It would not be wise to turn a Hispanic customer over to an assistant because this is an indicator that you do not believe their business is important enough for you to handle yourself. Use assistants behind the scenes, but make all calls and contacts yourself.
- Hispanics are reluctant to say "no" and may substitute "maybe" or "I'll think about it"—and may even say "yes"—out of politeness. Don't think you have a transaction until the papers are actually signed. If you are convinced that a certain property or negotiation meets the needs of the family, stress the benefits to the family.
- Establishing close relationships, trust, and favor are important. During salutations and introductions, a handshake and personal greeting are appropriate. A friendly inquiry about family is a common courtesy. After a couple of meetings watch for body language cues, and don't be

surprised if while shaking hands you are pulled in to follow through with an abrazo, or hug.

■ Treat Hispanic customers like a good friend and the reward will be a higher number of referrals than usual, since Hispanics do business only with people whom they trust. Community word-of-mouth is priceless.

■ These courtesies toward Hispanic customers will be greatly appreciated, but of course, the bottom line is to treat all customers as if they are the most important customers.

Copyright © 1999-2001 NAHREP. All rights reserved. Reprinted with permission.

Index